Contents

Who This Book is For 5
   How to Read This Book 6
Introduction 9
   Why I Wrote This Book 12
SECTION I: So, You Want to Start a Biz? 15
Chapter 1: Security Schmecurity 18
   The Traps Keeping You Stuck 25
   Getting Fired from a Job I Didn't Have 33
Chapter 2: The Real Cost of NOT Living Your Dream 40
   Don't Overthink It 43
   What You're Feeling is Normal 47
Chapter 3: Fears Keeping You Stuck 53
   How Will I Know What to Do? 55
   How Will I Know I'm Ready? 58
   Where Do I Start? 62
   How Do I Find Clients? 65
   What if I Can't Pay the Bills? 68
   What Happens When I Leave My Job? 73
Chapter 4: Psyching Yourself Up to Leave 78
   Learners are Earners 81
   Embrace Your Expertise 85
   Ask, Ask, Ask 91
   Play to Win 95

    Quitting Your Job 98

Chapter 5: Get the Right People with You 103
    Pre-Prospecting 105

    Permission to Be Your Badass Self 108

    Filter Out the Haters and Naysayers 116

    Accountability Buddies 122

SECTION II: Make Your Escape 126

Chapter 6: Getting Ready While Still Getting Paid 129
    Emergency Fund 131

    F.U. Fund 135

Chapter 7: Know Your Numbers 141
    Where to Start? 142

    Deciding What to Charge 146

    Get Your Head on Straight 150

    Taking Care of Business (Read: Busy Work) 153

Chapter 8: Punching Fear in the Face 162
    Facing Your Fears Head On 165

    When Your Brain is a Bastard 169

    Retrain Your Brain 177

    Separating Your Thoughts from Your Feels 183

    Find the Fear, Physically 187

SECTION III: Into the Unknown 189

Chapter 9: Prospecting 190
    Start With People You Know 191

    What About the Competition? 195

 Don't Be a Dick 196

 Converting Strangers into Prospects 199

 Specialist or Generalist? 204

Chapter 10: Business Realities 208

 The Business-Body Connection 209

 Be Available for What You Want 213

 Self-Management for Client Management 216

Chapter 11: Client Relations: the Good, the Bad, and the Ugly 224

 Setting Boundaries 226

 When to Stay and When to Walk Away 230

Chapter 12: Execution 238

 Knowing Where You're Going 239

 Doing the Creative Work 242

 Business Budgeting 246

 Raising Your Prices 248

Chapter 13: When It Feels Like You Don't Know What You're Doing 252

 Happily Never After? 254

 When Shit Goes Wrong 259

 Creators Create 262

 Be Willing to Walk Away 263

Chapter 14: Staying Sharp and Starting to Grow 266

 Trying New Things 267

 Finding the Fast Track 270

 Asking For (and Getting) Help with Grace 273

Chapter 15: Leveling Up 276

    When Doing Good Work Goes Wrong..277

    Outgrowing Your Solopreneur Business 280

    Your Inner Game 291

Chapter 16: Angie's Law 294

    Further Reading and Resources 299

    Acknowledgements..300

Who This Book is For

If any of the following sounds familiar, we should talk:

→ **You're creative, and love to draw or paint or take photos or create franken-recipes** that have your colleagues raving at the office potluck. But maybe (like I was) you're stuck in a soul-sucking 9-to-5 job where you feel like a cog in a production line, you can't get anyone to take your ideas seriously, and there's no end in sight.

→ **You don't have many (or any) real opportunities for real, meaningful advancement** and the higher-ups don't have any interest in your personal or professional growth. Or they care more about how many hours you park your ass in a chair, staring at a screen, versus the quality of work being done. The cubicle (or couch, in our post-pandemic, virtual working world) feels like a coffin, and your work hours and home hours start to blur together in a way that means you never fully disconnect.

→ **You yearn for something more… for freedom to do work that feeds your soul,** be paid what you deserve, and create a lifestyle you love. Yet you're miserable most of the time… overwhelmed by your workload, low pay, and responsibilities. That was me about a decade ago. And being stuck in a cube 12+ hours a day certainly wasn't what I dreamed my life would look like when I was a kid.

→ **You see others out there making YOUR dream happen—earning a living doing something creative.** Musicians, artists, writers, content creators, photographers, graphic artists, or pastry chefs… they seem to be running thriving businesses and you're left wondering what they've got that you don't.

Great news! Most of those people you admire don't have some mysterious "secret" that magically unlocks the door to success.

What they have is <u>permission to kick ass</u>.

They have a particular brand of stubbornness more commonly referred to as determination. They've developed a mindset that lets them punch fear square in the face, which enables them to trust themselves way more than some company or "boss" who never seems to have their back.

I imagine you want something similar for yourself, and that's why you're here. Hell yeah!

If you're just starting your creative freelance business, or even if you've already started and need a little shot of courage to hit the next level… this one's for you. I've experienced that paralyzing awake-all-night panic, and those quiet, nagging moments of self-doubt. I know how that feels, and I've dedicated my life to helping others break free.

I'm on a mission to create an army of badass creative business owners bent on changing the world for the better. So, gather 'round and let's get to it.

How to Read This Book

Let's get one thing straight, right here and now.

There's always going to be a reason NOT to do something.

This book exists to help you recognize when those reasons have become fear-based excuses that are only holding you back. Throughout the course of this book, I'm going to keep refocusing your attention on proof that this dream IS possible. There's evidence all around you, every day… but sometimes that fear kicks into overdrive and obscures everything, telling you, "But here are 4,059 different ways you could fail spectacularly, so you may as well not even try."

Yes, there's the possibility that you could fail. I failed the very first time I tried to start my freelance business... surprise! I was a decent writer who wasn't naturally great at business.

There's a learning curve with this, just like there is with all the skills you now possess, from walking to reading to feeding yourself. Imagine if we supported and encouraged our inner entrepreneurs the way we cheer on a baby learning to walk... then maybe we wouldn't see every failure as a sign we're not cut out to do this, but as something that had to happen to get us one step closer.

Failure is an event, it's not your identity.

And fear of failure is exactly why I'm writing this book. I call it a love letter to a younger me—and a guidebook that will help you forge a straighter path to your dream. This is all the shit that I wish I had known the first time I went freelance.

Back then I was afraid of everything... I didn't believe people would pay me. I didn't think they could afford my rates, so I'd offer discounts well before they ever asked. As I've grown my business and worked my way up in terms of better clients—and better projects with better budgets—I've learned the more I charge, the more people respect my time and expertise. The more I charge, the more likely my clients are to put my advice and my work to use and see results. I have shared stories here that were incredibly hard to put on the page... but if they help even one person, then I consider this a wild success.

Along the way, I will point you to the FREE companion guide that goes with *Permission to Kick Ass*. **Go download it now at permissiontokickass.com/guide.** These valuable exercises will help you apply what you learn in this book to grow your awesome new freelance career.

So, in the name of baby steps and fast action, I'm going to encourage you to go grab that companion guide right now. Do it because this is an important agreement you're making with yourself. Download it, print it out if you like… write your name in it and give yourself permission to take this seriously, to a point—this is a business book full of F-bombs, after all. Fun is an important part of business, too!

I hereby declare that you have Official Permission™ to get out there and kick all kinds of ass.

Now it's time to turn the page and see just what the hell kind of crazy journey you've just signed on for.

Introduction

"Why aren't you posting more?"

I was about five years into my copywriting career, and I'd just joined a membership site called Copy Chief. In case you've never heard of copywriters, think *Mad Men* - we specialize in sales and marketing writing.

I was stoked. A whole community of creative business people just like me? Hell yeah! The founder of the site is a man named Kevin Rogers, who would eventually become my mentor. A few months after I joined, Kevin invited me to a quick call to talk about my experience in the community. When he asked me why I wasn't posting in the forum, I was like a deer in headlights. I mean, sure I was a Senior Copywriter at my corporate day job, but this community had these amazing, brilliant, FREELANCE copywriters that I'd put up on a pedestal.

Here were a bunch of smart, successful freelancers sharing all kinds of incredible insights, and I was over in my cube being a boring corporate stiff. I'd never negotiated a killer retainer contract, or figured out how to run my own business—in fact, this job was my solution to the failure of my first business—so who the hell was I to give other people advice? I said as much to Kevin.

He was momentarily stunned. "Angie, you do realize there are people in there who would move mountains to get your level of experience, right? You're not exactly chopped liver, my friend."

Before that moment, it had never occurred to me that I might have skills someone else would want, or envy. All I knew was a picture in my head of what a "successful copywriter" looked like, and I was definitely NOT it. Yet I desperately wanted to figure out what I was missing. Here was this entire community of people, who were not trapped in a job, and who made this whole "freelance" thing work for them.

I was determined to learn their secrets and figured a little brown-nosery never hurts.

"I'm really excited to be here, I promise," I told Kev. "What I really want to know is how can I help YOU?"

"The best way you can help me is by sharing inside the community and making it a kickass place to be," he said.

"But I don't really have anything to say, not like those cool freelancers dropping knowledge bombs on a daily basis."

That's when he laid the whammy on me:

"I feel like you're waiting for someone to give you permission. And you don't actually need permission to help people if you know something that can help them. You can be a few steps ahead of someone and still help them solve a problem… and you don't have to be the world's foremost expert to share your solution. But just in case that whole 'needing permission' thing is holding you back, I hereby anoint you 'expert ENOUGH.' You have permission to answer any and all questions you can, and ignore all the ones you can't."

You might have guessed by now… that line inspired a massive shift in my perspective, and also the name of this book.

I took Kevin's advice and started answering questions, connecting people, sharing resources, and helping where I could. If I didn't know the answers to someone's question, I tried to point them in the general direction, reassure them the answers were out there, and let them know all they needed to do was go find them.

It wasn't long before people started messaging me asking for one-on-one coaching because they saw me as an elite expert… the same kind of elite expert I'd once thought everyone ELSE was. The same cool experts I'd found so intimidating that it kept me from participating.

I certainly didn't feel like "enough" of an expert, but I kept Kev's advice in my heart. I helped where I could, and the more people reached out to me for advice, the more I realized I wasn't the only person waiting for anointing before putting myself out there. Almost every creative person I spoke to—writers, photographers, painters, bakers, and all kinds of other creators—helped me realize there are a lot of us driven by this need for "permission" to pursue our chosen path.

If that sounds like you, I feel you on a deep, spiritual level. I've always had this idea of what a "creative" looks like, and that person somehow never looked like ME. Never mind that I spent all day, every day, writing at my job. Or that I spent evenings and weekends singing with my band, or afternoons sketching. My inner critic relentlessly screeched, *'You have bills to pay, you need this job to pay them, you can't get paid to be a Creative, you are NOT a Creative.'*

Can you see the bass-ackwards logic in that little tangle of terrified thoughts? Here's a hint: writers write. It's a cliché bit of advice, but it's the absolute truth. I was *already* creating, and I was *already* getting paid. All I had to do was figure out how to get paid on my terms—so I could have the freedom and flexibility I craved.

Turns out I had permission to do the things I loved doing all along—it's just that it came from ME versus an external "expert approval board."

If you're reading this, I'm betting something similar might be true for you. Maybe you've chosen a creative path and heard all kinds of garbage about "starving artists" and how you've got to be responsible and get that "steady paycheck." But something in your heart doesn't want the 9-5 lifestyle with all its commuting and corporate politics—been there, <u>fuck that</u>.

Maybe you're daydreaming about "someday," when you'll be able to live and work in another country, or take three months off every year, or set your own rates—and make a hell of a lot more money than you ever could as an employee. Whatever that "someday" looks like, it starts with doing what you're already good at, and getting paid for it on your terms.

If that's you, then Darling… Sugar… Pumpkin face muffin butt…

Come to mama. I gotchu.

Why I Wrote This Book

Before I got my bachelor's degree—the one that was supposed to help me get a "real job"—I kinda drifted along aimlessly, following whatever shiny object caught my attention. I did stints picking up trash at a waterpark, tutoring math, bartending, entering data, telemarketing, firefighting, teaching water aerobics, and even selling credit cards during the worst economic downturn in decades. If it sounded remotely interesting and offered to pay me, I tried it.

So, what changed?

I got tired of wandering mostly, but still had no idea what I wanted to be when I grew up. I did the one thing I knew I could do well: I went to grad school at Carnegie Mellon, where I earned my master's degree in Entertainment Industry Management (MEIM). The program's mission is to bridge the gap between the business and creative sides of entertainment—the money folks who'd bark, "It's show biz, not show ART!" and the artists who'd retort, "Without the art you wouldn't HAVE a business!"

I learned a little bit of everything while getting that degree: accounting, HR law, entrepreneurship, and screenwriting. And in the process, I thought I finally found my dream job—TV development. Those are the folks that find the shows and match them to the network brand. I wanted to become the next Shonda Rhimes and create immersive, irresistible TV shows. I worked my ass off to get that degree, and it was a cool program all around (shout-out to my fellow MEIMs).

My thesis was about how the future of entertainment was subscription-based digital streaming—nailed it. After graduating, I worked stints at Warner Brothers, CBS, TNT/TBS, NBC Universal, and the CW, but was having a hard time finding anything beyond temp gigs. As it turned out, finding that elusive, steady paycheck in Los Angeles was challenging—that is until I landed at the Oprah Winfrey Network just as they were getting ready to launch. My contract kept getting extended, and it finally felt like I was where I was meant to be.

Unfortunately I got laid off weeks before the network launch—and started wondering if I was ever going to make it. With money rapidly running out and subsisting on 39¢ tacos from Del Taco… I made the totally logical decision to spend $20 I didn't have on the book, *The Well-Fed Writer* by Peter Bowerman, because someone recommended it.

I discovered copywriting in the pages of that book—I literally fell into it after getting laid off from what I thought was my forever gig. But I was new to both copywriting and to business—so making money was slow going. With money running out and my roommate leaving Los Angeles, I decided to close the door on my entertainment industry career. Some super gracious friends in Silicon Valley agreed to let me crash on their couch, so I moved in with them in hopes I could figure out how to build my freelance business.

For ten months, I took every writing gig under the sun—business plans, live pageant scripts, websites. Whatever someone would pay me to write, I'd write. But still, I couldn't figure out how to get steady, predictable income. I wasn't even making enough to get me off unemployment! Eventually my friends decided they needed a bigger place, and I couldn't afford the rent to move with them.

That's when I found myself sitting alone on a mattress in an empty apartment, trying to figure out what the hell to do next. I had this dream of having a writing business, and by all appearances it looked like it was the end of the road. But something in my gut said the dream was possible… so I wound up making one of the hardest decisions of my life.

I chose to live in my car.

A word of caution to you, dear reader: if you choose to live in your car and pursue your vision, first of all be safe. Second, maybe hold off on telling your parents and loved ones about your decision until after you've recovered and landed somewhere safe.

I realize how fortunate I am to have wonderful, caring parents. Each of them invited me to come home to Texas and "get back on my feet." I still can't explain it to this day, but I knew I had to stay in Silicon Valley. Something in my soul told me that if I took the "safe" road I'd wind up waiting tables for the rest of my life.

As luck would have it, that gamble paid off. You could say I understand the power of the right idea at the right time, because it turns out reading a book changed the entire course of my life. Hell, it introduced me to a career I didn't even know existed! And if this book does for you what *The Well-Fed Writer* did for me, I can die a happy woman. I'm pouring everything into these pages that, if I could, I'd go back in time to bitch slap into my younger self—the stuff I wish I'd known the first time around.

That said, I'd love to tell you that reading a book magically fixed my life. The reality is, my journey's had a lot of fits and starts, a lot of hard lessons, and a lot of falling flat on my face. Your journey probably will have some fits and starts and stumbles, too. But my hope is that you may discover lessons within these pages that might lighten your load and shorten your trip.

You'll read about my struggles when I managed to land my first copywriting job, what it was like to walk away from a cushy salary and benefits and failing my way forward until I finally found my "thing." It's taken me a few at bats to find my dream gig, and even now I'm still figuring out the next evolution of my business… so trust me when I say if you're feeling like you're making it up as you go, you're not alone. But there's good news! You can still have an amazing business that supports the lifestyle you envision, even if you never feel like you've "figured it out!"

The key is not to just read and dream, but to take massive action… which brings me to:

SECTION I: So, You Want to Start a Biz?

I've got a bone to pick with the idea that "job = stable." But we'll get to that in a bit. Most people who talk to you about entrepreneurship and freelancing being "unstable" either have never started their own business or started one and failed (and given up on the dream, resigning themselves to the day job).

Let's get one thing clear: what they really mean by "unstable" is "unknown."

Unknown is new. Unknown is scary. Unknown has a lot of "ifs" and unanswered questions attached. It makes logical sense that the natural reaction to "New, scary thing OMG!" might be "No thanks, I'm cool where I'm at." That's fear talking. Even those of us who have failed at entrepreneurship, gone back to a job, and then left the job to try again, will tell you the fear never really goes away.

In fact, every time I made a massive leap forward in my life, it was immediately preceded by the most intense fear of my life. At some point I recognized that fear was driving me and making all my choices for me. I was too scared to try anything, too scared to fail… too scared to truly *live*.

It doesn't help that on top of what you might already be feeling anxiety-wise, the well-meaning folks who know and love you will start to question your decision, too. I know… it happened to me! When I first set out on this entrepreneurial journey, there were many times I felt crazy, or in over my head… and that was only reinforced by everyone around me, with their steady jobs and unspoken assumptions about what I was *really* doing hanging out at coffee shops on my laptop all day.

If I had a dollar for every time someone told me, "Just get a job, any job! You're fooling yourself with this writing thing," I'd be ridiculously fucking rich. I know they meant well, and they said those things precisely because they cared. I count that as a blessing for as much as it sometimes drove me nuts.

Eventually, I learned that I had to follow my own gut, rather than listen to people who had no idea what it was like to start or run a business (related note: finding people who are doing what you want to do will be critical for sustaining the dream—I go deeper into this in Chapter 5, where I talk about your "Accountability Buddies"*)*. Entrepreneurship is always going to look crazy to the 9-to-5 advocates, the folks who prefer "stability" and "security" to this whole business building adventure.

They may even throw scary statistics like these at you:

First-time entrepreneurs have an 18% success rate.
That's according to the article, "Startup Statistics—The Numbers You Need to Know" (on *SmallBusinessTrends.com*), which shares a lot of other interesting stats people often forget to cite.[1] For instance, that same study states they also discovered that the success rate increases with every subsequent venture.

Translation: practice makes perfect, even in business.

Sounds weird right? But it makes sense when you think about it, because we learn as much (if not more!) from failure as we can from success. So really, the key is being willing to fail your way forward. To step into the unknown with faith—not necessarily in a higher power—but in yourself.

---

[1] Mansfield, Matt. "Startup Statistics—The Numbers You Need to Know." Small Business Trends. 22 January, 2021. https://smallbiztrends.com/2019/03/startup-statistics-small-business.html.

By pursuing this entrepreneurial path, you're stepping into a world where every day is about solving new and interesting problems and thinking about interaction with your fellow humans in a whole new way. It's not for everyone, but if you feel called to this… remember:

Feel the fear and do it anyway.

Welcome to entrepreneurship, friend! You're in great company.

Chapter 1: Security Schmecurity

I walked out of my day job on December 16, almost a decade ago.

I shit you not, I exited to a slow clap and chants of "Angie! Angie! Angie!" I couldn't make that up if I wanted to.

The fact is I adored and believed in my team—the Creative Team. We did amazing work together. We could have done even bigger and better things. But I no longer believed in the company. It'd been toxic from the day I signed on, but for years I had this delusion of being able to help change the culture for the better. After all, you're supposed to be the change you wish to see in the world, right?

I studied negotiation, teamwork, and communications. I tried every trick in the book when it came to collaborating with the teams outside my department—presenting my case, bargaining, getting emotional, being totally dispassionate and borderline apathetic, letting them suggest or take credit for ideas—and no matter which tactic I tried, it never worked. The funny thing is, the challenges were never with my own core creative team—only with other groups, outside my department.

I'm not exaggerating when I say this place was toxic—I was once in a meeting where a VP said, "This company was better before we had copywriters," in front of about 30 people. Context: at the time I was the only copywriter on staff, so there wasn't really any ambiguity about who was being called out.

I was so stunned and caught off-guard that I left the meeting—without fanfare or fireworks, which is probably shocking to people who know me—to walk around the building and get my head on straight. When I was sufficiently calm, I quietly returned and sat through the rest of the meeting as if a so-called "leader" hadn't just publicly tried to humiliate me.

18

To add insult to injury, I later got called into my own VP's office and chewed out for how unprofessionally I'd behaved in leaving the meeting to cool down. I was bewildered. It's unprofessional for me to take a moment to compose myself, but totally acceptable for a vice president to single someone out? Wow.

Those were the "Stormy Angie" days, when I was often frustrated to the point of emotional outbursts. I've cried in meetings, lost my temper… you name it, I've had every "unprofessional" reaction under the sun, short of punching someone in the face. That's precisely why I was so proud of myself when I walked out of the meeting!

The moment I realized no one was coming to my defense or calling out the VP's terrible behavior, the three options that popped into my head were 1) sob, 2) shout, or 3) take a walk and cool down. I chose what felt like the most professional route, only to have my own department's VP come down on me for walking out.

Sad to say, that was inside my first six months on the job… when I was determined to prove myself, and it felt like getting fired would leave some sort of negative mark on my permanent record (hint: it doesn't. No one's paying that close attention to what you do unless they're stalking you). So, I vented to friends and bit my tongue and doubled down on the work. After all, if I busted my ass to deliver good work, they couldn't keep shitting on me, right?

What happened to me is exactly why so many talented people quit their jobs. I've heard it phrased as, "People don't quit jobs, they quit horrible bosses," and if that ain't the damn truth, I don't know what is. The *Harvard Business Review* did a survey of people that left Facebook and found that,

"They left when their job wasn't enjoyable, their strengths weren't being used, and they weren't growing in their careers."[2]

Ouch.

Turns out the corporate environment I walked away from is more the norm than the exception. In another study done in 2019, Dynamic Signal found that 80% of the U.S. workforce was stressed because of the same things that trapped me, including the toxic top-down culture where their voice was never heard, and they didn't feel safe to share their ideas.[3]

Man, I was so idealistic in those days… despite people in that company showing me exactly who they were, I stayed for almost four more years after that meeting took place. And trust me when I say, it didn't get any better no matter how hard I worked.

Maybe you've had a similar experience, where you were determined and positive and it didn't work out for you. But I'm going to encourage you not to sell the whole car and give up on your dreams just because you blew a tire. You've still got a lot going for you, so it's not worth throwing everything away over one bad experience.

Determination is an entrepreneurial gift. With practice, you learn when that determination will work in your favor and when you're better off walking away.

---

[2] Goler, Lori, Janelle Gale, Brynn Harrington, and Adam Grant. "Why People Really Quit Their Jobs." Harvard Business Review. 11 January, 2018. https://hbr.org/2018/01/why-people-really-quit-their-jobs

[3] Hannah, Robyn. "Dynamic Signal Study Finds U.S. Workforce Stressed And Ready To Quit." Dynamic Signal. https://dynamicsignal.com/2019/03/20/2019-employee-communication-and-engagement-study/

In my case, I wasted a lot of time, effort, and emotional energy trying to convince people to hear me out, who were equally determined not to listen. That was not an effective use of my creativity and persistence… it was stubbornness and ego. I wanted to be right, to be recognized as a brilliant strategist, so I was unable to look at the situation objectively and make a different choice.

Fear plays a huge part in this… it'll seize on those setbacks and use them as justification for keeping you where you are. For me, the voice of fear sounded something like, "Maybe you're not as good as you think, since no one will give your ideas a try. Maybe they know something you don't and if you try to go somewhere else, they'll laugh you out of the room and you'll wind up homeless and broke."

My struggles with my coworkers only amplified my fear of failure, which led me to stay way longer than I might have otherwise. Every time I thought about leaving, there'd be some tiny improvement in working conditions and I'd lock in on that, asking myself, *Is it really as bad as you're making it out to be? The teams had a joint picnic and people sat together and talked… that's a sign that things are improving, right? You got unsolicited compliments from that person who yelled at you in a meeting last week—that must mean there's a light at the end of the tunnel!*

Pay attention if you start hearing yourself rationalize like that. There's looking for the good in people and situations, and there's *denial*. I was in denial because I was afraid I couldn't do better. And denial and fear will keep you stuck in what I call the "job trap." It's where you believe this is as good as you're going to get, that you can't possibly build something better. And if you indulge in that line of thinking too much, you'll be right about not being able to do better—because you won't even try!

Now, just getting to this point of deciding to leave is an uphill battle. And it's not really your fault if you're having doubts. This is something we're all indoctrinated to believe—that you must get an education, find a good job, work your way up the ladder, save some money, retire after 40 or so years. That's the "formula" for happiness we've all been sold since we were old enough to read books or watch television. That may have been true in another era, but it's okay to want something more (or even something different!) for yourself.

You do NOT have to work five days a week for forty years just to get a shot at personal satisfaction and fulfillment.

Maybe your version of "happy" is living in the woods, off the grid, exploring the wilderness and getting up close and personal with nature. Maybe it's living in a Manhattan penthouse and eating at the best restaurants, dressed in the latest couture. Maybe it's working your ass off for six months to make enough money to be able to take off for six months.

It's a trap to follow someone else's recipe for your own happiness. It's tempting, sure… because when you don't have the success you envisioned for yourself, you get to throw your hands up and say, "I followed the plan! I don't know what went wrong, it can't be my fault!" That's not to say horrible things don't happen, or that everyone chooses misery, or even that everyone has the support in place to do something different. But I am saying we all are more resourceful than we give ourselves credit for.

We have more power and capability and choice than we often realize. And the first step in making a big change—like walking away from a job—is seeing the situation you're in for what it is and deciding it's not something you want for yourself. Admitting you don't want something starts the necessary exploration of finding out what you DO want. And that's the key that opens the door to your potential.

Let's get one thing clear, right here and now: it's not a bad thing to crave stability and predictability. It's not a bad thing to want a steady income, or even health insurance and retirement savings. It's not a bad thing to take ownership of your responsibilities, personally, professionally, and financially… and to want to pay your own way. In no way, shape, or form am I suggesting you shouldn't want these things for yourself. I will never talk smack about personal responsibility! As I once told a romantic partner, fiscal responsibility is sexy.

But I take issue with the notion that a "job" is how you get security and peace of mind.

As long as you work for someone else—at least without having any kind of side hustle or savings—you're basically handing over control of your life to them. That's not necessarily a bad thing—some trade-offs are worth it. But if you're bewitched by the siren song of steady pay and benefits, there's no guarantee that once you get those things, you'll keep them. That's the nature of business (and life).

Even with an iron-clad employment agreement, you could still get the shaft. Especially with big companies—they have the legal team in place to help them figure out how to undo the contracts they did. If you don't have a lawyer that can play on their level and negotiate on your behalf, you're going to be out of luck if they decide to change the terms. You could wind up in a job you love with a boss who hates you, even though you're awesome and make them look like a rockstar.

Humans gonna human, that's one universal truth you can count on. And wherever humans are involved, shit gets unpredictable *real quick*.

And there's the other big thing we don't talk about: if the company shuts down, none of this matters anyway. Your iron-clad contract doesn't guarantee you a job in a building that's been shuttered and sold. When I started writing this book, we were all blissfully unaware that a major global event was on the horizon. Back then, I had a note to myself about looking up stats and figures to prove the rates of business failures and layoffs because I knew I'd need to make a case for you to believe me when I say jobs aren't guaranteed.

Then in 2020, a pandemic swept the world, taking millions of lives, shuttering businesses, losing us millions of jobs and billions of dollars. Maybe you were personally impacted and lost a loved one or a business or a job (heartfelt aside: all my love to everyone devastated by the pandemic).

Here are a few realities that the pandemic made super-clear:

1) Way more jobs than were previously thought can be done partially or mostly online/from home. At the same time, we can't just hole up at home—as a species, we need human connection to thrive on a personal level.

2) A lot of people found out just how fast their jobs can go away due to forces completely beyond their control. Even A-players were suddenly without work because the company was suddenly without business.

Being let go can be devastating, not only to your finances, but also to your entire being (whether it's justified and expected, or you never saw it coming). Trust me, as someone who loves her work, who has trouble sometimes STOPPING the work, and pulls way more late nights than any human should… I get that your identity as a person can be deeply tied to what you do for a living.

It's bad enough when a job you hate lets you go—it's even worse when it's a job you love.

But your work is not your worth.

It's for all these reasons and more that I firmly believe everyone can and should get a side gig going, even if it's just to bolster your savings or float you through to the next job. I'm not necessarily advocating everyone working three jobs just to get by—but if you want to make some crafts or bake some cakes and hit up a local arts fair once a month to see what you can sell? Seems like a worthwhile endeavor to me.

The only person you can truly depend on, who will always have your best interests in mind... is *you*. That's not to say you won't have friends or family you can depend on, but they've naturally got to think about themselves on occasion, which means your security and happiness is on YOU, my friend. No one else can passionately pursue your future on your behalf. So, will you step up and try, even if it means the possibility of failure, or will you stay stuck because of the illusion of safety?

The Traps Keeping You Stuck

Now that we've thoroughly dissected this idea of "security," let's dig into the traps that keep you stuck holding onto your job like a kid with a treasured blankie.

The Money Trap

How to recognize this trap: you're panicking, worrying about how you'll pay the bills if you can't figure out how to make the business work. Or you find yourself thinking there's no way you can pay the bills without a job. I lived paycheck to paycheck most of my life and first learned the importance of savings in my late 20s... so it's fair to say I've been caught in a money trap, in one form or another, for most of my life. It's especially dangerous if your go-to behavior is to expand your lifestyle to match your income—meaning as you earn more money, you're also spending more money. That's no judgment, as I have also been repeatedly lured in by that fanciness.

These days I'm a HUGE advocate for living within your means (or even below your means) and aggressively squirreling away money for a rainy day. We're talking turning down dinner dates if you can't afford that steak, or moving in with roommates, or driving a car for a decade to get maximum value from your investment. In fact, I'll be ranting about money, savings, and the F.U. Fund more in-depth in Chapter 6, so stay tuned.

It was precisely because I didn't have any money saved that my copy career almost didn't happen. Remember my story about choosing to live in my car? I was between opportunities and living with my best friend, Alix, in Silicon Valley. Picture it: three adults, three cats, and a baby all holed up and crammed together in a one-bedroom, one-bathroom apartment. Alix and their partner were gracious enough to let me live on the couch while I was trying to make my first attempt at freelancing work.

For ten months I tried every strategy to get business, from signing up for freelance sites to dropping flyers and making cold calls. I even sent out my writing resume to more than 300 job listings trying to find something, ANYTHING in the marketing industry that would get me closer to my goal of being a copywriter. But ten months is a long time to spend in such close quarters. Eventually, my friends decided to get a bigger place. They even offered to find a space with an additional bedroom for me, but I couldn't afford the additional rent. So, a few weeks before the lease expired they moved out and I spent my nights sitting on a mattress in the empty apartment, sobbing while desperately trying to figure out my next steps.

It was at that point I recognized I had a hard choice: go home to Texas and live with my amazingly generous parents while I got back on my feet… or stay in California and live in my car. I still can't explain it to this day, but something in my gut told me to stay where I was or I'd wind up waiting tables for the rest of my life.

I chose living in my car, much to my parents' chagrin. I put what little I owned into storage and spent my last few days trying to find a safe place to park my car overnight. And then, the day I had to turn over keys… I got a call from one of the places where I'd applied and interviewed. They offered me a job and wanted to know where to send the offer letter.

The role was a junior copywriter position at an e-commerce party favor company. They offered just enough part-time pay to cover the bills, and while I did still have to live in my car and couch surf for a bit, it was thankfully only a matter of weeks before I spent my entire first paycheck on getting myself into a house with wonderful roommates.

The money trap is hard because it's super uncomfortable. Being stuck here means you have to make hard choices, and it may even feel like you have no options. Trust me, you do. Even if it's temporarily being between houses until you can figure out how to make it work.

Note: I'm not advocating voluntary homelessness or suggesting it as a lifestyle, nor am I implying that homelessness is a quick fix. Far from it—I recognize that I had certain advantages with friends taking me in, as well as owning a car I could sleep in.

My main takeaway from this time in my life is two-fold: people can survive and thrive even when thriving seems impossible, and sometimes the universe tests you to see how badly you really want the thing. I still have trouble believing that the DAY I lost the apartment is the exact same day I got the job that saved me. If I'd operated out of fear and played it safe, I would have been on the road to Texas when the job offer came through… and would likely be waiting tables instead of writing this book.

Fast forward about five years, and I'd managed to leverage that first part-time job into a full-time role with a cushy salary (the aforementioned toxic gig). After several years, as a senior copywriter who'd helped hire and oversee training of new staff and had several big (think: multimillion dollar) wins… I discovered my "cushy" salary was about $10,000 behind the curve for people with similar titles in my area. Not only was I behind the curve for Silicon Valley, but also the national average.

By this point, I'd expanded my lifestyle to accommodate my salary, and between the nice apartment, the credit cards, and the student loans, finances started to feel tight again. I took my salary findings to the company in hopes of leveraging it into a raise. Instead, I ran face first into a wall: the company had a single, annual merit-based salary increase… and that merit raise was capped at 6%. To get the full 6%—which was not anywhere near $10,000—I had to get a perfect five-star review. Except part of my review included company-wide goals, so if the company didn't meet its goals, there was no way to get a perfect score, even if I knocked all my own milestones out of the park.

Feeling unappreciated and taken advantage of, I made my plan to leave. But then my car broke down and I had a large, unexpected bill. Suddenly that fear about how the hell I'd pay the bills kicked in, and it'd be another six months before I finally walked out the door.

Eventually I worked up the courage to walk away from the toxic job. I went to my manager and said, "I wrote an email campaign that generated $8.4M, and a created catalog that generated almost $1M. Why can't I get more than a 6% annual raise when the value I bring to this company is so clear?" My manager, being the freaking awesome guy he is, went to bat for me with upper management. But as upper management tends to do, they came up with a bunch of excuses as to why they couldn't (read: wouldn't) pay more. That was the final straw, and when my manager delivered the bad news, I told him that meant I had to walk. He understood and wished me well.

How to loosen the jaws of the money trap: start saving if you're not already doing so.

There's always going to be an unexpected expense—that's why it's so important to start saving now, even if you don't feel like you can spare a single cent. When you've got money set aside, unexpected expenses don't become emergencies where you risk losing your home or going hungry. And I get that it might not be easy to get on the savings train, especially if you're barely getting by. I've been there too. Start small if you must, with a dollar at a time—something you won't really miss. Over time those dollars will add up and help you feel more secure in the face of the unexpected.

Then tap into your reason why.

Do you want to change peoples' lives? Do you have an idea for a new, disruptive, or innovative technology that you know will be fucking rad? Or do you simply want to build a comfortable lifestyle for your family, where you've got the freedom and flexibility that allows you to be present for the people most important to you?

The beauty of entrepreneurship is there's no real cap on your potential income—suck on that, upper management. If you want to make more or work less (or both!), there's a way to figure that out. Hundreds of thousands of people have done it before you, and they'll continue to start businesses long after you and I are gone. You might surprise yourself, but not without first working up the courage to try. What got you here will not get you there—meaning what's gotten you to this point is not going to take you to the next level. To get to that next level requires a change of approach, new skills, and a whole lotta faith in yourself.

The Creativity Trap

How to recognize this trap: if you feel like you could do your job in your sleep. That is its own special kind of hell for creative people.

For me, that first part-time junior copywriting role was supposed to have been freedom from money worries—plus, I got paid to write. My teammates were wonderful, and I even rode a horse for the first time at a team building event (crazy to think about since I'm from Texas).

Unfortunately, I quickly settled into a routine, verging on a rut. Every week I wrote two blog posts, four emails, and as many product descriptions as I could fit into my part-time schedule. How many ways can you think of to describe a paper plate? "Ooh, this one has yellow stripes, and this one has diagonal stripes, and this one has polka dots, *woo-fucking-hoo*!" And, "Ooh, it's a glass you can get monogrammed. Ooh, it's a bag that you can get monogrammed. And hey, here's a baseball cap you can get... you guessed it, monogrammed!"

That makes me sound a bit ungrateful. It was a really great job, and it proved to me that I could get paid to write. That's an essential piece of this creative entrepreneur puzzle—proving to yourself you can get paid. I learned a ton at that job and connected with some amazing people. But after a year and a half, I could tell that I wasn't growing. I was suffocating in a creativity trap, and my writing skills were slowly stagnating because I wasn't trying anything new or stretching outside my comfort zone.

On top of that, I wasn't invited to marketing meetings, so I didn't really have any say in my projects. It was a great opportunity, and the one that saved me from living in my car. But I had nowhere to go, nowhere to grow. That's not a great place to be for a creative person.

Another way to recognize the creativity trap is admitting when you're bored out of your skull. Don't get me wrong, there are some people who can do the same thing day in and day out, eat the same thing day in and day out, follow the same routine for 40 years and be completely fucking happy. If you're one of those people, you're probably having a hard time reading this book because I'm probably making your underwear catch fire with all the racy things I'm suggesting.

But if you're bored and you know there's more you can do, then why the hell would you stay at a job that's not challenging you to be better? One of my mentors says, "If you are the smartest person in the room, you're in the wrong room." You absolutely should be in a room where you're surrounded by smart people who are driven to accomplish great things... because they'll challenge you to step up and do great things too. And then they'll celebrate those wins with you—because most successful entrepreneurs I know are also some of the most generous, grateful, and uplifting people I've ever met.

How to get yourself out of the creativity trap: creativity thrives on exposure to new and interesting ideas, and fresh inputs. So, if there's nothing new happening at your job, find a source of stimulation—a class, a book, a daily walk, a trip to a nearby (or faraway) town. See if that renews your passion for your work. If not, it may be time to stretch outside your comfort zone and go in a new direction.

The Stress Trap

How to recognize if you're stuck in this trap: when getting up and going to work every day is causing you tremendous anxiety.

I noticed that after a while it was really hard to wake up. I would hit snooze and risk running late repeatedly—even though I'm one of those obnoxiously on-time people. That was my first indication something was wrong. Being late really bothers me, so when I noticed that pattern emerging, I sat down and tried to figure out why it was happening.

It wasn't just the 10–12-hour days and the one-to-two-hour commute… my body seemed to be doing everything it could to prevent me from going to the place where I felt a tremendous amount of pressure and stress. Even when I had a great night of sleep or drugged myself into oblivion and was totally relaxed, as soon as I woke up, I remembered I had to go to work. My shoulders would shoot up around my ears, and I was immediately tense and stressed, imagining the meetings I'd have that day and all the deadlines I'd have to hustle to hit.

I hope you don't ever get to this point because it's physically and mentally painful. But for me, in this job where I was giving my heart and soul and doing my best work, where I couldn't get a raise to match the value I brought to the company, where coworkers would come to my cube and scream at me… eventually it got to a point that my dread of going into the office greatly outweighed the excitement I got from doing the creative work.

A low-grade anxiety started to permeate every aspect of my life. It made me second-guess everything—*Is this a sign I'm not cut out for this? That I can't hack it in a high-stakes, high-pressure role?* I was also in physical pain all the time. My muscles were constantly knotted and tight, and I wasn't sleeping very well, leading me to start regularly napping in my car midday. Finally, I stopped exercising and fell into a depression. All the while I kept working until I burned out and had to take three days off work to sit on my front porch and stare at nothing for hours. That's not an exaggeration.

As an aside: burnout is no good for a creative person, or anyone, for that matter. One of my mentors, John Carlton, the Rebel Marketer, says, "There's no guarantee you will come back from burnout." So don't ever fool yourself into believing it's okay to keep going full steam ahead until you hit the wall, thinking after the wall you get to rest. Newsflash: if you can't slow down, hitting that wall may quite literally be the thing that kills you.

Back to this idea of anxiety and resistance—when you're having a really, really hard time convincing yourself to do something, that's something to pay attention to. Usually, your body and your subconscious brain is telling you that there is something wrong with this situation, and something needs to change. Because I can tell you, despite not being a morning person, these days I love getting up early and stretching, journaling, having a cup (or five) of coffee, thinking about the next steps for my business, and getting in some writing.

That brings me a great deal of excitement, even on my stressiest days when I've got multiple projects due at the same time. And the difference between the anxiety that I had at my old job and the performance-related anxiety that I have now is night and day. This is the good kind of anxiety—the kind of pressure that motivates me to step up and challenge myself to be better… in contrast to the job stress that stifled me and killed my creativity.

How to get yourself out of the stress trap: if you're going a million miles an hour and have no time to think, slow down.

Take time off if you can. If you can't, take walks, meditate, or do yoga. I used to make fun of meditation advocates and yogis because my southern Texas upbringing led me to believe it was "hippie dippy bullshit." What it really is, is a way to slow your heart rate, ease your stress levels, center your mind, and control the intrusive thoughts that lead to stress and anxiety. This allows you to think your own thoughts instead of having your thoughts racing out of control, which is especially scary since thoughts are the precursors to action. You might think you don't have time to fit this stuff into your busy schedule. To that I say: see the hitting-the-wall analogy from above.

How can you not have time to fit into your own damn life, my friend?

So, now you know the three things that might be keeping you stuck in a job: The Money Trap, The Creativity Trap, and the Stress Trap.

What are the traps you're facing now? I encourage you to write down all the reasons you have for leaving, all the things that make you hate your job. If you need a little inspiration, visit **permissiontokickass.com/guide** to get the companion guide. Check out the Reasons to Leave exercise inside. When you know why you need to go, you're in a much better position to give yourself permission to make your move.

Getting Fired from a Job I Didn't Have

I wish I was writing a book that told you all you have to do is quit your job, and you'll be instantly, wildly successful. I know I secretly hoped for overnight fame and glory. Combine that with the way I left that office to people literally chanting my name… that made it all the more painful when after months on my own, I struggled to make ends meet.

In my first 14 days as a freelancer, I'd billed five figures. I tracked it—starting on January 4th, it took me until the 18th to book five figures of work. I thought I'd made it and subsequently fell prey to one of the classic blunders that ensnare (and sometimes shut down) new freelancers: I stopped prospecting and promoting my own business to fulfill the client work I'd just booked. So, this one is a writer-downer:

Don't ever stop prospecting, no matter how busy you get. Better to turn away or refer out extra business than to not have enough (more on how to get clients in Chapter 9)**.**

When I finished the projects for my clients in early February, I was exhausted from working around the clock to do a good job. I took a week off to relax (which was a first for me). Then I started to promote my biz again. It took another couple weeks to ramp up—given the exhaustion and busy-ness from the first time around—and I was hesitant to hit my marketing as hard as I had in January. As a result, I booked less work and made less money. I kept prospecting, but the nature of the beast is it takes time—because not everyone is ready to book work when you're ready to do the work. So, I watched my income dwindle, my savings empty… and I started to panic.

Until I got a call from my old boss, who was still working at the retail company where I'd been a senior copywriter. We'd stayed in touch the entire time, and I'd even done some one-off project work for him here and there as I took care of other client projects. Now, someone on the team was going on vacation for a week, and he wanted to know if I'd come in and fill in for them on-site.

I ordinarily would have said "no" to the stressful commute, but my situation was getting desperate, and with not much support on the home front from my then-partner, I was feeling lonely, too. I was looking forward to hanging out with my old work homies again, so I agreed to the gig… commute and all.

Everything went great the whole week. I was enjoying the relatively easy work and reconnecting with my colleagues. Then Friday rolled around... on the last day of the 5-day contract at about 11 am, someone from HR walked over to my desk and said, "Your contract has been terminated. Please pack up your things and leave the building."

What the actual fuck?!

I looked at her and said, "Okay, I know that we worked together for years, but technically speaking, I'm a contractor who doesn't know who you are and what authority you have to remove me from the building. I am happy to respect your request if I hear it from my on-site supervisor."

"That's not possible," she said. "You have 15 minutes to collect your belongings and exit the premises."

She stood there like a hall monitor, refusing to move until I started packing. I looked around and noticed the department was suspiciously quiet, empty cubes all around.

"Tell me what is going on. I'm not moving until I talk to my supervisor," I told her.

Looking around nervously, she told me, "You'll find out soon enough."

Meanwhile, I was repeatedly calling and texting my supervisor, along with the creative agency that had contracted me to do the on-site work. With no one getting back to me (and the HR lady doing her best to loom over me like the Stay Puft Marshmallow Man from *Ghostbusters*), I packed up. Once in my car, I continued calling whomever I could, trying to find out what was going on.

After about 15 minutes, I finally got a text back from my old manager and on-site supervisor: "We all just got the ax."

That day, the company laid off the entire creative team and replaced it with an outside agency. To boot, the way they went about it was shady as fuck. They called the creative team into one room and gave them the news, trading severance payments for signing paperwork promising not to sue. In the room next door, the strategic marketing team was being served donuts and orange juice as they were being introduced to the agency team.

Then the company took it a step further and had the ENTIRE HR team standing by in the Creative department when the meeting ended. My friends and colleagues were given 15 minutes to clear out. You can't easily clean out years of desk junk in 15 minutes, nor is that enough time to collect sample work to help you build a portfolio. And they weren't even allowed access to their computers to be able to grab that sample work! I hung around to help them load stuff into their cars as best I could, until yet another HR minion came out and threatened to call the cops on me for trespassing if I did not immediately leave the premises.

Some of my colleagues had been with the company for decades, and they walked out with whatever they could throw into a box. Then they had to load up their cars and leave with HR standing in the parking lot supervising, as if these people they'd known and worked with for years actually wanted to come back into a place where they weren't wanted.

Stormy Angie definitely made an appearance after the trespass threat. I figured I didn't have a horse in the race 'cause I hadn't worked there for months. I yelled, insisting they could at least PRETEND they gave a damn about people they worked with for years instead of giving them the cold shoulder. Maybe they could even help load the boxes into cars if they were so fucking concerned with getting everyone off company property?

Because we were all shocked and feeling low, I actually wound up at a bar drinking my sorrows away with the rest of the team. I felt their pain, just as if I'd lost my job too. And considering how I didn't technically have a job at the company and was screaming at HR staff… can you imagine how riled up I would have been if I'd talked myself into staying only to be laid off four months later? I probably would have stroked out right there in the parking lot.

The fact is, when you're working for someone else, they're running a business and they have costs to consider. This is something you'll become super familiar with as a business owner, if you aren't already. When spending exceeds what they are bringing in, they're going to have to cut expenses. And even when you bring in money and are a revenue generator for the business, you could still be cut.

Somebody at the top might not understand the value or the money you're bringing in. I know because that happened to me. I made the company tens of millions and still had a hard time convincing them of my value. And that was the same job where the whole creative department (i.e., the people who made the advertisements that drove the bulk of sales) got let go. The company leaders couldn't see the forest for the trees.

Here's the thing: you could work your ass off to make the company money, put your heart and soul into the work… and they still have no obligation to keep paying you when they're losing money.

The most interesting (and sad) piece of this whole story is that their efforts to save money didn't end up helping… about a year after the creative team was let go, the entire chain was shut down. This was years after the Great Recession of 2007-08, and before the massive job losses that happened in 2020 during the pandemic. An entire company shut down during a period of relative economic growth. And it really didn't have anything to do with Angie and the creative department, or how good we were. It can happen to anybody.

By contrast, in my business, I'm the only one that can fire me… unless I sell what I've built to a publicly traded company where the board could conceivably fire me. But if that's the case, then I'd only have sold my business if I'd be making so much money that I wouldn't really care if I got fired. My point still stands… walking away is within my control. No one can stroll into my home office one day and tell me it's over, pack your things and get out.

If you get nothing else out of this rant, remember that the big boys are in just as much danger as any of the small companies out there. People depended on that company for their entire livelihood, and they were devastated when someone had to make a numbers decision that didn't really take the employees' lives into consideration. That's why the only safe bet that you can make is on yourself—because you have control over how you move forward, how much you have in savings, and what steps you can take next. You can pivot and do things in a way that these big companies can't.

At first I was scared to make the leap, but I've come to love having my own business. It's how I took back power over my own life. I took a big risk… and while building my business, at first, I certainly didn't have steady income or a 401(k). What I did have was control. I could control how much I prospected for new business, how much new work I took on, how much I charged for that work, and how I structured my business. If a client went away or a payment was missed, I could hustle a little harder and make that income up way easier than trying to beg someone in corporate to advance me money or give me a raise.

I didn't know it on the day I got fired from the job I didn't have, but I'd harbored this secret thought that, *I could always go back if this freelance thing didn't work out*. Then the safety net was pulled out from under me, and I had to commit or quit and start hunting for a new job.

So, I went all in and bet on myself.

It occurred to me that when I bet on me, "me" had to take care of business or give up her freedom. I knew I could figure out how to bridge the income gaps between what I was bringing in and what I wanted to make. It turns out I'd outgrown the three big traps that kept me stuck for years, and being let go wound up being the proof I needed to believe I was on the right path as a freelancer.

I knew enough successful freelancers to understand that when I'd figured out the client-getting part of it, I could get help and get better at business. And that's exactly what I did. For every challenge I encountered, I invested in resources, training, and coaching to help me get to where I wanted to be.

Over time, as I grew my skills as a business owner and freelancer, my income leveled out and gave me back the so-called "stability" I was missing from my old day job. In fact, I was making more than most in my family had ever made at a day job, working half as much. That's not to brag… it just goes to show you that often, stories you tell yourself wind up being true simply because you don't see any other options beside the one you've told yourself is "real."

To quote Ron Swanson, "Don't half ass two things. Whole ass one thing."

Commit. Take the risk. Invest in yourself.

If you're going to play, you might as well play to win.

Chapter 2: The Real Cost of NOT Living Your Dream

I had an aunt who deeply understood the cost of not living your dream. Aunt Chris didn't get her Master's degree until she was in her 60s. Here's how she described her decision to go all-in:

"I was always going to turn 60, whether I had the degree or not. Might as well have the degree!"

I love Aunt Chris. She taught me so much, and though she's gone, her lessons live on and inspire me just about every day. Look, I get how tempting it is to indulge the inner drama queen and think, *It's far too late for me, save yourselves!* while falling onto a fainting couch.

I have a bit of a contrarian approach to this though—*late is infinitely better than never*. This is true whether we're talking about starting a business, getting an education, meeting new people, or opening a savings account. If you're still breathing, you've still got time to get out there and kick ass, whatever that looks like for you.

Resist the urge to indulge in "it's too late for me" thinking. We're not talking about a plane that takes off and leaves you behind, we're talking about your life. If life is a plane, it's YOUR plane… and it's up to you to get on board. Presumably, if you're reading this book, you're alive.

So long as you're alive, now is as good a time as any.

Now I can't promise you that just by putting yourself out there and following your dream you'll have instant and lasting success. However, I can tell what will happen if you DON'T follow your dream—maybe you won't be any worse than you are now, but I'm willing to bet you're not going to be that much better off either.

Unfortunately, everything you've done that got you to this point will not get you to the next stage. The next stage requires change, bravery, and facing the unknown. And that resistance to change is exactly what keeps so many talented people stuck in a situation that no longer works. It's not your fault if you resist change—it's scary! It requires pain and risk.

You don't get bigger muscles by lounging on the couch and dreaming up your ideal workout plan—you get stronger by getting your ass to the gym (or at least doing some pushups at your own house). The same goes for relationships. You don't make new friends, or find the love of your life, by holing up at home and refusing to communicate with others.

That means if you want to fill a real bank account with real dollars, you'll have to do more than dream up a hundred ways to make money—you'll have to take action on one (or more) of those ideas.

And yes, with great reward comes great risk.

You could pull a muscle or get injured during a workout. You could lose money on a bad investment (or by lending it to a friend—that's a rant for another day). You could have your heart broken. While these things are painful, none of them have life-or-death dire consequences (even if it feels like they do).

If you pull a muscle, you take time to recover, and then maybe next time you hire a trainer for a couple of sessions to help you figure out how to build muscle in a way that minimizes your risk of injury. If you make a bad investment, you dig deep into what attracted you to the opportunity (and what made it fall apart), and you use your newfound wisdom to better evaluate future choices. As my stepdad, Bob, is fond of saying, "It's just money. I can always make more."

This goes beyond business. Every decision you make can be unmade. That doesn't mean it will be EASY—but it can be done.

If you wind up in a bad relationship, you can leave it. That's not to minimize the experience, but as someone who's survived an abusive relationship, I can tell you that betting on myself was the best choice I could have made. I'm a million times happier on my own, living life on my terms, than I ever could have been trying to figure out how to live under someone else's rules—especially when the goalposts changed every week.

I can't give you solid numbers to show you what you are missing out on when you don't take a chance on your dream, at least not along the lines of fancy compounding interest formulas a financial adviser might have. Because the scary part is that I can't guarantee any specific results or outcomes. Business is kind of like a computer in that way—sometimes it just doesn't work, and the reasons are countless.

Things not working as you'd hoped doesn't mean you got everything wrong, or that you weren't meant to do this.

Sometimes it's timing. Sometimes it's messaging or pricing. Hell, I have a friend whose new product wasn't making sales. On a lark, he stopped his paid Facebook ad campaigns, duplicated those ads, restarted those ads using the duplicates, and suddenly started making sales. I never in my life thought starting a business could benefit from the old IT trick of "turn it off and turn it on again," but apparently, that can be the case when it comes to paying for advertisements.

Now that's a little more advanced than you need to worry about right now if you're just starting out. Running ads is another skill you can add to your arsenal as you grow as an entrepreneur. But for our purposes, money loves action and speed. You don't need to know everything there is to know to get started, so don't get stuck in endless planning loops.

The bottom line is… what you're feeling is normal.

If it was easy to follow your dreams, everyone would be doing it. But it's not easy, so the majority settles. My hope for you is that you're as inspired by my Aunt Chris as I am… and that you try—even if you're scared—and especially if you worry it's too late. If you try, you might fail, but if you don't try, there's zero chance you'll ever realize your dream. I don't know about you, but I'd rather risk failing and being that much closer to the dream than give up before I even get started.

Don't Overthink It

At one point during the six months of limbo, when I was waffling about leaving the toxic gig, I had a colleague reach out and offer to talk me off the ledge. We set up a phone call, and one of the first things he asked me to do was break down the reasons I needed to leave my job. He patiently listened to my theatrics, and worries-gone-wild, for the better part of a half hour, and then he gave me the kind of advice I call "a loving ass-kicking."

He told me, "Angie, you could find a part-time job if you're worried about covering your basic bills. But as long as you're writing all day at work, and then coming home and writing all night… you're not giving your best to either your job or your clients." He was right—I could only sustain this pace for so long before one of them would have to go. I was holding onto the job to create stability for the business, but so long as I was tied to the job, the business couldn't grow—I didn't have the bandwidth.

This is an easy trap to fall into—getting stuck worrying and overthinking. If I had to guess where it comes from, I'd say the school system (at least here in the United States). We learn how to memorize facts for tests and how to perform a series of tasks that equals good grades—but we don't really learn how to fail or solve problems. That much became clear to me during my least favorite (at the time) class at Carnegie Mellon—Entrepreneurship.

In Entrepreneurship, the professor assigned an absurd amount of group projects, and we worked with the same 4-5 people all semester. Our first project was a practice pitch deck, where we did a mock presentation to venture capitalists (VCs) to get funding for our hypothetical business. Of course, my group was full of A-driven overachievers. We were hell-bent on getting top marks and nailing this presentation.

We spent all week on our first pitch, working late into the night on slide design, scripting the presentation, and rehearsing. We delivered it flawlessly and got a B+. We were floored (and frankly, pissed) because we knew one of the other groups had pulled an all-nighter and thrown together their presentation at the last minute, and got an A. It didn't make any damn sense to me that someone could put less time and effort in than I did and make a better grade.

So, when we got assigned another practice pitch, we collectively leaned into the feisty butthurt feelings from our first project and deliberately waited until the last minute to throw our presentation together. To our utter shock, we got an A. It took me years to stop being bitter enough to figure out that the class I hated the most—because I couldn't figure out the "right" steps to get that coveted A—taught me the most about how the real world works. The real world doesn't care whether you worked your ass off. It only cares that you delivered.

And sometimes delivering can be a lot simpler than you might think.

Years later, after starting (and failing at) my first freelance business, I realized what went wrong in that first pitch (and in my business)… overthinking it. We would debate and challenge each other, tweaking and tightening until we got something that felt "perfect." We changed things around, doubted if our choices were right, and frankly, obsessed over all the wrong things.

In our singular focus on getting that good grade, we lost sight of the bigger picture—how to please the hypothetical VC, versus pleasing the professor. When we had to think on the fly for our second presentation, we lasered into what really mattered in a good pitch without getting distracted by ancillary bullshit. Now, I don't advise putting off work until the very last minute as a general strategy for success. But I do hope you got the big takeaway here, and that is:

Working harder isn't the same as working smarter.

Case in point, back to Entrepreneurship class for what would be the final project. One night, the professor came in with a fistful of $50 bills. She divided us into our groups and gave each group one of the bills. "Using this money, and ONLY this money," she said, "you have two weeks to go out and make me more money. You are not allowed to add your personal money to this seed fund. You ARE allowed to reinvest what you make back into your business. The group that makes the most money in two weeks gets to keep all the money made by all the groups. Now go."

I was all jazzed up to win—because my group had quickly figured out that the building where our class was held didn't have a café, only vending machines. You had to go to another building to get food. As the daughter of a pastry chef, I offered to make cookies and other baked treats so that our colleagues could grab a quick snack between classes. One of our members was a musician, and she put on shows, and made CDs and sold them. We held an art workshop in our hall so folks could have a creative outlet. We hustled HARD for those two weeks and managed to haul in around $350.

The winning group came in with around $450. They had also noticed the lack of food options in our building, so they took their seed money to a local restaurant. They bought $50 worth of food, resold it at a marked-up price, then went back and bought more, and repeated that process for two weeks until they won.

That group made more money than we did, and they did it with a lot less effort. They took our idea and did it better. I took a little comfort in the fact that the professor made the winning group buy the whole class dinner before formally collecting and awarding them all our hard-earned money. And true to form, the winning team partnered with their preferred restaurant for an economical (and wonderfully tasty) buffet dinner.

My group members had put in a lot of time and heart. Each of us spent hours creating what we sold, not to mention the time staffing the sales table, running the workshop, and advertising our products. We'd essentially recreated our pitch deck fiasco all over again, and years after the fact, I was able to see that we had this deeply embedded idea that "making money is totally possible, but you have to work hard." It makes total sense that the plan we came up with was possible, but hard. The winning group showed that making money was possible and could be simple when you don't overthink and over-plan.

This isn't just true for business—it works for creative projects, too. In a different class, screenwriting, I struggled with every script assignment because I thought I had to be some sort of brilliant, 100% original world builder who dreamed up everything out of thin air. Each week I'd tried my damnedest to invent amazing worlds and stand-out characters, and each week when the class read them out loud, my scripts would fall flat—to the point I seriously started doubting my writing ability.

Perhaps sensing my frustration, the screenwriting professor told a crazy story of something that'd happened to her that she wound up incorporating into one of her scripts. "You can't make this shit up," she said. "Odds are, the stuff you see happening in your favorite TV show or in the movies happened to the writer or someone they know. You want to tell good stories? Become a good observer. The best stories come from real life." *Easy for you to say,* I thought.

A week or two later, she'd given us a comedy script assignment. It just so happened that in the span of a few days, I'd had a series of conversations with different people about quirky grandmothers. One person's grandmother had discovered the wonderful world of online dating but would only accept dates with men named Jim. Another took her daily medicine religiously at 5 pm—and that "medicine" was a shot of Jack Daniels. Another had found an at-home, non-surgical facelift kit, where she attached small pieces of tape to her scalp around her hairline and literally pulled her face back with strings hidden by her hair.

I rolled those stories into one character, creating one over-the-top grandma who took her "medicine" every day at 5 pm, dated only men named Jim, and taped her face up in a self-fashioned facelift every day. When we read the script out loud, the whole class was rolling. It was the first time I'd gotten any kind of reaction from my work, and that exercise forever changed the way I create. These days I'm an observer of life. I write what I know, and I pay attention to what's going on around me. And in consciously making that choice, I started noticing what a weird and wonderful world it is, and how we can find inspiration all around us on any given day if only we pay attention.

So, heads up—when you go for your dream, odds are you will want to overthink this. Don't. Building a business certainly isn't easy, but it doesn't have to be hard. Keep it simple as you're getting started. My Lemonade Stand model will help with that (more on that in Chapter 3).

What You're Feeling is Normal

By now, you may have noticed a lot of feelings swirling around whenever you start thinking, *Maybe I should start my own business!* One minute it's, *Oh hell yeah, these people have taken advantage of me for far too long, and now I'm going to show 'em*! And the next it's, *What am I thinking? I'll have to go crawling back!*

Congrats! You're experiencing the entrepreneurial emo rollercoaster. Welcome to the club, because this is how most of us feel on any given day, even after doing this for years. Need proof? Check out my podcast, Permission to Kick Ass. I've interviewed over a hundred entrepreneurs who tell similar stories of feeling like they're floundering even when they're winning by every definition of the word.

I'd be lying if I told you that you eventually gain enough confidence for these feelings to go away. Unfortunately, stepping out of your comfort zone will become a normal part of doing business, which means you develop a certain level of comfort in never really feeling like you know what you're doing. To you I say…

What you're feeling is totally normal.

Some of the most successful people you know, maybe even people you really admire, feel like this from time to time as well. If anything, that should help you know you're in the right place. If all entrepreneurs feel this way at some point, and you're feeling this way… doesn't that make you one of us?

I know I felt like a fraud, especially in my first few years. The first online copywriter community I found (before Copy Chief) was a hyper-macho, super competitive place where bragging was the name of the game. That made me feel even more insecure… so I played along. Even though I didn't have the steadiest business out there, I boasted and bragged and showed off my swagger with the best of them. Then it backfired in the best possible way.

Someone in the community clued me into an upcoming event for copywriters called the Action Seminar. It was put on by an industry leader whose writing I really admired (John Carlton) and who promised all kinds of invaluable education. I expressed interest in going and suddenly, all the dudes in this community were saying, "See you at the Action Seminar, Angie!"

I knew that the high-level people I wanted to meet—the people who really did well in the copywriting world—would be there. I figured I could drive six hours to San Diego, no problem, but there was also the issue of the $600 ticket price to get in. At that time, I didn't have that kind of cash, but all the people I knew and admired were excited to see me there, and I wanted to meet them in person. Suddenly, broke-ass, posturing Angie had to figure out a way to pay for this event she couldn't really afford.

At the time, I was super embarrassed at what I did next, and I hid it for years because I saw it as a sign of failure that I couldn't pay for things with "my own money." Now I see it for what it is—doing what I had to do to get where I felt I had to be. Basically, I created an IndieGoGo crowdfunding campaign. I didn't know it then, but there was something transformational about turning myself into the kind of copywriter and freelancer that pays her way to an event and becomes the real deal by doing so.

Even though I convinced myself I was begging for handouts at the time, I actually sold my way into the Action Seminar. I offered personalized, handwritten haikus for $5, dedicated songs at karaoke or band gigs for $20, and promised copywriting packages at a serious discount. I even had people reaching out to me privately for custom writing jobs because they saw my IndieGoGo campaign and didn't need what I offered but wanted to know if I'd work with them in some other capacity. That's the power of putting yourself out there, even if you feel silly.

In the end, I made about 200% more than I asked for (and that was a good thing, because I hadn't factored travel expenses into my initial budget). The money I earned was enough to buy the event ticket and pay for a hotel. This is critical because I sold the dream not only to my supporters… but also to myself.

Fast forward to the event, where I put on my best "Angie knows her shit" mask and pretended up a storm, hoping desperately that no one would figure out I was broke. That's where I first met my mentor, Kevin Rogers. I saw him speak on stage, and I wanted to be in his world. That night I found out where the speakers were going for drinks, and I dragged my then-boyfriend to that bar. I couldn't afford drinks, so I told the bartender to serve me water with lime and keep it coming. I was hungry but not about to pay $16 for sliders. I just wanted to rub elbows and show the A-listers that I belonged.

That weekend, even if temporarily, I was living the dream. I was in the room with the people I knew in my gut would help me get to the next stage. And if they could see me as a total pro, I was sure this was my ticket to that stability and writing success I craved.

My Action Seminar fantasy would be short-lived… a few weeks after I got back from the conference, I was in an accident and suddenly found myself in need of cash to replace a totaled car. Eventually, the need for cash got so desperate that I swallowed my posturing pride and reached out to a friend I met at the Action Seminar to let him know what happened and ask if he knew anyone who needed help with copy. That person ended up connecting me with a $2,500 writing gig (which was the biggest project I'd booked to date).

At the time, I was embarrassed that I "needed" a friend to refer me and felt that it was somehow shameful I couldn't find that $2,500 gig on my own. I was pleasantly surprised when that friend didn't unleash judgment on me like I'd feared. It only took that one genuine connection to change my whole perspective on outreach—talk about an investment that literally paid for itself!

Caveat: there was no way to know it would pan out that way before I went. And you can't realistically evaluate business and networking events on the money you expect to earn. The value is in what you expect to learn and the connections you expect to make. Events are a long-term play.

The point is, none of those projects would've happened if I hadn't decided I needed to be in the room, then done what it took to get there.

Sure, it was risky, but something in my gut told me I needed to do it, and I'm so glad I listened. I can trace years' worth of relationships and ongoing business back to the people I met at that one event. And once I got over the shame I held around having to crowdfund my way into an event, I started sharing this story and hearing similar ones from other entrepreneurs—they'd been scared and made a calculated risk, which paid off in unexpected ways.

I hope this story shows you the realities of the shame-elation rollercoaster that many of us experience on the business-building journey. When you choose to become an entrepreneur, some days you're convinced you're the fucking best, and everybody better recognize. Then the pendulum swings, and you might find yourself feeling lower than garbage, like you were stupid to ever believe you could have a business. Neither of these feelings is 100% true though… the reality is somewhere in the middle.

Now, I'm not saying avoid the emotions. When you feel doubt or confusion, or other negative emotions, feel them and deal with them as best you can… otherwise they'll pop up at inconvenient times and demand to be dealt with. Those feelings don't mean you ought to stop or shouldn't try. But whatever you do, don't cave to the emotions and let them steer your ship—because they're temporary and will pass.

I once experienced some wild emotional swings in the aftermath of a breakup and was trying to figure out what to do next with my business. My good friend Marcella Allison told me, "HALT. Never make decisions when you're Hungry, Angry, Lonely, or Tired." That's phenomenal advice. You need a clear head to make rational and logical decisions that will benefit you in the long run.

Feel the feelings, find the one that propels you in the direction you want to go, and strap in, baby. It's probably going to get bumpy. But trust me and Aunt Chris, it's WORTH it.

Chapter 3: Fears Keeping You Stuck

If I'm being honest with myself, I've been an entrepreneur since I was a tiny tyke. There used to be this company called Olympia Sales Club that would advertise in magazines like *Highlights*. The idea was to go door-to-door selling candles and other kitschy home goods. During 4th and 5th grade, I sold for Olympia in south Texas—dripping with sweat in the after-school heat. This was back when kids could wander their neighborhoods unsupervised, knocking on random doors without folks calling the cops on working-class parents (that's a rant for another day though). My mom worked nights back then, so my sister and I were expected to stay outside until the streetlights came on so Mom could sleep.

For some reason, I was all in on that sales club. It never occurred to me to care if someone didn't buy the candles, and I didn't feel that their "no" somehow reflected on me as a person. I'd shrug it off and go knock on the next door, because those prizes weren't going to earn themselves. I didn't even worry about whether I was selling the "right" way. I just kept asking people and figured it out as I went. Not for a phone or a bike, but for an alarm clock. It was a clock RADIO, and I really wanted that thing for reasons I still don't quite understand... especially since I've deliberately crafted a life around NOT needing an alarm clock.

I'd go on to make keychains and homemade baked goods and sell them to kids at school. I have no idea what the profit margin was on that stuff since mom bought all my supplies, but I sure as hell felt R-I-C-H with that sweet, sweet $10 burning a hole in my pocket. Back then, I was trying things and seeing what happened as if it was an experiment. I think that's the key—instead of putting life-or-death pressure on any one opportunity, try it out to see what happens. Maybe give it a couple different tries before deciding you weren't meant to do this. Take it from kid Angie (who eventually DID get that sweet ass alarm clock).

Let's do a quick thought exercise: imagine what might be possible for you if suddenly all the fears were gone. They vanished overnight, and there was nothing left blocking you. Instead of psyching yourself up to go to work because it's what you've got to do to pay bills and support the family… you're practically leaping out of bed because you GET to go to work. You're doing work you love, making the kind of money that excites you.

Maybe that seems like a stretch, or something totally unrealistic… but then again, it's exactly what kid Angie was doing back in the day, before "adulting" took over. Maybe it's more possible than you think—the only difference is the amount of money to bring in ('cause even I can admit $10 and an alarm clock ain't gonna cut it in the 21st century).

I'm going to encourage you to keep that vision in your mind as a reminder of what's possible when you remove the obstacles (to the best of your ability—you'll never remove them ALL, but we can get rid of more than we think). The reason is simple yet powerful: when you focus your mind on the shitty parts of life instead of the possibilities, you're indulging in a self-fulfilling prophecy because you're training your brain to only spot stuff that sucks. When that's all you see, it's easy to feel overwhelmed and unhappy and like everything feels wrong. Of course it feels wrong—you can't see anything good happening around you!

I don't want you to get stuck in that place where fear takes over your life, so let's work on refocusing and reconfiguring what you see. You've got to remember your reasons WHY (instead of your reasons why NOT) and look for examples of people doing the thing you want to do. I promise they're out there—and they may even be looking for someone like you to partner with. I'm not suggesting that success is as easy as visualization, because it's not.

But the first step to achieving anything is believing that you actually can.

Until you think it's possible (and truly believe that you can do this thing), you'll find new and inventive ways to forestall trying. That makes this perhaps some of the most important prep work you can do for yourself—reframing what you see and training your brain to look for more reasons WHY to do something.

So that's exactly what we will do in this chapter—dig in and find the real root of the fear so we can address it and keep moving. And since fears often pop up in the form of questions-with-no-answers-stuck-on-a-loop, I will do my best to answer the most common ones I hear.

How Will I Know What to Do?

Unfortunate truth: you won't until you just start doing things.

Basically, you don't have to have it all figured out upfront before you make a move. You can learn as you go—most of us do.

Some things you do will feel good or produce a result that excites you. Some things will feel not so good or produce a negative result (thus teaching you what NOT to do moving forward). Some things will produce zero results whatsoever, and you might feel like trying was a giant waste of time. Try not to go there—because all of this, the good, the bad, and the not-a-damn-thing-happened—it's all good data. This is your on-the-job learning.

I don't like asking, "What should I do?" It's a blocker question. It's so open-ended, and has so many possible answers, that asking it often leads to something called "analysis paralysis." That's when you've got a bunch of different options to choose from, and the thought of choosing one is so overwhelming that you don't do anything. Good news, though—there is a cure, and that's action.

Action is the antidote to overwhelm.

Action narrows down infinite paths and possibilities and gives you just the one path in front of you and the limited options that branch off that path.

Analysis paralysis is a close cousin of overthinking, and it's common when starting out—it feels like business is this complicated thing that others have figured out that you can't possibly know. The truth is good business is simple—it's showing up every day with something of value to offer and making the ask or sale. Some folks wind up failing because they make it way more complicated and lose sight of the consistent little daily actions that lead to long-term success.

Especially at the beginning of the entrepreneurial journey, it's easy to get overwhelmed with options:

Do I need a bank account?

Do I need a tax code?

Do I need to incorporate?

Do I need a website?

Do I need an assistant?

What about business cards?

Should I sell a product or a service?

You get so involved in coming up with questions that you don't necessarily have answers to… AND you don't necessarily even need to answer now. That overanalyzing stops you from acting, the same way overthinking can kill creativity and innovation.

So, when you're feeling overwhelmed by options, the trick is to recognize the anxiety and get out of your own head.

Talk to people in your network. Reach out to mentors. You don't need a contingency plan for every fork in the road before you get moving. And you don't need to know all the answers. The questions don't all need answers now. Many of them can wait.

I think there's a reason many aspiring entrepreneurs feel like they can't get support from their employee buddies. It's rooted in the perpetual dreamer trope... that stereotype where someone is stuck in fantasyland, picturing that perfect business they'll have someday when the stars are aligned. But taking the steps to make that vision a reality is scary because failure is a possibility. So, many people get stuck in that dreamer space, where they overanalyze and never act. They get caught up in creating a plan and a backup plan and a backup-backup plan and researching all the options.

If you want success in life, you've got to be willing to step forward, fall on your face, and think, *Well, that hurt. I guess I'm going to do that differently next time.*

I continually learn this lesson, not just in business but in daily life too. I once had the opportunity to take a course called "French and Snow" in northern Quebec. As I'm sure you can guess, the point was to get good at conversational French while indulging in outdoor winter sports—in January in northern Quebec. The challenge? I'm from south Texas and, at that point, had seen snow maybe twice in my entire life.

So how could I have possibly known you shouldn't wear cotton socks (or really cotton anything) in cold, snowy places? I made that mistake on my first day in Quebec and quickly made my way to the store in search of wool ones. Wool wicks moisture away, keeping your skin dry and toasty. Cotton absorbs moisture, keeping it close to your skin and making you feel colder.

There wasn't really a way for me to wrap my head around that until I experienced it for myself.

That's what I mean when I say some things you simply won't know until you experience it for yourself. There is no way, growing up in south Texas with our 115-degree summers, that I would ever have had the chance to learn that wearing cotton in the snow is not a great idea. That wasn't anywhere in my worldview. Snow wasn't even real as far as I was concerned because up to that point, I'd never seen "real" snow (the kind that sticks versus melting as soon as you breathe on it).

Once I got into snowy weather, I learned about it pretty quickly. Did my foot get frostbite and fall off? Thankfully no… because I asked for advice from folks who lived in areas with cold weather and took myself out to buy new socks so that I could be more comfortable. And it's the same thing with building your business. That's all it is—learning by doing, adjusting, pivoting, and moving forward.

Be gentle with yourself—learning to think like a business owner is a new skill.

How Will I Know I'm Ready?

I've got news for you. You probably won't ever feel ready, at least not like you're hoping. There's no flashing red sign that pops up, cartoon style, to let you know, "The time is now!" There's no wise old master who pours their knowledge into you, puts you through a series of tests, and proclaims you ready. The tests you go through to get ready are the ones you create for yourself by acting despite the uncertainty. Make peace (to the best of your ability) with feeling uncertain. You're ready ENOUGH.

We're pretty much all making it up as we go, so jump in and give yourself permission to figure it out on the fly.

That's exactly how you get the experience you're looking for. So many of my own personal leaps forward came from following this advice, so I want you to know I eat my own cooking here. Years back, when I was two weeks into my first full-time role as a salaried copywriter, I was going through the training and learning more about the company. The Creative Director (my boss at the time) came up to me and asked how the holiday catalog was progressing. Figuring I must have heard him wrong (because this was the first I had heard of it), I innocently asked, "What holiday catalog?"

"The one we're reviewing on Friday. You know, Christmas, gift giving, holiday time. Where are you at on writing the catalog?" At that point, I'd never written a catalog. I'd never worked in the special layout software the team used to create the catalog. All I knew was that I had three days to write a catalog, so I didn't waste time wondering how to do it—I just did it! When I didn't have the luxury of time to worry and stress, I taught myself the software and cobbled together a good-enough first draft to keep things moving and eventually get my first catalog out on time.

Was it my best piece of work? Absolutely not. Did I learn a ton? Hell yeah! And then I became the go-to catalog writer for the company because they knew I could crank out that copy, even on totally unreasonable deadlines (a fact that would later come back to bite me in the ass. Ah Angie, you were so young and naïve).

The best part was I got PAID to figure it out, my friend.

They didn't tell me to graduate from some catalog writing class before I was "good enough" to write. I didn't have to get certified as a catalog writer before they let me near their precious pages. They trusted me to figure it out, and I did.

The same is true of you and your business and your clients. As a business owner, you won't have a "boss" telling you what to do—you'll have to figure out what the next step is. And when you trust yourself to do the work, you usually find a way to do it.

The good news is that most people you work with won't know you're making it up as you go—and those of us who do (because we are too) are rooting for you to succeed. A rising tide lifts all boats. Now, I'm not saying you should promise someone you can achieve certain results when you're not even sure you know how to do the project. But have faith that you can figure out HOW to do the project.

Take a page from my brilliant friend's book. (I wish I'd learned of this sooner because I'd be even further along than I am). He'd sell a client on a big, ambitious project, something he really wanted to learn and level up to. Then he'd go hire an expert in that kind of project to show him how it's done and coach him through it. He sacrificed most of his project fee (sometimes all of it) in paying that pro to walk him through the process, but he also knew from that point forward he had the knowledge and experience to take on that project again… and command top dollar for himself as an expert.

That's a way to figure it out versus "faking it until you make it." Buy yourself a little extra time and do one of three things:

- Get thee to Google and figure it out through trial and error.
- Ask your network for solutions and pick one that seems like it'll work.
- Invest in hiring someone to coach you through.

Let's also reframe the question from "How will I know I'm ready?" to "How can I start scared?"

You can't expect to get it perfect the first time around. The odds of you becoming an overnight success are about as likely as you winning the lotto.

Don't count on it happening to you. You can certainly play the game and hope for a big payday, but you better have a backup plan.

This is the long game, not the lotto. And the same rule applies: you can't win if you don't actually play. It's not very realistic to think that you're going to figure out everything in advance, hit the ground running, and achieve massive success with no struggle whatsoever. So, get rid of that fantasy—because that's all it is, a fantasy. If it happens to anybody out there, that is pure and utter luck, and you can't build a future on luck.

And I want to shatter a persistent myth here and now: "Overnight success" is not a thing.

It sells more magazines and clicks to talk about how someone skyrocketed to success, coming out of nowhere to become a media and investor darling. But the reality is most "overnight" successes are ten years in the making. Even 20+ years, in some cases.

In the real world, luck happens when preparation meets opportunity. In other words, you make your own.

Another way to think of failure is in context. Take Thomas Edison and the light bulb. Granted, there's a whole debate over whether he or Nikola Tesla deserved credit for the invention. However, I love the quote attributed to Edison. It was a struggle to get this thing made, and essentially he said, "I just found 2,000 ways not to make a lightbulb; I only needed to find one way to make it work."

What could you achieve if you used every failure as proof that you're getting closer to success?

Put another way: if you tripped and fell flat on your face, would you lay there and wait for death? Let's lean into this a bit, really indulge in the drama. Picture leaves falling in piles around your prone (yet still living) body. Bicyclists running over you like some weird sentient speed bump. Snow drifts rising up around you as the seasons change.

Does that sound a little ridiculous? I certainly hope so. And yet it's how so many would-be entrepreneurs treat their business… as if any mistake means instant and lasting failure. Or like failure goes on some sort of permanent record that follows you around like a poltergeist, throwing things and shrieking any time you even think of trying again.

Why so serious, yo?

Be proud of those failures. Collect them. Treasure them. They're going to make for an amazing story someday as you sit around with other entrepreneurs, comparing scars. Because trust me, that's where the best stories come from—failing spectacularly.

Where Do I Start?

My answer may sound a little overly simplistic, but I stand by it. First, a little context: when I was a kiddo, making money was as easy as starting a lemonade stand on a hot day. You only needed a table in a busy neighborhood, cold lemonade, cash for change, and thirsty people.

Think of your business, at least in the early stages, in a similar fashion. Start simple, with just four basic things:

1. A product or service to offer
2. People who want to buy that product or service
3. A way to take money (cash and PayPal count—I'm serious about not complicating it)
4. Email address or some other way for them to get in touch with you

That's it. That's where you start. Seems like there should be more to it, I know... but people do it every day in online marketplaces and at flea markets. Think about it—they basically have something for sale, a way to take money from people, and people that want to buy the thing they're selling.

This applies easily to online or service-based businesses too. The bare minimum that you need is an email address where people can contact you, something that you can sell, and if that's a digital product, a way to send it to people. You could keep that digital product as a file on your computer and send it to buyers via email. You could also use that same email to sign up for PayPal so you can easily take payments.

I could make you a much longer list of crap you might hear about and think you need, but the reality is you don't need all those things to get started. You can always add websites, business cards, and a professional email address without "Gmail" in it after you start making sales.

You don't have to start fancy, but you do want to focus on bringing money in as quickly as possible. I promise that will motivate you a hell of a lot more than having a perfect website or beautiful business cards, both of which cost more than they earn you (at least in the beginning). That's the thing to focus on in the early days, especially—is this making me money or costing me money?

It's going to be trial and error once you've got your basic lemonade stand business set up. Once the money starts coming in, you can use finances as another data point to help you make better decisions (you remember me saying this is all good data, right?). You'll be able to evaluate, "Okay, am I making enough money to support myself? Am I charging enough to be profitable or am I losing money?"

And if the idea of "profit" makes you feel squeamish, stop that shit right now.

There is absolutely nothing wrong with profit. Profit is a natural reward for the risks of starting a business, and it's something to think about even in the early days. Don't aim to break even and make just enough to cover what you put in. Aim for enough to support you and your business—and then that little something extra. You've earned it for the (smart) risk you've taken in betting on yourself and starting a business.

By the way, you'll develop these skills over time as you encounter different growth situations in your business. They come largely from paying attention to cues like, *do I have to hustle and struggle every month? Okay, maybe I'm not charging enough. Maybe this thing isn't high enough value to sustain me, and I need to create something else I can charge more for*.

I'll say it again—a mistake is just another data point. It's not that the most successful people never make mistakes—they own it and then find another way forward.

Successful people learn from mistakes instead of pretending they never happened.

All this stuff is figure-outable. You need four bare minimum things to start a business: a product or service, people who want that product or service, a way to take money, and a way for people to contact you.

If you want to make it a little bit easier for yourself later on down the road, you're going to want to think about things like opening a business bank account, which in many cases, you can do virtually. **You absolutely should not use this as a reason to stall on starting to make money but do have this high up on your radar**—it's really going to help with taxes, which get complicated if you've got all your personal AND business income and expenses coming from the same account. You may need a business license for a business account with some banks, which you can easily obtain by going to your local city government, filling out some paperwork, and paying a fee.

The amount of that fee (and the paperwork, for that matter) depends largely on your local regulations, so it's best to Google "Start a business in [YOUR TOWN HERE]" to determine your next best steps. I've started my freelance business in towns from Northern California to Northeastern Florida, and the search engines never steered me wrong. Sometimes the local websites were confusing as fuck, and I'd have to call their office to get clarity, but that's how it goes.

The paperwork for a straight-up service-based freelancing business tends to be fairly straightforward—especially if you're not manufacturing, serving food, handling dangerous chemicals, or providing financial advice (all of which involve a whole lot of regulatory bodies, required insurance, and whatnot). For working out of your home and doing some freelancing on the side, the paperwork is pretty easy. Just find your local small business governmental office, file the paperwork, pay the fee to get your business license, send that license to the bank, and bam, you've got a business account.

How Do I Find Clients?

Let's start with a reality check: you can't (and shouldn't) be for everyone.

Yes, even if your product or service could truly help every person on the face of this earth, you shouldn't be for everyone.

Why? Because who you LIKE working with counts. Your preferences matter. And paying attention to your own likes and dislikes gets you that much closer to finding your ideal customer.

What do I mean by that? It's totally okay to decide you want to work with (or avoid) people in a certain industry. It's also okay to aim for (or avoid) a certain personality type. I can't work with flaky or dishonest people. And folks who think business is OMG SERIOUS will not like me and my "We can have fun AND make money" approach.

All of this is good data. There are literally billions of people on this planet, and you don't have to like or work with most of them.

Most of us go through a phase at the beginning when we want to help anyone with a need, convinced that we can help the whole world and all its inhabitants. But it's okay to design your company to suit you and your preferences. Forget the people who don't like you. You don't have to become someone they like, especially if you wouldn't like them much either!

Not everyone willing to hand you money will be a good client. And not everyone who needs what you offer will like you. Good news: you're not starting a business to be liked! You're starting a business to make a living, and not everyone will be supportive (or even nice about it).

Rather than stressing about working with someone who's not your cup of tea, free up that mental space for finding, connecting with, and serving someone you DO like. Don't waste any more time, emotion, or energy than you have to on people who aren't a fit—because even among all the people you would truly enjoy working with, you can't possibly personally do work for them all.

Translation: there is more than enough work to go around for ALL of us, even if we serve the exact same groups of people.

Personally, I don't work with doctors, lawyers, medical equipment manufacturers, financial advisers, or pickup artists. It's not that I don't like the PEOPLE doing those jobs. I'm just not a fan of the industries. Here's what I don't like about them (and I'll stress that this is my own personal opinion after having either worked with or met with potential clients to talk about projects):

- Doctors can often be too jargony, technical, and dispassionate.
- Lawyers tend to be too legal and focused on risk mitigation.
- Medical equipment manufacturers could be very dry and spec-sheet focused.
- Financial advisers are too heavily regulated (and some sectors are frankly predatory).
- Pickup artists (especially those who teach manipulative tactics) are just plain "ew."

Are there exceptions to those broad generalizations? Absolutely. I'm not saying those are bad industries to be in. I don't personally enjoy doing that work, so I don't do it. If someone in one of those industries comes to me (and they're not an exception), I connect them with people I know and don't even entertain the idea of doing that project. Why would I set myself up to face every day doing work I have no interest in?

This is my business, and I have agency over the work I choose to do. So do you.

By the way, all these preferences are things I learned "on the job," by taking projects that sounded interesting until I dug in and figured out they weren't my cup of tea. So, I'd finish the work as promised and use the experience as data to help me make better decisions in the future.

Some of these things you won't know until you experience them, so don't be afraid to take on projects and gigs just to see what happens. You may find a surprising new passion or have another "not interested in this" industry to add to your list. If you think of it as experimenting, especially in the beginning, learning what really excites you to do the work can be almost fun. And passion counts for a lot—otherwise, you might as well stay at the day job.

With my business, my love of writing is what kept me going when times were lean—because writers write. Whether I was getting paid or not, I was writing. So, consider: *what's that thing you'd do all day, even if you weren't getting paid*? And before you fall into the trap of thinking, "I love it, so if I do it all day for a job, I'll hate it," recognize that for what it is: a fear response. It's your brain trying to keep you safe and comfortable.

That's not to say you'll definitively love it or hate it if you make your passion into a vocation. Frankly there are downsides to everything. I'd be lying if I said I love writing 100% of the time. Sometimes I'm really frustrated with being a writer (for example—sitting down and making myself write this book with all my swirling fears about how it will be received). But 80-90% of the time, I'm thrilled to be able to pick up my laptop, go wherever, and bang out some thoughts. So, writing is a good choice for me. What's a good choice for you?

Now's a good time to go check out the Dinner Party Exercise in your companion guide (download for free at permissiontokickass.com/guide). That's where we'll go deeper into identifying your ideal customer.

What if I Can't Pay the Bills?

No doubt, you've been hoping we'd talk about money. This is where a LOT of the fear is probably coming from. I know that was the case for me, especially growing up relatively poor. In this section, I will cover more of the emotional and fear-driven responses to money, and later in Chapter 6, I'll share my practical strategies for saving money so you feel more comfortable taking short-term risks.

Let's do a quick thought exercise: if you had a $10k per month trust fund, do you think you could figure out how to make more money? If all your bills were paid, and suddenly the pressure to profit or perish disappeared, how much would that change your tolerance for taking risks? Do you notice a visceral feeling shift in your body when you imagine starting from, "Oh god,

I need this to work" versus, "Okay, I've got enough to pay the bills, so now let's see what happens"?

The first stance is one of desperation and subservience, and the second is one of power.

Here's the counterintuitive thing no one tells you about going into any project or partnership with an "I need this to work" approach… you may never say a word out loud about your shaky financial situation, but the clients will still get the message loud and clear. The reason is, you'll send out subconscious signals and do things you ordinarily might not, all because you're in the grips of fear about not having enough money.

I've seen folks answer emails at 3 am and when I challenge them, excuse it with, "Well, I WAS up at 3 am, so why wouldn't I answer?" Because you're sending an unconscious (and literal) message that they can contact you at any time they damn well please and expect a response, that's why! That is not a reasonable request from any client, ever. Period.

This is where many creative freelancers get stuck… working with predatory clients who see they can push you because you need the money they have, so they feel entitled to ask for more, take more, and be dicks about it.

Here's the thing: if you're working with people who treat you like shit—it's because <u>you let them</u>.

You set the standard for how people treat you, and you have to be deliberate and thoughtful about it. That's not to say you should come in acting tough, throwing your weight around, and generally behaving like a big jerk trying to "lay down the law." Just remember—where you lead, they will follow. I'm certainly not leading them to think I'll respond at 3 am just because they reached out, even if I AM awake. You'll hear from me in the morning if this is a business day, and first thing next week if it's not.

Desperation is an energy, and it will lead you to make emotional decisions that aren't based on fact or logic.

It forces you to react instead of being proactive and operating from a place of empowerment. When you can remove as much of the emotional part as possible, then every situation isn't profit or perish. And survival is a huge, huge emotional component that will make you act irrationally if you think you (or your home and finances) are in danger.

Our brains still haven't evolved to the point where we can distinguish between a tiger attack and a tiny paycheck. We look at a lack of income and interpret it as an indicator our life is about to end. If you don't know how you're going to pay your bills this week… if you don't know how you're going to afford food? That feels very visceral, and it can make you do stupid things that will self-sabotage your future progress.

And I've been in that anxiety spiral myself to where I was literally waking up every 30 minutes in the middle of the night thinking, *Oh my God, how am I going to pay this bill? I'm going to have to live in my car. How the hell am I going to feed myself this week?* Just constantly, constantly cycling. It reminds me of a line I heard in *Van Wilder*, a Ryan Reynolds movie: "Worry is like a rocking chair—it gives you something to do but doesn't actually get you anywhere."

Anxiety is the opposite of an empowered, ass-kicking frame of mind, which is why we want to refocus on what's within our control whenever anxiety takes over.

One thing you can control? Keeping your situation close to the vest if you're struggling. I'm not saying you need to pretend everything is okay but remember they're hiring you because you're a pro and an expert. That's not the time to let them know your life is falling apart—because that isn't something that instills confidence.

No matter what you're going through, remember that this is temporary, and you're working hard to change your circumstances.

Then take a deep, calming breath, put on your best "I'm a pro" face, and get yourself out there. You might just find that doing the work and growing the business takes your mind off your situation in a productive way. That's one way to give yourself that little bit of a foothold to level up into an area where things aren't quite as desperate.

Remember, you never have to say a word about how badly you need the money. If you're approaching a project with that thought in the back of your mind, you're going to unconsciously take little actions like being a little bit too naggy about that invoice and how you really need that paid before you can start the work. However, when you have a bit of money in savings and you're not desperate to get more into your account, you're free to treat clients like humans and give them a little grace (at your discretion, of course).

Because when you can pay your bills, AND you've got anticipated money coming in, you can relax and just be human with your clients. Not only does need make you unconsciously naggy, but it also drives you to stay on them about being paid (to the point of obnoxiousness) and changes the whole dynamic of your working relationship to be about money. It also makes you prone to overreacting, making assumptions, and judging a situation you know nothing about—because you're reacting from a fearful place versus acting from a confident place.

I want you in a position where you don't need any ONE client or ONE project.

Count on this: as soon as this opportunity goes away, no matter how awful or amazing it is, there will be another one. What's that old saying about "When one door closes, another opens… but often we spend so much time looking at the closed door that we miss out?" That applies here. If you're thinking, *I've got to take this one because who knows when the next client will come along*? I want you to stop that self-limiting bullshit thinking right here and now.

There are eight BILLION people on the planet—there will always be another project or client. That means your goal is to survive until you find that next project or client.

Embrace this idea to take back your power: *shit happens*. It will probably be uncomfortable for a while as you figure things out. There might be moments of quiet desperation. There might be moments of high stress. There are going to be unexpected expenses. All these things may happen, and none of these things may happen. Either way, make sure you're prepared with some money saved up in the bank because your ability to walk away is the only real way to take back your power. I can't remember where I heard it, but I fell in love with this quote: *shit happens so the SHIFT can happen.*

The whole focus of this chapter, if you take nothing else away from this, is that **you don't have to give away your power**.

And every day, you're making decisions that add to your power or take away from your power—whether you're doing it consciously or unconsciously. Not having a financial cushion is one of those situations where you're giving your power away. You're literally handing over control of your destiny to any unexpected expense that comes along, to any client that has trouble paying their bills right now, and to any equipment failure that means you must go back to the day job because you can't afford to pay for a new computer.

So that's a long-winded way of saying… my answer to, "What if I can't pay the bills?" Don't expect to. At least, not at first. Have a savings cushion that can support you for a few months so that you can better take smart business risks. If you haven't started saving, do it now—a dollar at a time.

Sock every unexpected extra bit of money into that savings account, and don't touch it.

With money in the bank, you will be better able to distinguish between a tiger attack and a tiny paycheck.

And you'll be able to look at a tiny paycheck and objectively think, *Well, crap. That's not enough to meet my monthly goal. What can I do to recover from this?*

When you can evaluate your situation like this, you'll know you're reacting from a true businessperson's perspective. *This is falling short of what I expected. Here's what I need to do to recover.* End of story. No panic necessary.

What Happens When I Leave My Job?

First, now's as good a time as any to let you know… don't burn bridges.

No matter how much you hate your old job, you may benefit from those connections with people in the future (and you may be able to help them as well). If the relationships are toxic and abusive, then by all means cut ties, but don't go nuclear. You never know what will happen.

Case in point, when I left my day job, I didn't anticipate that I'd wind up back there doing temp work. And I certainly did not anticipate being laid off alongside my old team after I took that fateful temp assignment. Every day will bring a new challenge, a new situation, or a new problem to solve. And sometimes your old colleagues are the perfect people to help you solve that problem.

Wherever possible, keep good relationships with the people you enjoyed working with. That network may just come in handy as you grow your business.

Second, let's talk about something many of us love-hatingly refer to as "the entrepreneurial rollercoaster" (not entirely dissimilar to the emo rollercoaster we talked about earlier in the book). Especially as you're starting out (and often recurring every time you try to grow and expand), you'll experience busy times and slow times—times when you're flush with cash and times when you're running really lean. You'll have frustrating clients and moments of joy and extreme gratitude that have you wondering how in the hell you got so lucky to be doing this for a living.

It might take several months or years to develop a winning strategy you can rinse and repeat to succeed. You might even have to try a few different business ideas before finding the right one. That's all totally normal. It means you're on the right path because you're doing the work.

There will be things you can only figure out by jumping in feet first. When I first hit the road on my digital nomad journey, I had to figure out a whole new system for being productive and staying motivated—especially since it was easy to sit around in PJs binge watching my favorite shows, only leaving the house for more food.

I had to figure out how much money I needed to make to support my preferred lifestyle and how to allocate that money between personal pay and living expenses, business expenses, profit, and taxes. I had to figure out which service offerings brought me joy and which made me miserable. It's all good data and part of the growth process.

The first time I tried (and failed at) freelancing, it felt like jumping off a cliff. I had a rocky landing because I didn't know what I didn't know. I didn't really have a support network, and I wasn't very well prepared. The second time I went freelance (when I left the toxic job), I was a lot more comfortable. This was partly because I'd hired a coach to bolster my business building skills and I'd grown my support network. The second time was more like an experiment—let's see if this little machine I built can fly! And sure enough, I doubled my take-home pay from the day job within the first month of leaving.

Newsflash: that's not luck. That's growth.

And that means, in many ways, we can create our own "luck." That's not to say we all have equal access to resources and opportunities. I think that's the thing that pisses me off most about business—that different groups of people struggle to do the same things the members of the "old boys club" often accomplish fairly easily. But make no mistake: if you did the work and worked up the courage to leave your day job, you took on the risk of betting on yourself, and you deserve every good thing coming your way. There are folks out there looking to give you opportunities, because they were also once given opportunities.

The fact is, we've been sold a great, big fat lie by the perpetuators of the "American Dream" fantasy. Work hard. Keep your head down. Do what you're told. Eventually, you'll get what you want. *No fucking way.* Here's why:

1) No one knows what you want until you tell them, so stop expecting people to read your mind. If you want to work 5-hour days, and your company has a strict 8+ hour a day policy, well… that ain't happening. Plus, getting what you want starts with knowing what you want. Most of us have never slowed down enough to really think about what we want, so we just follow someone else's lead. If you cannot articulate what you want in the first place, how on earth do you expect to get it?
2) That's how you make OTHER people rich. And since you have the skills to make THEM rich, why not use those skills to make yourself rich instead? And when I say "rich," that's a loose definition at best. I don't necessarily mean bank accounts full to bursting… money is not the only

thing that counts. Time. Creativity. Freedom. Relationships. All of those are also indicators of richness in your life.

You may not figure it out the first time around. I didn't. But if you do a quick search for "failed entrepreneurs," you might be surprised to see what good company you're in. Many of the most successful people out there failed repeatedly before they found a way that worked for them. Hell, I just did a search to see what popped up, and page one results turned up names like:

- **Vera Wang, who failed to make the Olympic figure skating team,** then left her job at Vogue when she was passed over for the role of Editor-In-Chief. Now she has her own fashion line and is renowned for her signature wedding dresses.

- **Steve Jobs, who was once ousted from Apple (yes, that Apple) over his perfectionism** and antagonistic leadership style (he fired talented folks for coming up a tiny bit short and killed nearly complete projects for the same reason). When he came back to the company, he'd learned a lot about controlling his perfectionism and leading others, helping Apple become what it is today. That's after being fired from the company he helped found.

- **Oprah Winfrey, who overcame a childhood of poverty and abuse to rise to fame** in a time when opportunities for Black women were even more scarce. Even after she established herself and became a billionaire, her first movie *Beloved* was a commercial flop. Years later, her cable TV network, the Oprah Winfrey Network or OWN (yes, the company that laid me off!) would struggle for years after it first launched in 2011. Despite the criticism and pushback, she kept going until it turned around.

Yeah, that's who you're sharing space with when you fail, my friend. You're welcome.

The key is these people didn't take "no" for an answer. They didn't see failure as an indication they should stop. They trusted their own compass and vision, and kept moving forward despite the odds and the setbacks.

Often the difference between those who succeed and those who don't get anywhere is sheer, bullheaded stubbornness and refusal to give up. It's not about avoiding failure. It's about LEARNING from failure and setting yourself up to absorb the failure without quitting.

Failure is an event; it's not your identity.

Chapter 4: Psyching Yourself Up to Leave

Here's something fun: just when you've worked up the courage and convinced yourself to do this big, bold new thing… that's when it seems like the universe is conspiring against you, taking extreme pleasure in keeping you stuck.

I know I certainly felt that way, especially as I was getting ready to leave my job. As I finished a draft of my resignation letter and resolved, "Today's the day I give my notice," all those little fears would pop up and rationalize staying instead. These thought trains went something like this: *You're just being dramatic… it couldn't possibly be THAT bad. Sure, you got screamed at in another meeting, but isn't this the price you pay for being successful?*

Newsflash: you do NOT need to put up with abuse to be successful. Nor do you have to abuse others under some misguided notion of making them "pay dues."

Every single time I wanted to leave, there was a tantalizing reason not to. That's no exaggeration—first the company dangled a potential bonus, then there was an irresistible campaign that would look awesome in my writing portfolio. Things temporarily got better between the teams, and people stopped screaming at me. HR even promised to go after some of the "problem children" who regularly bullied the creative team. And these little wins would prey on my fears that, *Maybe it's not all that bad, and maybe you should play it safe and stay.*

I tapped into my support network to get past those doubting internal voices, and asked my friends and colleagues to hold me accountable. I found a few people I trusted and respected, and told them, "I'm leaving. This is my final date, and I need you to hold me to it." I knew that I'd be much less likely to break a promise to friends than to myself. Saying your intention out loud and including other people in the vision can be a powerful step in the right direction because it puts pressure on you to take action or stop talking about it.

To be a person of your word, you must make the change or stop griping about what you *would* do if only you *could*.

Even with a support system, though, it took me the better part of six months to finally work up the courage to leave. During that time, I took on side projects to build up my savings and give myself a longer runway to get my business off the ground. All the while, those fears tried to chip away at my resolve and convince me to stay in my safe-but-miserable role.

Looking back now, it makes sense. When you're about to make a big change, your brain starts screaming, "Look, over there (where you want to go) is dangerous and unknown!" It's so critical to remind yourself WHY you're doing this and why it doesn't make sense to play it "safe." Remember, we already established that "safe" and "secure" jobs are an illusion.

When you feel that fear kicking in, instead of letting it paralyze you, let it be a sign that you might be onto something. Like I mentioned back in Chapter 1, almost every time I've had a big leap forward in my life, it was immediately preceded by the most intense fear of my life.

As those uncomfortable and scary feelings pop up, try leaning in to see if they might be indicators of good things to come, if you have the courage and faith in yourself to act anyway.

In fact, leaning into the fear is exactly how I got past the blocks that kept me from advertising my business when I first got started. I really indulged my inner drama queen and deliberately took it way past "What if I fail and wind up homeless?" all the way to "What if, by doing this thing, I unintentionally bring about the end of life as we know it?"

Lest you think I'm joking, I legit came up with a scenario that started with me advertising my business and ended in nuclear winter and total annihilation. Let's walk through it step by step, shall we?

It made total sense because, through a natural mix-up, my advertisement would wind up at the business owner's home instead of his office. When he read my letter, he'd obviously fly into an instant rage. He'd wad it up and toss it as he slammed the door, muttering to himself, "What the hell is wrong with this woman? What a stupid, insignificant asshole of a writer, thinking she can pitch me at home! I'm going to make sure she never works in this town again!"

He'd get in his car, already pissed (thanks to me), and road rage his way to work. As he exited the highway, he would sideswipe a bus and run it off the road. Of course, Little Timmy would be on that bus that day, and he'd be hurt. Bad. Timmy would be airlifted to the hospital, and the staff would contact his dad, a grand high muckety-muck at nearby Lockheed Martin, the defense contractor located at the Moffett Airfield in Silicon Valley. Timmy's dad was so high up, he was one of those guys that has access to "The Big Red Button."

When Timmy's dad heard the news, he would be understandably grief-stricken and consumed with worry for his son's welfare. His wife would FaceTime him from the Intensive Care Unit, where he'd see little Timmy hooked up to all these scary looking machines. In a moment of despair, he'd throw his arms up in the air and wail, "Oh, my god! My son!" His hands would come down, landing right on The Big Red Button. Within minutes, the missiles would launch, and we'd be thrown headlong into nuclear winter.

All because Angie had the sheer audacity to start a business and advertise it.

If you're laughing at my anxiety-driven story, good. I laughed at myself, too! Taking it to the extreme ultimately broke the tension and helped me learn to remove the life-or-death pressure from every forward step. I still felt the fear, but I was able to send out my letters because at least I knew it was highly unlikely I'd kill us all in the process.

Now let's dive deep into those fears. That's what we will cover in this chapter—those mental pep talks we all need from time to time to kick us out of anxiety spirals and put us firmly on the "Permission to Kick Ass" path.

Learners are Earners

Whatever skill you have—talking on the phone, cooking food, running outside without falling on your face—everything that's not covered by the autonomic nervous system (you know, stuff like breathing and pooping) is a learned skill. Once more for those in the back: **if it's not an involuntary bodily system keeping you alive, it's a learned skill.** By that same logic, you can learn business skills, too. The thing is, learning is uncomfortable for many of us because it's messy and awkward and embarrassing.

I'm willing to bet you busted ass in hilarious ways when you were learning how to walk. I'm guessing you didn't let that stop you, and you probably don't remember the embarrassing moments in gloriously cringey detail. This is a thing most of us can do, and we often take it for granted. I mean, when you think about it, walking is pretty fucking hard. Look at all the survivors out there—badasses who have experienced setbacks and tragedies, coming back from car accidents or cancer or worse, relearning how to walk as adults. Or even folks who have never had the ability to walk and had to find other ways to move around in the world. It's incredibly hard… and yet it's doable.

Many people have done whatever it is that you're trying to do since well before you came along. And many will continue to learn and practice that skill long after you're gone. So maybe it's time we embrace that inner child and say, *What the hell! If I'm going to fall down, I might as well see if I can bounce. Then I'm going to pick myself up. I won't lie on my face and wait for death... there's too much fun left to be had!*

The reality is that for all the skills we pick up, we learn to be fearful, too. Fear isn't something a lot of kids are born with. Sure, there are some naturally shy, cautious kids. But most of us discover what "hot" means by getting burned. Or maybe we break a bone and vow never to ride a bike again because we associate it with pain. Or maybe we fall off a floatie and sit at the bottom of the pool waiting for our cousins to pull us out, and subsequently develop a fear of water and drowning. Okay, that last one might be just me, but still.

We learn to be fearful.

Now I'm not saying be *fearless*. By all means, if a tiger attacks, run first and think about whether you should have run away later. At least you'll be alive to do the thinking! But if you feel those feelings and don't spot an immediate threat to your life, it's time to sit with it. Let the fear flow through you without resisting it and don't act on it. It'll pass. Your heart rate will slow. Eventually, you'll be able to look more objectively at how your brain hijacked you and ask yourself how you'd like to proceed. Are you genuinely in danger of losing your life, or are you afraid you'll fail or make a fool of yourself? Those last two are embarrassing, true... but life-threatening? Nah.

Just like you can learn to be fearful, you can also learn to face your fear. I mentioned above that when I was a kid, in a moment of rambunctious playtime between cousins, I got pushed off a pool floatie. We were splashing around in an above-ground pool in the heat of summer, and suddenly I was sitting at the bottom of the pool.

I distinctly remember the rippling sunshine filtered through the clear blue water—I could see everyone suspended above me, but I didn't know how to get back up to them. Finally, someone realized I was sitting at the bottom and pulled me up. For a long while afterward, I was scared to get in the water.

Yet summer after summer, all my friends and family would be in the pool splashing around and having a blast… and nothing bad happened. Eventually, I got envious of all the fun they were having and decided to do something about it. I learned to swim—just doggy paddling at first. I'd dart to the edge of the pool at the slightest hint of water coming over my face. Then I started swimming underwater. In my teens, I took swimming lessons to improve my technique. Then I became a lifeguard. In college, I'd go on to become a swim instructor and a lifeguard instructor.

By the time I finished my lifeguard instructor certification, I was no longer afraid of drowning—I knew I could get myself out of the water if I was conscious. You could say my childhood experience came full circle because, at one point toward the end of the certification process, I found myself sitting at the bottom of the deep end of a pool with a dive brick in my lap. I remember looking up at the surface and watching as one of my lifeguard trainees made their way down to "rescue" me and complete their certification.

When you approach those scary situations from a place of curiosity, you might just find yourself more willing to act.

One more story, and this one's for everyone who's afraid of making a fool of themselves. I wanted to sing with a band, but for years I couldn't bring myself to try out. I was terrified that I would get on stage and forget the words, bust a note, or otherwise make an ass of myself. Eventually I worked up the nerve to audition. I got a trial run at a real, live, actual gig where they gave me a four-song set.

I got on stage, the music started, and I promptly forgot the words to my first song. I stood frozen in panic. Thankfully the guitarist gave me a side-eye glance and quickly figured out what had happened. Then he jumped in and started singing. That was enough to jog my memory, and I jumped in on harmonies like I'd meant to do that all along. Then it was time for song two… and the same thing happened! I forgot the words again. The guitarist saved me again. Songs three and four went well, and even though I screwed up half of my audition set, I must have done something right… I wound up getting the gig!

That experience taught me you don't have to call attention to or apologize for every mistake. You don't have to stop what you're doing and start over from the beginning when you mess up.

You can absolutely keep going and recover on the fly. Most people aren't paying enough attention to realize you screwed up if you don't hold up a big flashing red sign saying, "Hey, I fucked up, and I'm really embarrassed!" Keep going. Learn what you can from the experience and do better next time. They're not watching you as closely as you think they are.

A few months later, with the band, we'd just finished a set with a high-energy rendition of "Tush" by ZZ Top. We announced our break, left the stage… and I realized I'd left my drink and purse up there. I returned to the stage to grab them and promptly tripped and fell on my face. It gets worse. I was wearing a cute, flirty skirt and high heels that night. When I wiped out, my skirt flew up over my backside, and I flashed my ass at people I'd just serenaded with a song about butts.

I was mortified. But what was I going to do, go hide in the bathroom and refuse to sing for the rest of the night? I got up and said into the mic, "Apparently, I can't sing 'Tush' without showing you mine. We'll be back in ten minutes!" We all laughed at my little mishap, and the show went on. Maybe a couple of them remember that night almost two decades ago, but I'm pretty sure I'm the only one. And yet that didn't end my musical career. Neither did telling you this story just now.

You can make an incredible ass out of yourself, whether intentionally or unintentionally. It's all recoverable. Pick yourself up and learn what you can from every failure. Have a sense of humor, and treat yourself with grace. You're learning and don't have to get it perfect.

By the same token, try to treat people around you with grace and kindness, too, because they're also going to mess up. Think of a time when you screwed up and had someone you respect look at you and say, "It's alright, we can fix this. Not the end of the world." You can be that person—so give people (including yourself) that space to learn.

I'm a fan of telling people I've coached that I can't teach you the attitude—you must bring that yourself. I don't mean attitude like sass or being a self-important jerk to all the "little people." I mean a good attitude, that spirit of really wanting to help, of wanting to learn, of "no job is too small," and of not being "above" any particular job.

Start with a willingness to be less than perfect at first. You can't just wake up one day and say, "I know Kung Fu! I'm going to go be a Kung Fu instructor!" You have to put in the reps and get your ass handed to you a time or two before you're ready to teach others. So, remember… building or growing a business is a skillset, and one you can learn. But you've got to get that learn-and-experiment mindset right first. Otherwise you risk forever studying and never actually doing.

Embrace Your Expertise

It's a common misconception that for someone to see you as an expert, you must have all the answers. The reality is that it's very rare that someone expects you to know everything. What they really expect is for the person they hired to be able to figure out a solution, and they don't always care how you got to the solution so long as the problem is fixed.

By that logic, if you can figure out the right questions to ask, you can find the answers. Therefore, if you're the kind of person who's resourceful and takes action, you have a lot more capability to help people than you're probably giving yourself credit for. Even if you're on the beginning end of the spectrum with your skillset, it won't be long before you're leagues ahead of most.

That might seem like a bold proclamation, so let me give an example of how I've seen it work repeatedly in my field of expertise, copywriting. If a brand-new copywriter spends every day studying copywriting for half an hour and another half an hour practicing their writing—and the client doesn't—at the end of one week, that "new" copywriter has seven hours' worth of practice and expertise that their client doesn't.

At the end of two weeks, the "new" copywriter has spent 14 hours learning copywriting that the client hasn't. By the time the end of the month rolls around, our "new" copywriter friend has 30 hours of experience they've put toward their development. The client still has zero hours and minimal understanding of copywriting and marketing—at least not to the level the new writer does. According to the old adage of 10,000 hours makes an expert, this newbie is well on their way to expertise with just an hour a day.

The clients stay at the same baseline level of knowledge in what you do, while you're learning, adding more skills and strategies to your repertoire, and getting better over time. Plus, you only need to know a little more than the people you are trying to help. I liken it to climbing a mountain. The people at the top of the mountain really don't remember what it's like to be where you are if you're toward the bottom. They don't remember what obstacles were in the path. They don't remember where the path took a certain turn.

But someone who's a few steps ahead of you can say, "Hey, look out, there's a little crevice you need to jump over there. Make sure you don't trip over that branch. Watch out for that doggie doo bomb some asshole forgot to pick up." Maybe they even reach back and grab your hand to help you move through the challenging parts with a little more certainty. Whereas the expert way up at the top of the mountain doesn't have the same perspective. They might not even be able to see you because they're so far up there.

New freelancers tend to have skewed definitions of what an expert is—the lone guru on the mountaintop. But now you know everyone on Guru Mountain can turn around and help the people behind them on the path. Yes, I mean you, too.

If you're a beginner or new to your field, you might look at people at the top who seem like they know all there is to know and have solved all there is to solve, and you might be tempted to compare yourself to them. That comparison would not only be inaccurate, but it would also be unfair. I don't want you to compare yourself at all, but if you must, then compare "beginner you" to "beginner them" and realize you have way more in common than you think.

Remember, the experts you admire are human beings, just like you and me. At one time they were beginners learning the ropes and using whatever knowledge and skills they had at the time as the foundation for their current business. They did the same baby step process every brand-new business owner goes through. They made mistakes, had setbacks, and had to think around corners. You can take that same path.

And remember, when scaling Guru Mountain, very few people have the ambition to get all the way to the top. Many will find a cave or an oasis along the way and build a home there. Others will camp out somewhere for a while, decide they don't like it, and come back down to find another mountain. Some will look at that mountain and nope right out of there—never even start climbing. Everyone's journey is different.

Start where you are and consistently do your thing well. Rinse and repeat. You'll level up and grow your expertise with practice.

And what if you're still new to your field? In the eyes of your potential clients (most of whom are either just starting out, or have very basic beginner questions because they're not experts in your field either), you know enough to help them. Be their expert.

I was intimidated the first time I was asked to speak on stage at an event with over a thousand entrepreneurs. The event host wanted me to do live copy critiques—that is, evaluate people's website text, look at their emails and sales videos, and give my opinion on what they could do to improve and get a quick win.

Because this was such a big event, I was bracing myself to cover super advanced strategies and high-level concepts. Then I saw the submissions and was shocked. Everyone, and I mean every single one, needed copy 101 help—NOT the advanced stuff I had assumed. I helped a lot of people that day, just covering the basics.

A good foundation in the fundamentals is often all you need to build a solid business helping people.

Now that I've shown you that you have more expertise than you think, that doesn't mean you have to spend all your time talking *at* people. Too many people think they must "prove" their expertise, so they drone on and on, throwing qualifications and accolades at people in a desperate bid to hide insecurity.

I have a tip to help you look super smart when talking to potential clients—only do about 20% of the talking.

Let them tell you what they need, and what they're going through, and you chime in from time to time with smart questions that zero in on what their problem is and how you might be able to help. That's how you grow your expertise while learning "on the job."

There will always be beginners coming into your field who need your help, even when there are already more established people talking about the same thing. It may FEEL like you're in competition with bigger brands and fancier experts for a limited number of available clients, but that's not the reality. You might work with people that find the top expert too technical and hard to understand. And there you are with everything you know, ready and willing to help.

There are billions of people out there, and they don't all need help from the most advanced folks.

Not only that, but by connecting with other entrepreneurs and freelancers in your field, you have resources you can tap into and people you can ask questions to fill in the gaps. You can do the research when you get a question that stumps you. Here's the funny thing: you can learn something for someone and say, "Hey, that was such an interesting question I hadn't even thought about, so I went and did a little digging and talked to a few people I know, and here's what I learned." That's how to look like an expert and reframe a question when you don't have all the answers.

We should talk about impostor syndrome here, too. I believe everybody feels fake when they first put themselves out there as an expert. If anything, the fact you're feeling like that should make you feel part of the Cool Kids Club™. Because the people you admire most, the biggest megastars out there, they're also afraid that one day they're going to make a misstep, and everybody will discover that they had no idea what they were talking about all along. And the reality is that even the world's premier experts make mistakes.

That doesn't mean they don't know what they're talking about; it just means they're human.

Plus, if you have a natural aptitude for something like design, don't discount your experience just because doing the work feels "too easy." What's easy for you isn't easy for everyone. For instance, if you're thinking, *I'm a great graphic designer, but can't everyone just use Canva?*

No. Absolutely not. Plenty of people struggle with even "beginner" level graphic design platforms, and you can be their go-to expert by offering to share what you do that works. Tips that feel super-obvious to you because of your experience can be huge ahas for newbies. Think about it like this: if what you can do in 15 minutes generates huge results for them—is that more or less valuable than a non-expert who spends 15 hours trying to do the same thing and gets nowhere? Would it have been worth it for them to hire you?

Look at the fact that you're working on your skills and expertise every day, growing a little bit every day. That's not fake. Focus on getting 1% better every day and imagine how good you will be at the end of the year… then at the end of five years, at the end of ten years.

Being an expert doesn't have to be all or nothing, like you never make mistakes and only people who are perfect are experts. Making a mistake in public doesn't make you an impostor. Get over that fear and **give yourself permission to make a misstep and course correct.** I said it in Chapter 3, and I'll say it again now… if you make a mistake, if you fall flat on your face, you're not going to lay there and wait for death. You're going to pick yourself up, clean off whatever scrapes you have, and keep moving forward.

Impostors really don't exist. Well, I mean I guess they do, but I'm not sure why you'd want to worry about someone who'd impersonate a business owner—they're probably doing it as part of a scam.

The freelance world is mainly filled with people that are trying, and that give a damn. They want to help people, so they start a business. If you make a mistake, don't lay down and wait for death. Don't take that as a sign that you were never meant to be in business and you suck. Pick yourself up, figure out what needs to be cleaned up, and know that you can move forward.

Everything is fixable as long as you're alive to take another breath. Every day that you wake up is a day to try again and do a little bit better.

Ask, Ask, Ask

When I see new freelancers getting stuck either trying to create a business or solve a problem for a client, there's something I've noticed a lot of them don't do—ask for help. And that's not a judgment. Capitalist society, particularly in the United States, places a ridiculous amount of value on the "self-made" brand of success. To that end, many of us have grown up believing that asking for help is weak or entitled or rude.

Unsurprisingly, some don't know where to ask for help, and some don't know when or how. It doesn't shock me that many people assume they're not "ready" to invest in their education or pay for help. When you're not stuck in it, it's easy to see how pride and ego interfere in this critical step on the path to success.

Too often, I see newer entrepreneurs spending hours and days trying to figure out how to do a thing on their own to save money… only to feel frustrated and overwhelmed when it doesn't turn out as they hoped. The examples are countless: building your own website if you're not a techy person, creating your own graphics if you're not a designer, and balancing your own books if you're not great at accounting.

Look, we all start somewhere. And at the very beginning of your business, you'll likely have more time to spend than you have money. You'll spend something either way, so it's okay if DIY is where you have to start. But recognize that there are diminishing returns to doing it yourself—spending four hours trying to get a web page just right isn't the best use of your time when you could earn $200 (or more) an hour.

If you're trying to do things on your own and getting stuck, there's no shame in finding someone to help out so you can move on to the next thing. Here's some truth for you: no one that got anywhere, or achieved any level of success, got there without help.

Being successful doesn't mean that you get everything right, and it doesn't mean you figure out everything by yourself.

I suppose it's technically possible to build a business figuring out absolutely everything on your own with zero outside input, but I feel like it'd take 20-30 years to gain significant traction. If that's how you like to do things, low and slow, no judgment here. But I'm just not that patient. If you're reading this book, I suspect you'd like to see some sort of success inside the next year or two, rather than waiting decades for things to click.

In some instances, it makes sense to go it alone. Just don't make that the entirety of your business. While it's true you can go faster if you go alone, you will go a hell of a lot further if you go together with the right people. For those of us who want to enjoy the fruits of our labor while we're still young enough to do it, there's a way to shorten the learning curve—getting good at asking for help.

Talk to people who have done what you're trying to do. Ask them questions about things you're struggling with. Ask for meetings and introductions, and favors. Seek out tips and tricks that will help you get to success just a little bit faster. I guarantee that most experts asked questions of someone ahead of them on the path—and as a result, many of them are more than happy to help someone who's asking questions (read: someone who's doing the work and helping themselves).

Make the ask—the literal worst thing that can happen is the person you ask says, "No."

Awesome, now go ask somebody else. Keep asking because you'll probably find someone who can help you well before you run out of people to ask. And if you're worried about people being super mean with their "No," know this: most of us don't waste energy on going out of our way to devise an elaborate humiliation scheme. For most professionals, "No" is enough. There's no blacklist. No one is keeping score. And if someone is rude when you ask questions, that speaks more to their character than yours.

I'm from the South, so I get this. We've got a particularly stubborn, insistent cultural dogma that goes something like, "No, I got this, I can do it on my own. I don't need any damn help." But the reality is, smart people ask for help. And they keep asking until they get answers. They don't just stop if someone says, "No," or if they get an answer that doesn't makes sense to them.

In case it's not clear by now: you're not a superhero and you don't HAVE to be.

We've established that you need to ask. Now let's talk about doing it. There's an art to doing it well, and I like to think of it in two parts:

1. **The first is knowing which people to ask**. It's seeking out advice from a smart person who's done what you are trying to do, who genuinely wants to help, and who cares about your forward progress. Don't ask people who don't know what the hell they're talking about. Would you ask your neighbor Joe-Bob, the landscape architect, how to run a fashion show? No.

    Don't ask broke people how to make money. Don't ask single people how to find the love of your life. And don't ask wantrepreneurs how to build and run a business. Find someone who's doing what you want to do… and doing it *successfully*. That is the person you want to ask your questions to.

2. **The second is trusting the process.** Sometimes, someone who's a few steps ahead of you on the path gives you advice that doesn't make sense to you in the moment. And when it doesn't immediately make sense, your brain does this funny thing. It goes, *Yeah, but…* and shuts that idea down. *Ok, well, it works for this person because they've got all these advantages that I don't have. It's never going to work for me because…*

   How do you know? Often people ahead of you can see around the corner, where you have little to no visibility. So, of course their idea wouldn't make sense to you… you don't have enough context to see the full picture. This means sometimes you must try something in good faith, without knowing what will happen next.

The reason is simple: you cannot possibly know what will or won't work for you until you try.

Even if it's an idea you've tried before that didn't work, it doesn't mean it can't work now, or it never will. Just like there are hundreds of potential solutions to every problem, there are a hundred reasons something might not have worked. Trying it again under different circumstances might pleasantly surprise you.

Ask. Take the advice that makes sense to you. Disregard what doesn't feel good—you absolutely do not need to (and can't possibly) take every piece of advice you get. Do challenge yourself to act on stuff you don't understand, especially if someone you trust tells you it'll help.

By getting out of your comfort zone, you make progress. And with the help of others, you'll go further, faster.

Play to Win

There are two ways to approach this: you could play to win, or you could play not to lose. I want you to play to win. Period. Full stop.

But Angie, couldn't you wind up winning in both instances? Yes, you might, dear reader. But one of those mindsets is defense, aimed mainly toward barely edging out the competition and doing just enough to stay in the game. The other is offense and is about going all in, not just barely getting by, but also achieving incredible things.

Look, every time you take a risk and put yourself into the game, it's scary. It's a big personal challenge. But you have to push yourself beyond your comfort zone and do something different from what you've been doing up until now—that's the only way you'll get different results. And once you enter this game, why would you play defensively? Why would you aim low and go for "not losing?"

Why would you play it safe and do the absolute minimum that you can do to say that you played the game?

You're not Bill Murray in *Space Jam* (1996). If you haven't watched the movie (shame on you), he spends most of it trying to convince Michael Jordan to add him to the Looney Tunes basketball team. He laments how he could have been great if ONLY someone would give him a chance. Repeatedly, he practically begs, "Put me in coach, I'm ready to win!" And, of course, he eventually joins the team and helps them win the game. At that point, Michael Jordan acknowledges that Bill Murray has some skills… and Bill announces that he's retiring untied and undefeated.

Granted, we're talking about a fictional battle between Martians and the Looney Tunes/NBA here. But if you think about it, you probably know someone in real life who's done something similar and always had a goal.

As soon as they got close or got to the first step, they quit rather than keep going.

If they kept going, they might mess up! They might lose! They'd rather have the "perfect" reputation than chance failing. Those aren't the people who grow; those aren't the people who achieve great things. Those aren't the people who win. They're the ones kicking back with their feet up talking about, *If I only had a chance*, or *If only I'd gotten my big break*. Recognize that lotto ticket thinking?

If you're going to jump into entrepreneurship, you might as well bring your A game and play as if the championship is on the line. Take a chance and believe in yourself. Go all in on YOURSELF. Trust yourself to figure things out (and to ask for help when you can't). Understand that if you fall, there's always an opportunity to get back up.

Real talk: the people that came to win will wipe the floor with those doing "just enough."

Do your best, not the bare minimum. And if you're not sure how to do your best, or you're feeling stuck, most of the time it's because there are too many options. Your main goal is to get back into action-taking mode, and to do that, you have to get as simple as you possibly can and make decisions quickly. That's what entrepreneurs (AKA bosses of the company) do.

If you suck at making decisions and always seem to waffle, narrow it down to your two best options and flip a fucking coin.

It might seem silly but trust me on this one. Here's why it works: you're either going to have a gut reaction as soon as that coin goes into the air and know which one you hope will win… or you'll see it land and be disappointed it didn't turn out like you hoped. Either way, that's your gut telling you which step to take next. The more you exercise your decision-making muscle, the stronger it'll get. And you'll learn way more by acting and letting the real world tell you whether you're on the right path.

With trial and error, you'll start to learn about yourself and say, "Oh, now that I'm doing this thing I found exciting, it's totally a different thing than I thought it was." Or you might find a solution that you didn't even know existed. But those things are only possible when you focus on acting.

If we could will things into existence just by thinking about them hard enough, I think we'd live in a drastically different world. Unfortunately, we live in the real world, where things only change when you act… when you put yourself out there and ask for help. You'll make connections and allies and find solutions you didn't even know were possible.

Remember: nobody expects you to know everything.

You are expert enough, here and now, to go out and try to do this thing. You can learn anything you don't already know. Stop trying to be perfect. You can still create amazing things and have an amazing life without ever having achieved perfection. If you're plagued by perfectionism, focus on what you ARE (instead of what you're not). I'm certainly not perfect, and here I am, still trying to share what I've learned and make your life better.

I've had (and still DO have) all the same fears that I'm talking about in this book. I've wondered who I am to teach these things. Why would somebody want to learn anything from me? I don't have a life coach certification, yet I keep putting stuff out and teaching and coaching to the best of my ability. I know I'm helping people… because they TELL me I'm helping them. And not one of the people I've helped has asked me about my certifications because they can tell I've learned everything I know through trial and error and by putting myself out there.

You've got life experience, and that counts.

One last rant on playing to win: there's never been a better time to start a business in the history of mankind. Right now, you've got incredible resources at your fingertips. You can go to a library and access free high speed wi-fi and get answers almost instantaneously. You can go to a local community business meeting and ask dozens of questions to experienced local business owners. You can hop on a video call with someone you respect and get answers immediately.

And you don't have to figure it all out yourself. You can do it with a couple of mouse clicks and a credit card payment over the internet. No buying a building, no creating signs, and no massive campaigns. You don't have to put yourself hundreds or thousands of dollars into debt.

With enough passion, drive, and resourcefulness, you don't have to be the smartest person in the room. Life is a series of figuring out how to solve problems. The solution to one problem creates another problem that needs to be solved… which creates another problem that needs to be solved, and so on and so on, until we die.

If you can solve problems, you can achieve damn near anything.

Go into this knowing that you can do it… because that's what you've been doing every day of your life thus far. You've survived everything life has thrown at you to date. Go you! I like your odds.

Quitting Your Job

And now we've come to one of the biggest challenges most would-be freelancers face. This may not seem like it applies to you if you're not currently employed, but this same info applies to side gigs, part-time jobs, and even paying client work that's become a slog.

When you need to make room for your new freelance hustle (or a new client), eventually, there will come a point in time when you'll want to leave your job (or old client).

That can feel like an impossible task given all the unknowns, and there are some things you can think through in advance to be better prepared. This is all about working up the nerve to follow through—which is arguably one of the hardest parts.

First, if you're worried that coworkers will screw with you or retaliate or make you look bad for leaving, I've got news: that can happen whether you stay or go. If you let their potential reaction dictate your future, you're giving away all your power and personal agency. They don't have to like what you're doing. And if they get mad or threaten you, I say that's even more of a reason to walk.

In or out of a job, people are going to threaten to damage your reputation all the time when they don't like what you're doing. We live in an age of outrage. People are going to be pissed off, and they are going to run their fucking mouths until the rage has passed (or until something else happens that sets them off on a different warpath).

You're going to upset people, whether intentionally or unintentionally. That's life. Sometimes, it's because of something you did, and sometimes, it's because they are having a bad day and you're a convenient target. But let me be clear, only one person can damage your reputation, and that's you. The rest is just gossip.

So long as your choice isn't hurting or endangering people, you've got to let go of what their reaction might be.

One of my friends used to say, "You can't make them dance the way you want them to." I love that quote so fucking much. It opened my eyes to how, in trying to control someone else's actions and feelings, I was really being controlled by the situation. When I let go of the outcome and did what I thought was right, with a lot of caring and compassion, the situation always resolved itself, one way or another.

You can't let other people's reactions determine your destiny. Because if you conduct your business and your life according to how other people think you should live it, you're setting yourself up to be mighty disappointed.
Your opinion of yourself is a hell of a lot more important than other people's opinion of you.

You've got to think highly of yourself (or at least feel like you are trying and doing your best every day, and that trying your best is enough). You don't have to be perfect; you just have to try. And you have to genuinely give a damn.

Okay, we've talked about angsty feelings; now let's talk about tactics.

It's customary (at least in the United States) to give two weeks' notice when you're leaving. That gives them ample time to put up a job posting and start screening candidates, ask for your help describing job duties, and potentially interview someone or even train a new hire.

Forewarning though: some companies will say, "Thank you, goodbye," as soon as you give notice. You might not have the opportunity to finish your two weeks, so be prepared. Have any files or relevant samples you want to save (plus any contact info you want to keep) stored somewhere other than your work computer when you turn in your notice. See Chapter 1 for an example of what can happen when you don't regularly save samples, good reviews, and contact info.

Another thing that can happen is getting a counteroffer. I think that's a shitty deal. If they weren't willing to reward you for years of loyal, hard work before you decided to leave, they're not really valuing you now either.

100

They're just afraid to lose you. They're playing not to lose versus playing to win.

If they were playing to win, they'd have been thinking strategically about how to keep you on board and happily producing high-quality work for them all along. Ask yourself, *Why didn't they proactively try to keep you and give you opportunities for growth and pay increases before you decided to leave?*

Let's dig in a little deeper and really pick this one apart. After they find out you were on your way out, how long do you think it will be before they start looking for someone else? It happens more often than you might think—your willingness to leave shows them they have a gap, and they start wondering, "What if Angie decides to leave again in six months?"

If they offer you more money, I say don't take it. They should have thought about that well before you decided to leave. If they threaten to give you a bad recommendation, who the hell do they think they are? God? This isn't that Netflix show *Black Mirror,* where you have a literal rating floating in the air above your head for everyone to see.

I hope we never get to a public rating system where if people are having a bad day, they can go, "Fuck you—one star!" and doom you to wander around forever, branded as LESS than five stars. But, I mean, what will the folks at your job really do? If they go nuclear and do everything in their power to slam you, it makes them look unprofessional, obsessive, and even a tiny bit unhinged. You keep your cool and keep moving forward and let them do what they will.

Another reminder, because I can't say this enough: you are not safe as long as you work for a company built by someone else.

Yeah, it's a little bit of a risk to bet on yourself. But you know what? I like those odds much more than putting my life, my stability, my future, and my potential in someone else's hands to control as they wish, to treat me as if I'm less than a person. To not give a shit about my family the way that I give a shit about my family.

If you're telling me that you can't do this because you have people to provide for, I say that that's even more of a reason to do this. As an entrepreneur, you can build an incredible life for the people you love that you couldn't when you were toiling away at someone else's desk.

If you're going to work that hard to make someone else money, you can figure out how to work that hard to make money for yourself.

Chapter 5: Get the Right People with You

A while back, Mark Timm, the CEO of Ziglar Family, spoke to the Titans Masterclass (a marketing mastermind I was a member of) about the importance of mentorships. He said, "If you see a turtle on a fence post, you can guarantee he didn't get there by himself."

It's such a silly little visual thinking of a turtle on a fence post, stuck up there all wiggly. Why would you even do that to a turtle? I digress...

If there's anyone at the top of your industry that intimidates you, maybe think of them like the turtle. They didn't get where they are without help. Think about all the acceptance speeches that start with, "I'd like to thank," or "I wouldn't be here without…" That's someone at the top of their game recognizing and acknowledging the assist, really valuing the people who helped them step up.

There's this wonderful phrase I hear a lot in business, and that's to "send the elevator back down." That means those of us who have had any kind of success have a duty to turn around and help others get to our level. None of us gets anywhere without help, and so many successful people make it a point to try and be that helping hand for someone else (especially if that someone else reminds us of a younger version of ourselves).

There's so much good news here. You can let go of the notion that you have to do this all yourself. You can trust in the fact (let me reiterate: FACT) that there are people out there who will be more than happy to help you hop up and join them on that proverbial fencepost. This is why we talk about networking being so important in business.

Your network is how you find those helpful people.

The flip side of that coin is intentionally removing people from your network who aren't on your side. It was tough for me to build my business when I was getting advice from my family. I love them and they are wonderful, caring, wildly hilarious people who taught me a ton about life and love. But when it came to becoming a writer and starting a business, they were worried for me. They were scared I might fail, get hurt, or worse… live the starving artist trope.

Here's the deal: I understand why they were concerned, and that's because none of them had done what I was trying to do. They didn't even know people who had done what I was trying to do. So, from their perspective, this thing I wanted wasn't a smart risk. My goal was completely foreign to them—a totally different reality. I didn't figure all this out until years later, but I get it now.

Of course, becoming a freelancer doesn't make sense to someone who doesn't know anyone who's become a successful freelancer.

It's highly possible your friends, family, and everyone in your go-to support network will have that knowledge gap too—especially if they're all employees. If they can't get behind you and don't understand what you're trying to do, make sure you're at least getting involved in online entrepreneur communities. Surround yourself with people who not only believe that this is possible, but who have achieved the kind of success you want to achieve. Those are the ones who will show you that what you're trying to do isn't just a pipedream, but is totally achievable.

At one point, I had a partner who not only didn't believe in my dream, but actively worked to sabotage and prevent me from going after it. He was mean, belittling, and not at all supportive. Unsurprisingly, we didn't work out in the long run. And what was the main reason I chose my freelance dreams over staying with an unsupportive partner? I had a community where I could see other writers going out, finding client work, and making a consistent income.

They were learning how to position their expertise and get better and better projects, making themselves more and more money. They showed me what was possible, and when I recognized that, I knew I could choose who to believe (hint: it wasn't the ex). When you surround yourself with people who show you what's possible, it becomes almost impossible NOT to succeed. They challenge you to step up into a better version of yourself because they understand what you're going through on a deep level.

A lot goes into building a kickass network, so let's dive in. Here, we're breaking it down into pre-prospecting, filtering out the haters, and finding what I call your "Accountability Buddies."

Pre-Prospecting

The first step is to reflect on who's already in your network. I struggled so much initially because I thought cold-calling and reaching out to strangers was the only way to "build my network" and get work as a freelancer.

Cold calling and cold emailing can work, but they're not the fastest (or easiest) way to get started.

And the reasons are simple: credibility and timing. When you're reaching out to people cold, you must establish some sort of connection and trust factor with them, which takes time. Even when you've built that connection, that doesn't mean they're ready to buy, which means nurturing that fledgling relationship and keeping in touch until they are ready.

I'll give you a scenario: imagine you're cruising LinkedIn, minding your own business. Some rando messages you and asks if you need any help with your brand photography. If you don't know that person from Bill Murray, the most likely answer is "Nope."

Now imagine you're at a conference (could be in person or virtual) and you meet someone who geeks out about photography, and you have an interesting conversation. Then they reach out afterward, and because of your connection, you're seriously considering whether it's time to redo those headshots. Or you're remembering a friend who was talking about getting new photos done, and you make an introduction. All this from connecting with one cool person you like, and wanting to do something quick and nice for them.

Once you've got the right people in your network, you'll find that referrals for business can be that simple. I can't tell you the number of times I've been idly talking to someone, and they said something like, "Oh, I need to get my website rewritten" or "Yeah, I'm thinking about new graphics. I'm about to rebrand." Often, I offer to introduce them to people I know, and more often than not, they gratefully jump on that intro offer.

If I've got a good relationship with someone who needs what you do, and I connect you to that person, you've got borrowed authority and credibility from me. You're instantly promoted above "stranger danger," and there are less barriers for you to overcome in this trust-building process. If it's not obvious, I love referrals, and they've become my preferred way to seek out new business.

Now this doesn't mean I want you to go mass emailing everyone whose hand you ever shook (eliminate "BCC" and "blast" from your vocab right now). If you do it the "efficient way" (that is, BCCing, copying and pasting generic templates, or "blasting" to save time), you're way more likely to get blocked than get business. That's why we're going to do a little pre-prospecting work before you start reaching out to folks.

You'll take inventory of who you know that you could reach out to, including former colleagues, people from volunteering or social clubs, friends, and family members. It's okay if it's been years since you connected with them, so long as that connection was real. If you regularly attended meetings together, took the same course, or volunteered together, great! If you only spoke once in passing or while standing around the water cooler, they're probably not someone you want to add to the list.

Really dig deep—don't just count on your own memory for this. Look through your phone contacts, email contact list, and social media accounts for who's following you, etc. I have a friend who recently helped someone from high school start her business—and they hadn't spoken since band camp, 1997.

So, if someone you knew at some point in your life might be interested in what you're trying to do, put them on the list. This includes anybody in a field related to yours (for instance, when I started freelancing as a copywriter, I included everyone in any kind of marketing role) or anybody you simply miss having in your life and want to reconnect with. Announcing something new in your life is a great way to break the ice and start a conversation, even if years have passed.

Create a spreadsheet (or notebook, or CRM, or whatever helps you work best) with their names and contact info. Add some additional context if you can. Any little detail that will help you connect, person to person. Who do you know that works in your industry? Those are people you might eventually ask if they have projects you could help with, or if they know someone who needs your skills. Who may work with your target clients? There are people who might offer different but complementary services to your ideal customer.

In copywriting, for instance, I might look to connect with designers and videographers. I can write website copy and video scripts for my clients and connect them to folks who can make those words come to life with amazing graphics or video. And odds are, those designers and videographers will send me work, too, since their primary skills aren't writing.

Who has a skill you may need, such as bookkeeping, copywriting, website design, etc.?

Be thinking about whose businesses you might support as you grow yours. Who just really likes you and would help you no matter what? I bet you've got more solid contacts than you think.

I know that reaching out to people can be scary as hell, especially knowing that you will eventually ask them for something.

Don't skip adding someone to your pre-prospecting list just because the thought of contacting them makes you want to run and hide. Right now, all we're doing is making the list.

Give yourself permission to include every name that might even remotely be interested in your new direction. We'll go deeper into who to contact, when to reach out, and what to ask when we cover prospecting in Chapter 9.

I break pre-prospecting down in even more detail in the companion guide (download for free at **permissiontokickass.com/guide**). Get it and go check out the Kick-Assets Cheat Sheet.

Permission to Be Your Badass Self

Quick disclaimer: I know it's hard for some of us to own the term "badass" for various reasons. Maybe you haven't had a chance to accomplish much in your field… yet. Maybe this is a big transition, and you're feeling a little insecure since you can't see into the future. Maybe you really don't like the word "ass." All good, I know some folks are not natural swear word users and that my language is not their favorite.

I want you to embrace this sentiment though, because to better serve your clients, you've got to be that badass they need. You can't come at this from a wishy-washy place where you're introducing doubt into their mind about whether you can help them. And I'm not saying you have to come at this 5,000% confident.

Commitment and conviction come before confidence.

And even before that comes the voice of your "inner authority," as my friend, psychotherapist Dr. Julie Helmrich, likes to say. That's the little voice inside that reminds you this is totally doable and gets defiantly uppity when someone questions your capabilities. The voice that says, "It's okay, I can figure this out," when faced with a problem. Call it your gut, your shoulder angel, or even your mini me.

That little voice that's convinced you can do great things… that's the one to listen to.

You just have to learn how to turn up the volume on that little voice, so eventually, you get comfortable using it to drown out the naysayers. Another way of thinking about this is looking for reasons you CAN instead of reasons you CAN'T.

When I first started, I had all kinds of doubts as to whether I was a legit writer. Who am I to think I can get paid for this? Then I did the exercise I'm about to share with you and uncovered a whole bunch of writing experience that I wasn't giving myself credit for while I was busy focusing on all the skills I thought I lacked. I sat down and dug into my memory banks, and counted every bit of writing experience I had, big or small, paid or otherwise. And when I took this exercise seriously, I discovered that I'd been writing since I was a child—no joke.

There was the time when, on a family walk, I almost slid down an embankment into a stagnant pond full of mosquitos. My dad and his cat-like reflexes made a desperate grab for me, managing to catch my hand, sacrificing his seam in the process. Five-year-old Angie thought this was absolutely hilarious—that my dad split his shorts saving me from the mosquitos—so I wrote a five-year-old's equivalent of a short story and shared it at school.

In sixth grade, I entered a short story contest. I was so excited about potentially seeing my work in a book that I had the story typed up (computers and printing were still fairly new in those days), printed, and pasted into a physical book. Even if I didn't win, I had this little physical book with my printed name glued to the front cover. I was practically an author!

Then in my first couple years at college, my peers wasted no time informing me how jealous they were of my ability to crank out 20+ page research papers in a day. Several offered to pay me to do it, and around the same time I saw some paper writing services pop up online. I had a nice little side hustle going for a few years, and while I wasn't exactly comfortable putting "people paid me to do their writing homework" on my resume, I could say with absolute confidence and truth that I've been paid to write since my teens.

On top of all this, I took several undergraduate courses that were explicitly about writing or in which I did a lot of writing. So, when I was thinking about grad school, it made sense that I'd go for my Master of Fine Arts (MFA) in Writing. I actually applied to two different programs at Carnegie Mellon University—the MFA and another program I wound up getting into, called Master of Entertainment Industry Management (MEIM).

Guess what: I got accepted AND rejected by the same university for grad school.

That just goes to show you that one place may say no, and then the one next door says yes—so you can't take it personally. You have to keep trying. Now, I did take the rejection from the MFA program pretty hard, but in my defense, the letter was also snarky as fuck. It laid out all the ways I fell short—too little experience, portfolio wasn't strong enough, voice undefined—and told me to try again in a few years.

When I made it into the MEIM program, it took all I had not to walk into the dean of fine art's office and tell him I didn't need his fucking acceptance or his stupid writing degree. The thing is—I doubt he would have even remembered writing that letter to me, let alone who I was. Thankfully, logic prevailed, and I focused on getting my degree versus getting revenge.

I shared this last story because when you go through this exercise, when you really reflect on your experience to create your backstory—whether you're looking for examples for your baking, scrapbooking, photography, writing, or floral arrangement experience—you're also potentially going to run into not-so-great memories that can introduce an element of doubt. The contest you lost. The snarky rejections from someone probably having a bad day.

In recalling those painful memories, you might be tempted to shrink. I challenge you to see it as an opportunity to rewrite your story and prove the naysayers wrong.

Look at all you've done despite the setbacks. When you do this, you become the bullet-proof freelancer who can take future rejections with dignity and grace. The fact is, not every proposal you send will get accepted, and not every client will be happy with your work. Those are fixable problems, and it's totally possible to kick ass anyway, despite things not being perfect.

So, are you ready to try this exercise? Set a timer for at least 45 minutes and cut out all distractions. No phones, no internet. Start making a list of everything you've ever done that's related to the work you want to do. No experience is too small, and everything is fair game, including:

- Church
- School
- Internships
- Hobbies
- Personal website or blog
- Special interest groups and clubs (Meetup.com anyone?)
- Networking groups
- Volunteering
- Teaching at a kids' camp
- Your own YouTube channel
- That one project at work where they let you design the flyer or write the email or otherwise do something related to your field of interest

It all counts, even if you feel like you were just winging it, or it was all amateur hour. It was you putting in the reps, and that's the thing that matters. Make a list of everything you've done until the timer runs out.

Then go find whatever proof or examples of that work that you can. We're talking digital files, print copies, recordings, and whatever is relevant. Gather it all in one place. You could even make everything digital and save it all in one main "experience" or "sample" folder.

If you gave this exercise a good-faith try (that is, you didn't sit there the whole time playing games on your phone or making excuses as to why every instance you can think of doesn't count), and you still have nothing? Well, now's as good a time as any to start practicing—start a blog, take a class, join a club, and start building those skills and gathering those samples.

If you already work in your field, that's fantastic. You probably have way more samples than you know what to do with. That's the position I was in after I left that copywriting job. If you aren't working in a creative field and you're looking to leave to start a creative freelance business, you might have to do some digging. Go through all the work you've done and old emails, and find an example of what you can do. And you really only need one strong example. But even if you find one that's embarrassing, you can always improve it knowing what you know now, and then use the improvement as a sample of your work.

Start with one sample. The reason is simple: too many people use "I need samples and/or a portfolio" as an excuse to stall putting themselves out there.

Get one strong sample and start reaching out to people you can help. You can create better, stronger samples as you go (while getting paid to do so!)... and that's a total badass move. Remember, we're only working on landing that first client to prove you can get paid to do this creative thing. We're not jumping from the bottom of the mountain straight to the top. Unless you're Superman or have a fully functional jetpack, you will have to take it a step at a time, just like the rest of us humans.

You don't need a big fancy portfolio or a ton of stats to get started— EVERYONE starts from nothing, even the gurus you admire.

Start being the new you. Just pick that one sample. Eventually, you'll replace old samples as you get newer and better ones. Start where you're at and grow from there. I know the one-good-sample approach can work because when I applied to my first in-house copywriting role, I didn't have any on-paper, bankable copywriting experience that I could point to. I worked for that college paper writing service. I did some internships in the entertainment industry with tasks like reading scripts and writing summaries for busy executives. I had a handful of freelance projects from various online marketplaces—everything from production scripts to websites to business plans.

So, my samples weren't 100% applicable to copywriting. But it was the writing experience I had, it was part of my backstory, and it showed I could write. Then I figured out the rest—and since I got the job and you're reading this book, you now know this approach can work too.

In the interview, I managed to take all the above experience and spin it. That's not to say I "spun" it in a deceptive or tricky way—instead, I connected the dots between my experience and what I was trying to do in a way that showed them what I did had value and could be applied to their situation.

Think of this as a creative exercise on its own—you can almost always find a link between what you've done in the past and what you're trying to do in your future, even if it's pretty thin. The point is to find a way to show that the skills that you have can help your client (or the company you're trying to work with), help them move forward, and help get them closer to their goals.

That's how I essentially created a copywriting career out of nothing—by cobbling my previous experience together in a way that helped people see my skills and trust in my ability to figure things out. To reference something that you may well be too young to remember, using a piece of chewing gum, some duct tape, and a string, I MacGyver-ed together my whole career.

With no formal writing education, no special advantages, no crazy connections, and no handouts, I basically willed this shit into existence through sheer stubbornness and failing over and over and over again, until I found a way NOT to fail.

In many ways, this is a book I'm writing to a younger me. You don't have to make my mistakes if you don't want to. Please don't read this book and say to me, "Yeah Angie, but all these other people, they're trying to get me to do all this other complicated stuff to start my business. What you're saying sounds way too simple." Ask yourself who profits from your stalling and making things overly complicated. They may be trying to get followers or to get money out of you by teaching you their "proprietary" way of building a business.

Building a business certainly isn't EASY, but it doesn't have to be HARD.

Start where you are with the simplest possible methods and models. Get money coming in as quickly as possible to validate your ideas. Don't take out loans and put things on credit if you don't have to. Pick your gurus wisely. Consider whether they're about helping or selling you more and more—there's nothing wrong with selling, but intent matters. If your gurus would be okay seeing you lose your house or go hungry to get you in their program, that makes them a shitty guru in my book.

Listen—I made things harder than they had to be for years because I thought solutions had to be complicated to be valuable.

Instead of trusting myself, I would clam up and be a quieter, watered-down version of myself in an attempt to look "professional." But I'm here to tell you, it doesn't matter if you're wearing a hoodie if you solve their problem. That's where the value is—your skill and willingness to help someone—not in your looks, or your tech toys, or the way you talk. All you have to do to be valuable is solve the problem, and a simple solution is just as valid as a complicated one (hell, most of the time it works better too).

Okay, now you've got your backstory, and maybe even some samples cobbled together. You've got an idea of how your experience connects to your future goals. And if you want to sprinkle some extra magic on that shit, take a moment to write down all the reasons you fucking rock. What's awesome about you? What do people come to you for? Don't be afraid to ask supportive friends for perspective on this if you're not great at hyping yourself up and talking about yourself in a positive way. They'll be a loving mirror, reflecting your awesomeness back at you.

Write down all the reasons you have what it takes to succeed in your chosen field and what you bring to the table. Maybe you're a great listener and advice giver. Maybe you have a very systematic way of approaching things that helps you get clarity super-fast. Maybe you have a talent for combining flavors or ideas in a new and unexpectedly delightful way. Write it down. Believe it. Own it. Know it's true and that you have what it takes to figure it out. When you genuinely believe in your own badassery in this way, you're giving yourself permission to get out there and kick ass.

Filter Out the Haters and Naysayers

Let's talk filters. I use that word because realistically, it's unlikely you'll be able to fully remove all negativity from your life. You can easily mute or reduce negativity to something you can manage (if not ignore) by understanding that not everyone who talks to you (or about you) deserves your attention and consideration.

This is especially true of people I not-so-affectionately call "the haters." These folks aren't misguided people who may have a point. They're miserable, stuck, and their thrills come from pulling people down because misery loves company. Those people don't deserve a second of consideration from you.

Easier said than done… I'll be the first to admit to that. When I first committed to producing a podcast, I was terrified that people would hate it and I'd get dragged through the mud on social media. It's a ton of time and effort (not to mention money) to produce a podcast—truly a labor of love when you're first getting started, especially if it's not immediately making you money. For months I stalled even committing to a launch date because I was so scared of the imagined hate I'd be getting for daring to stick my neck out.

Thankfully I tapped into my support network, committed to getting the show out, and have since launched it to rave reviews. But then that old fear popped up again when I started advertising it: *Surely, the haters will come out and shit all over my ads*. After much hand wringing, I ran an ad anyway, and sure enough—they came out in full force.

They commented on my ad, telling me I was a spammer, a scammer, a piece of shit, and just about every other nasty thing you can imagine. Only when I saw it, I strangely wasn't hurt… I was amused. I had this vision of a grumpy old asshole sitting alone in his living room watching TV, and yelling, "SPAM! SPAM!" at every commercial break, instead of, you know, changing the fucking channel.

Suddenly, 14-year-old troll Angie, who used to hang out in chat rooms, crack jokes, and poke fun at everyone, was awakened… and she was *thrilled*. Troll Angie replied to every single one of those comments and thanked them for bumping my ad up in the algorithm and getting my podcast in front of more people. I imagined their heads exploding from my gleeful responses to their fury.

Before long, my friends found the ads and started commenting to bump the ads up, too. That thing I'd been terrified of doing for so long quickly became one of my favorite stories to tell. In fact, I probably enjoyed trolling those guys way too much. And I learned to adjust my target audience to exclude "grumpy old men."

This is part of the gig. When you put yourself out there, people will have opinions on what you're doing, whether you ask for it or not. They'll gladly spew venom and bullshit at you after forming a half-baked thought from seeing two seconds' worth of your work.

I think many of them are just profoundly unhappy and believe snarking at someone else will "put them in their place." Many of them are secretly offended by someone daring to pursue their dream… so instead of trying to do it themselves, they try to get you to stop because you remind them of all their failures and shortcomings.

You can't live your life for what will or won't please the haters.

This is where one of my favorite quotes comes in. It's from Teddy Roosevelt, and he says (my additions in [brackets]):

"It is not the critic who counts; not the man who points out how the strong man stumbles, or where the doer of deeds could have done them better. The credit belongs to the man [or woman, or person] who is actually in the arena, whose face is marred by dust and sweat and blood; who strives valiantly; who errs, who comes short again and again, because there is no effort without error and shortcoming; but who does actually strive to do the deeds; who knows great enthusiasms, the great devotions; who spends himself [or herself or themself] in a worthy cause; who at the best knows in the end the triumph of high achievement, and who at the worst, **if he [or she or they] fails, at least fails while daring greatly, so that his [or her or their] place shall never be with those cold and timid souls who neither know victory nor defeat."**

The critics' opinions don't count if they are unwilling to do the work themselves. In fact, in all my time in business, I have yet to meet a successful businessperson who actively criticizes or goes out of their way to hate on other business owners. It's a waste of time and energy, and most entrepreneurs have better things to focus their efforts on.

Most of the people hating on others have too much time on their hands, and if they were out there creating their own stuff, they wouldn't have enough hours left in the day to find people to shit on. That's why I say their opinions really don't matter. That's not who you're creating your art for. Feel free to ignore them entirely (or gleefully troll them for more algorithm juice if that makes you happy).

Now let's talk about loving doubters. In Chapter 4 I talked a bit about the support system needed to help you quit your job. That may or may not include friends and family, depending on whether the people in your life are stuck at day jobs. If they don't know anyone who's done what you're doing, or if they're stuck in dreaming (but never doing) mode, you've got to take their advice with a grain of salt. A lot of what they have to say will be fear couched in concern—and really, it's a projection of their own fears onto you.

You get to decide who gets a spot in your inner circle, so consider how they show up for you when you talk about your dreams. Are they encouraging? Maybe they stay. Do they criticize you or tell you it's impossible or risky? Maybe they go (or maybe you simply no longer talk to them about your business goals).

It's not hiding the truth or lying by omission—it's filtration. People around you get the information they need to know, especially if you already suspect they'll be less than supportive of your work. Be intentional about being around people who can show you the way and help you step up… versus people that constantly try to focus your attention on the risks.

These days I weigh my decisions not on whether they're risky or not (they are—that's life). Instead, I ask myself, *At the end of my life, will I regret not doing that thing*? **If so, I do it.**

Look, you've got to accept that a significant number of people in the world don't get entrepreneurship. They can't wrap their heads around what you're building. That doesn't mean they're bad people. I remember bringing home boxes from the office about two weeks before I left that toxic day job.

I'd been talking about leaving for over six months at that point and had kept my then-boyfriend apprised of everything as it developed—my decision to leave, the request for a modified schedule, the denial, my notice, everything—and he was still surprised when I came home with those boxes. I think my jaw actually hit the floor when he casually said, "Oh, you were serious about quitting?" as if I was playing some random prank that involved packing up someone else's shit and lugging it home. That relationship ended about six months later.

That unsupportive ex was a special kind of dream stomper. I hold no ill will toward him and am grateful that his disbelief and lack of faith didn't scare me away, but rather pissed me off and made me even more determined to follow this path. On the other hand, my family is full of awesome people who just didn't understand what I wanted to do. Entrepreneurship wasn't something that made sense to them, at least not at the time.

I remember one particularly tearful chat with my dad when he told me, "As your father, I can't say I'm glad you're choosing to live in your car with your cat. I don't know how you're feeding yourself and staying safe, and that's scary. But I've never gone after my passions. Who am I to tell you how to find your happiness? Sweetheart, if anyone can do this, you can." I had tears streaming down my face. My family had an understandably mixed bag of fear and faith in me, so I focused more on their belief in me, even when they didn't understand or agree with my choices.

I'm happy to report that since I first started talking about going down this path, my mom and my sister have each started their own side hustle, and it's been so exciting to see them grow! Maybe they just needed to see someone start a business so they could see it was possible for themselves. That reminds me of another favorite quote of mine by Marianne Williamson (my emphasis in bold):

"Our deepest fear is not that we are inadequate. **Our deepest fear is that we are powerful beyond measure. It is our light, not our darkness that most frightens us. We ask ourselves, 'Who am I to be brilliant, gorgeous, talented, fabulous?' Actually, who are you not to be?** You are a child of God. You playing small does not serve the world. There is nothing enlightened about shrinking so that other people won't feel insecure around you. We are all meant to shine, as children do. We were born to make manifest the glory of God that is within us. It's not just in some of us; it's in everyone. **And as we let our own light shine, we**

unconsciously give other people permission to do the same. As we are liberated from our own fear, our presence automatically liberates others."

I've always loved that quote. Using my flame to light someone else's candle doesn't diminish my flame in any way—and it makes the room a little brighter. Then what if they turn around and light another candle, and another? Before long, the light will be blinding in the best possible way.

Keep filtering and filling your network with people who encourage you to shine your light. Find people you trust who are either working toward the same goals, or believe in you and want to see you succeed. Find people you can report to and who will hold your feet to the fire when fear starts to creep back in.

Now I'm fortunate enough to have figured a lot out, achieved a few things, and made strong connections with people I adore. Because I've been ruthless about filtering out haters and naysayers, I have even more faith in my ability to find a way forward—regardless of what happens.

I could send out an email series tomorrow and make sales from my own products. If I find myself in a tough spot, I've got an amazing network and can reach out to friends and connections to get work quickly. None of those people doubt I'll succeed, and their faith bolsters me on down days.
I know I can control my own destiny, regardless of what life throws my way. I want that for you, too.

Be ready to put yourself into some uncomfortable situations and trust that people will show up along the way to help you. This is why it's so important to ditch the idea that you need to fly solo or that you have to figure everything out on your own before you can make connections with the people around you.

Don't isolate yourself and hide, but don't blindly share your dream with anyone—not everyone has earned the right to be in your inner circle.

And remember, life's too short to give a damn what the haters think.

Accountability Buddies

You may think I'm fearless—I've been told that a lot from people who don't know me well, who hear the way I speak and tell stories on stage.

In real life, I'm probably one of the most anxious people you'll ever meet. I get myself so worked up that all my worst-case scenarios end with total annihilation. That has paralyzed me and inspired more than one round of feet dragging when I'd promised I would act. But there's one thing that forced me out of excuse-making mode and into action—I did it both when I first left my job to go freelance and again when I started writing this book and tossing around the idea of a podcast: I told people what I was planning and asked them to hold me accountable.

About six months before I walked out the door at that toxic job, I tried to get a more flexible working schedule. My goal was to avoid working myself to death—while also carving out time to build my business and save up money. I proposed a common working arrangement of 4/10s, meaning I'd work ten-hour days Monday through Thursday and take Friday off. I planned on using those Fridays to focus exclusively on business growth.

I spent a week obsessing, endlessly researching, writing, and rewriting my proposal. I figured it'd make perfect sense, especially since the company's east coast headquarters had published flexible working policies on their site. But alas, the west coast headquarters (where I was located) shot my proposal down with, "If we did this for you, what would we do for everyone else?" I didn't really care what they had to do for everyone else—that's someone else's job and not mine to figure out. After my proposal was denied, I had to figure out my next move. I tell you that story for a reason—it was my final test.

It was my last-ditch effort to see if the company cared enough to keep me.

Given flexible work was technically a benefit offered by the company, it should have been a no-brainer. But for whatever reason, they decided to contradict their own policy and turn me down. This is a situation I think a lot of employees find themselves in—asking for something and not being prepared to walk if they don't get it.

If you ask for a raise or workplace accommodation and tell them you need this or you'll leave, and you don't leave? You've just backed yourself into a corner. Now they know they can take advantage of you because you won't follow through. So, when my boss sat me down to tell me HR had denied my request, I looked at him with tears in my eyes and said, "You know this means I have to leave."

I was terrified just saying that out loud. After all I'd given to the company, the denial felt like a slap in the face. After quitting, I doubled down and went to a group of four to five copywriter buddies that I trusted. The great thing about this group was that all of them were freelancers with their own businesses. They were all doing the thing I wanted to do. So right after the proposal was rejected, I told them, "I made the call. I am leaving December 16th so I can enjoy a nice long holiday break with my family and start fresh in the new year. Hold me to it."

Natural curiosity took over at that point. Over the next several months, as I made my plans and took on side projects, those friends would reach out to me and ask, "So, what are you doing? Where are you in the process of leaving?" They forced me to think about it and make plans versus sinking into fear-based avoidance. I started calling them my "Accountability Buddies," something I still call them to this day.

I gave my notice in September, about three months out from leaving. I wanted to give the company extra time to find a new writer because I really cared about the role and wanted to train my replacement. My boss was hamstrung by the higher ups, and they never hired someone to take over my role. They just divided up my workload between the remaining staff (and that workload, as previously mentioned, was already close to unbearable). That should tell you something about whether I made the right choice.

I kept collecting evidence that I was making the right call and working on my escape plan and saving money. Then I upped the ante, made a semi-public announcement inside the Copy Chief community, and wrote a post telling people I was leaving on December 16th, and I wanted everyone to hold me to it.

I knew how I wanted them to see me—as a peer and colleague—and telling them was my way of forcing my own hand, pressuring myself to act and not just talk a good game. Essentially, I made myself accountable to people I knew would hold me to my word. And since I consider myself a person of her word, it's very important to me not to break a promise I've made to friends and colleagues I respect. I think accountability partners are important. The reason is simple: it's easy to make excuses when you're only making promises to yourself.

I don't say "make excuses" in a judgmental way here. I want to shine a light on the shame many of us carry, weighed down by so many broken promises to ourselves. I can't tell you how many times I've committed to a new workout routine, then… *Well, today I had a long day, it's raining out, and I'm tired. I'll just do it tomorrow.* Before you know it, I've skipped my workout for three weeks straight because there was always a reason not to do it.

If you look hard enough, there will always be a reason NOT to do something.

I'm a big fan of giving yourself every reason you can TO do what you want to do, especially if it's a big scary thing with a big potential reward. Sharing it with others (rather than keeping it to yourself) is one way to get support and encouragement to keep going, especially on days you don't want to.

You don't necessarily need to make the public announcement I did. You'll know what feels right by trying different things and seeing what works best for you. But I encourage you to 1) find at least one person you trust to hold you accountable and 2) share your plans with them. Don't make them "someday" plans. Make them as specific as possible, and add dates where you can. A certain kind of magic happens when someone is counting on you to show up—and it's a great way to overcome even the most stubbornly persistent fears and get moving.

Now let's make your escape plan…

SECTION II: Make Your Escape

We've spent a bit of time digging into your why, facing fears, and getting people in your corner—this is all crucial prep work because it's not circumstances that'll stop you so much as what's happening in between your ears. In this section, we'll get a little more into the nitty-gritty of planning out your escape from the job, how to start your business, what to do about money and pricing, and more.

As you go through this, I want you to keep your big "why" in the back of your mind. This isn't about "stability" (although you can absolutely build a business to provide the stability you want). This is about your goals, income, lifestyle, and time. It's about working just as hard for yourself and your clients as you would have worked for your employer—only this time, instead of begging for raises and time off, you get to set the rules.

Unfortunately, there are many people who want to be able to set the rules without taking any risks.

Now, if you haven't started a business before, it stands to reason that you don't know what to expect. The first time that unknown is terrifying. But trust me, the further you go, you might even find yourself getting addicted to the excitement of launching a new product or starting a new company. The first time is the scariest; after that, it can be an adventure if you let it. Because even if you have started a business before, the next one isn't a guarantee—though you do get better and better at spotting opportunities and trends the longer you do this.

So many people get hung up at the start and never move beyond planning simply because of those unknowns. They don't know what to expect and constantly talk about the dream but never do anything about it. Lack of action is one of the biggest heartbreakers of all, at least to me. How many life-changing, world-changing products and services and companies don't exist because the dream died before someone acted?

Forewarning: no matter how carefully you plan, the level of detail, the double-checking you do with people you trust, the endless studying and strategizing... none of that will prepare you for the reality of the rubber meeting the road.

One of my mentors is a big fan of saying that no battle plan ever survives direct contact with the enemy. And granted, I really don't like to think of business as a battle—the fight is not between you and your clients (who are most certainly not your enemies). If anything, it's with yourself, your motivation, your ambition. So maybe this is less battle and more lining up all your duckies—and I don't know if you've ever seen ducks walk across the road—they're never in a nice, neat little row. If you try to herd them, they'll go wherever the hell they feel like going, despite all your careful preparations.

Plan because that's better than winging it, and it gives you something to fall back on. But know that the plan will change regardless of whether you're ready for it, or even want it to change. It's time to trust yourself to be the adult that you are, who has survived 100% of the shit thrown your way to date. Believe that you'll be able to figure out a solution to any problem you encounter. And the reason is we will set you up for success in this section.

One more bit about mindset before we get into business planning: I challenge you to ditch any thoughts that might pop up that sound like:

"I already know this is not going to work."

Or…

"I've tried that before…"

Or…

"I don't agree with you, that doesn't make sense to me."

That's a great way to screw yourself over and shut down possibilities before you've even explored them. There's a reason I keep hammering on simplicity—because you can literally follow the path others have set before you and see damn good success without having to reinvent the wheel. You get to put your own spin on the wheel, obviously. But don't make this harder than it has to be by shutting down seemingly easy solutions.

I've literally been at mastermind meetings where folks turned on a $2MM revenue stream like they'd turn on a water faucet. They had a product idea, and their customers had practically been begging for it for years. They kept thinking, "It can't be this simple, I've got to create something that's really going to wow them!" Long story short, we convinced this business owner to try it, and at the next meeting, they were grateful for the push.

If you recall, in Chapter 3, I mention starting as simply as possible with the "Lemonade Stand" model of your business. From there, you can grow and evolve it into something more sophisticated that can eventually run without you (if you want) or that you can sell (if you want). But the steps you take to get there aren't the same steps you take to get going. Start simple.

Here we go…

Chapter 6: Getting Ready While Still Getting Paid

I was finally holding this 112-page catalog in my hands... this thing was supposed to be a crowning achievement of my career. And instead of being proud, I only wanted to light it on fire (and maybe throw myself out the nearest window). I could barely stand to look at it.

Not surprising, considering I'd been working 12+ hour (sometimes even 19-20 hour) days, seven days a week, for four months straight. I was commuting an hour each way every day, and I regularly had two to six hours of meetings on my calendar and an eight-hour workload to tackle as soon as I walked out of the conference room.

I had gained upwards of 60 pounds from stress eating and grabbing whatever I could from the cafeteria. I was constantly running out in the middle of the day to nap in my car. And when I got home, instead of understanding and support, I had to deal with a partner who wondered aloud about my sanity in staying in such a toxic environment.

I'd asked for more staff to help with the workload... *no budget*. I'd asked to scale back the number of projects we were working on, limit the revision requests, or at LEAST prioritize all the requests that came in haphazardly from seemingly every person in the company with an email address. *Nope*.

That catalog was the last straw. It was probably the most gorgeous thing I'd ever had a hand in creating, and despite the early excitement, it never got the full promotion it deserved. It made around a million dollars in sales with no discounts, and I knew it could have done even more if we'd been able to really make a big deal out of it, but once again, corporate ego interfered with good marketing sense. I started planning my exit.

Some months prior, I'd gone through a coaching program for freelance writers about learning how to create a business that supported you (instead of hiring yourself as an employee of your freelance career). My mentor, Kevin (the one who gave me permission to be an expert) taught me the foundation for becoming an in-demand freelancer. I figured going out on my own—and potentially failing hardcore—had to be better than staying in that toxic place. ANYTHING had to be better than that place.

I started pre-prospecting and contacted folks who could help me find side projects while I kept the day job. I needed enough in savings to help me feel comfortable getting out… just enough to make sure I could pay the bills for the first few months while I got my freelance business off the ground. As you're getting ready, I highly recommend getting your Emergency Fund squared away, and then getting three to six months' worth of living expenses in your F.U. Fund (more on Emergency and F.U. Funds in the next section of this chapter).

Unfortunately, I inadvertently wound up digging myself in deeper… I mean, who does a two-hour commute, a twelve-hour day, and then comes home to write for two to three more hours before calling it quits? Me, apparently. Instead of confidently earning cash and getting repeat clients I could turn to once I left the day job, I was burning the candle at both ends. The quality of my work suffered—both at the job and with my side projects. I was fast approaching burnout and beginning to wonder if I was even cut out for this writing thing or if I was just fooling myself thinking I could start a business.

Be realistic with yourself if you are considering taking on side work to boost your savings—are you disciplined enough to carve out time to get the work done? What other avenues are available to you for making a little extra money and stashing it all away? Maybe it's side work or consulting. Maybe it's selling stuff, or tutoring, or even Ubering. I can't tell you the right way to side hustle… but I can advise you to try out different things, find what feels right, and be gentle with yourself because there will be a learning curve with everything you try.

Things will get a little bit tough from time to time, and sometimes it'll be your own decisions that land you in a pickle, and sometimes it will be totally out of your hands—hello, global pandemic! Any time you're stuck in the shit and wondering if you'll find a way out, remember that this is for now, not forever. What got me through that "burning the candle at both ends" phase was the knowledge that this phase was temporary. It helped me remember why I was working so hard—to save money to quit that job and get my freelance business up and running.

I have been freelancing since 2017 and making a comfortable living. I've had ups and downs and surprises along the way, but every time I've worried about running out of money… somehow, I never do. My take-home pay is more than it was when I was a corporate stiff, and I work about a quarter of the hours. And it's work I like! I spend my days working with clients, coming up with new ideas, and growing my business. This isn't a reality I could have imagined before I took that leap of faith and figured out what was truly possible.

So, whatever you're going through right now, take care of yourself as best you can, and remember that it's only for now, not forever.

Get yourself through and hang in there. And in the meantime, hold tight to that dream. And let's get down to planning…

Emergency Fund

First, we've got to talk about finances.

Not having enough money is probably the root of 90% of the fears people have when it comes to starting a business.

I bet it wouldn't be nearly as terrifying if you had a $50,000 a month trust fund to try out whatever you wanted. Sadly, most of us don't have that kind of cash. In fact, according to SpendMeNot.com, 69% of Americans don't even have enough money in their savings to cover a basic emergency. And granted, there's no way to know when an emergency will happen or what the extent of that emergency will be. But by nature of being human, you can probably expect that something will happen at some point.

So that makes it smart to expect the unexpected.

You might wake up with a flat tire. You might trip and wipe out on the stairs. Me and my clumsy ass have done that plenty of times. It's a wonder I haven't broken my damn neck, but I have sprained an ankle before. That's an unplanned expense at an unexpected time. You can't live with your money stretched so tightly that any potential disruption is catastrophic.

Between when I first wrote the first draft and the second round of edits of this book, a pandemic swept the globe, destroying companies, lives, and savings accounts. You never know what will happen—I don't think anyone could have predicted that (other than maybe Stephen King in his book *The Stand* or Steven Soderbergh in the movie *Contagion*. I take it back, I guess the Steves saw it coming).

There are plenty of non-pandemic emergencies, though. Prime example: a couple of years ago, my computer hard drive crashed in the middle of a big project. I'm incredibly fortunate since I had a backup laptop—because first world problems. But then my backup laptop also crashed within a day of my primary laptop. It had been glitchy for a while, but I'd assumed that was part of its charm… it always started eventually. Until it didn't.

I had to email my clients from my phone and tell them, "I'm offline because my computer crashed," and run to the electronics store. I bought a spare laptop to use while they sent mine out for repair and agreed to return the replacement laptop once mine was ready. But if I hadn't had money in my account to buy that temporary laptop, I literally would have been out of working commission. Or I would have had to go to the library and use outdated computers.

You need an emergency fund to protect yourself.

I don't say all this to freak you out and make you give up the entrepreneurial dream. This is about strengthening your resilience muscle. Everything is survivable, especially if everything is not also an unaffordable emergency. Put some money away to prepare for that so life doesn't keep you perpetually afraid the other shoe's going to drop.

I'm a big fan of socking a thousand dollars away as your Emergency Fund. A grand is enough to cover most of those unexpected expenses I mentioned above. The key is to make sure you put it in a place you can't touch it. You've got to pretend it does not exist. It's not there to be used for anything but an emergency or an unexpected expense that needs immediate attention. Now, an unexpected expense is not going, "Work was rough this week, beer's on me, dudes!" Nor is it buying Pampered Chef from your best friend. You must treat that fund with respect.

So how the hell do you find a grand when your budget's stretched to the max? A dollar at a time, my friend.

You don't have to get a grand in the bank by tomorrow, but it's important to prioritize it. One thing that helped me was any time I got unexpected cash—one of those random class action settlements, birthday money, a tip in my band's jar… that went into the Emergency Fund until I hit that magic $1,000 mark. And if you're fortunate enough to not be living paycheck to paycheck, it's time to practice living on less. Whatever money we bring in, we tend to expand our lifestyle and use up the extra money.

Now the name of the game is going to be taking money off the top, so you never even see it. We call this paying yourself first. Try automatically funneling 10% out and see how that feels. If you brought in $1,000 per week, that would be $100 in savings, or $400 a month. You'd have your fund full in just two and a half months! For many people, $100 is a cable bill or a fancy dinner out. Stash that money away, pretend it's not there, and keep it somewhere you can't easily reach it. Adjust your lifestyle downward as much as you can comfortably afford and put that money in your Emergency Fund.

I've had my Emergency Fund for about fifteen years now, and I've had to dip into it maybe three times for a blown tire, an unexpected medical expense, and an unexpected vet expense for my cat, etc. Every time I dipped into that money, my priority was to stop spending and start saving again to replace what I took out.

I keep that account at $1,000 at all times, outside an actual emergency. And I don't use it for anything other than unplanned emergency expenses. I'm not using it to buy myself clothes or go out to dinner. And I'm not taking that money from my Emergency Fund without putting money back in.

One last note on the Emergency Fund: when I first started mine, I went into "maintenance mode" with my monthly budget. I was spending just enough to survive to save up as quickly as possible. Do that if it feels right to you but remember not to get so strict that you never enjoy your money at all. As you're saving, you can, and absolutely should, keep some room in your budget for activities that bring you joy.

Even if you're working two jobs and exhausted, you can find little things that bring you joy. Walk in nature or take yourself out to a cheap movie—I am particularly fond of my local theater chain's five-dollar movie Tuesday. When I'm feeling burned out, I can sit in a theater full of people that I don't have to talk to and explore another reality for a couple of hours.

You don't have to be 100% stress-free to indulge in little moments of happiness.

It's a celebration of your hard work. We all need that reminder regularly—that life is worth living, this goal is worth pursuing, and all the highs and the lows are temporary.

F.U. Fund

Now, let's talk about my favorite thing ever—the F.U. Fund. Yes, it stands for exactly what you think it does.

I learned this one from John Carlton, and it's like your Emergency Fund on steroids. Why? Because this account will float you through lean times and help you sleep a little easier as your business grows. It's also what I like to call your "freedom fund."

Having this money set aside means you can afford to walk away from anyone or any situation that's no longer serving you.

Without that freedom, you wind up living in a perpetual state of anxiety. And when you're in that state, you can't possibly produce your best work. Not only that, but anxiety over money makes you beholden to your clients. That's like hiring yourself for another shitty job, except instead of playing in your genius zone, you have to do all the work yourself—from finding clients to collecting payments to cleaning toilets.

When you don't prepare yourself financially, you're giving your power away to other people because they have the money, and you need it. That puts you in a position where you feel you have to do anything your client asks so that the money will keep flowing. So, I strongly advise (read: I'm badgering) you to fully fund this account as soon as humanly possible. It's going to free you from ever having to depend on any one client or any one deal to survive.

When you have an account with a lot of zeros in it, you might be tempted to see it as a cash reserve, but don't treat yourself to an all-inclusive vacation at Sandals—create a vacation fund for that. You're not using the F.U. Fund to save up enough to buy a car with cash. It's there to save your ass in the event shit hits the fan, and to give you enough buffer to figure things out. What you're buying with this fund is *time*.

That's usually what leads people to making bad decisions and screwing themselves over—they're running out of money, and they're running out of time.

Let's talk specifics: six months of expenses is the target. You could go for nine or twelve if that makes you feel more comfortable, but for most of us six is enough. That's because if you're working hard every day at meeting new people and growing your business, you will meet people who will pay you to help them within that time frame.

And I mean doing the work of meeting people and prospecting, versus staring out the window, going out to three-hour lunches with friends, doing mindless busy work, or puttering around the house. Money loves action, and there are just too many people out there struggling with too many things for me to believe you can't find ANYONE you can help for money inside six months.

I urge you to have a specific number (six, nine, or twelve months) AND a target date in mind when you reach this step. The reason is, I've met people who use "I need to build up my savings" as an excuse to avoid acting. I've known quite a few people who've been saving up… and saving up… and always finding a reason to stay at the day job. Every time they get ready to leave, that number in savings suddenly doesn't feel big enough, so they keep hustling and keep stashing money away. Then they're devastated by a layoff they never saw coming. It happens way more often than you might think. Set a number goal and a timeline and let your Accountability Buddies know your plans so they can hold you to it.

The F.U. Fund buys back your power, your time, and your headspace—because now, one lean month doesn't mean you're in danger of going hungry or losing the roof over your head.

Here's another way to think of the F.U. Fund: it's an investment in your future success. There will be lean months that are no fault of your own.

Economies change, priorities shift, budgets adjust, and clients make last-minute decisions—all these things could leave you bringing in less than you planned for the month. That's when your F.U. Fund kicks in. It gives you time to ramp up prospecting and freedom to avoid taking on a bad client. You don't have to put up with anyone treating you like shit, and all this month's bills are still paid.

And if a project goes sideways (which a few will inevitably do), you won't devolve into panic and a funk, thinking you're a failure, or spin your wheels trying to drum up business OMG yesterday, only to wind up with another shitty client that makes you miserable. Trust me, it happens—shitty clients can smell desperation like a stinky cologne.

To determine how big your F.U. Fund should be, come up with the number that'll float you six (or nine, or twelve) months, then add 20% for unexpected expenses. And when I'm talking about covering monthly expenses, I'm not talking about barely scraping by on ramen noodles. I want you to take stock of what it actually costs to run your household—including groceries, gas, fun money, savings, and more.

If you're currently spending $3,000 a month on living expenses, then your minimum F.U. Fund is $18,000 ($3,000 a month in expenses times six months = $18,000. Plus, another 20% = just over $21,000). Keep it simple. I recommend using the same strategies that worked for your Emergency Fund savings and keep living that way until your F.U. Fund gets to where you feel comfortable with it.

Then DON'T FUCKING TOUCH IT.

Are you (or a family member) bleeding? You can touch it.

Is your house and/or computer on fire? You can touch it.

Do you have no projects on the horizon? Get to prospecting and touch the money.

THEN PAY YOURSELF BACK. Don't let yourself go below that target figure except in case of a dire emergency, or if the only project on the horizon means you have to work with a major dillhole who's going to make you miserable. Walk away from the dillhole, refocus on prospecting, and **breathe a sigh of relief that it's urgent but not an emergency**.

Depending on your individual circumstances, you may or may not want to have a fully funded F.U. Fund by the time you leave your job. You may be able to move in with parents or friends and not need quite as big a stash. On the other hand, if you're carrying a mortgage (or renting), you'll probably want to save as much as you can.

I know that was true for me when I left my job—at the time I lived in the San Francisco area. I have since moved, but at the time, it was (and still is, as of the writing of this book) the most expensive metro in the United States. I had a three thousand dollar a month mortgage payment that I was jointly responsible for. My partner at the time was terrified that when I left my cushy eighty-grand-a-year gig, I wouldn't be able to pay my half. And that's a valid fear, so I wasn't mad. Hell, I was scared too! So, I took the slow and steady approach and gave myself plenty of time to scrounge up extra money before I left that job.

And then, as your business grows, make it a habit to feed more money into that F.U. Fund continually. The more you save, the less likely you'll be trapped by problem clients as you build your business. When you have that money, you can walk away from any situation that doesn't suit you. You can even pivot your entire business and decide, *Oh, I thought I would be an email writer for a while, but you know what? I think I want to be a novelist.* Then you've got enough money to go out there to change directions and prospect for new clients.

Having my Emergency Fund and my F.U. Fund did a lot to ease my anxiety. I knew I wouldn't be homeless. I had enough saved to get a roof over my head one way or another, and then plan my next step. It was enough cushion to still pay the bills and still have time to hustle for new clients. And let's be honest, in this day and age of business, it doesn't have to take you months to get business. You could have a signed contract in as little as a week (sometimes even faster!) if you're out there having conversations and presenting yourself as someone who really wants to help someone else with the skills that you've got.

Should you stay in the job until you have a fully funded F.U. Fund?

Not necessarily. I prefer it that way, because that's my level of comfort. But some people fare better when they take sudden, drastic action to "clear the slate." These folks are much more risk-tolerant and would likely feel safe quitting a job whether or not they had savings in the bank. Nothing wrong with that approach—it all comes down to your comfort and risk tolerance as to how much you need the F.U. Fund to get started on this path.

I will say this about going for it without a safety net: there is a special kind of magic that happens only when your back is against the wall, and you have to produce OR ELSE.

It gives you a lot more freedom to overcome things you might have otherwise been scared to try: networking tactics, putting yourself out there, and advertising your services. You have to. You don't have a choice. You don't have any income coming in, and you must promote yourself.

That's one way to get comfortable with discomfort in a hurry. When you jump in without savings, you don't have the runway to try a little thing and see if the idea works, and then go a little bigger and see if it works, and then a little bit bigger. When you quit and take away the safety net, it's go big or go crawling back to the job. That's why I personally recommend the F.U. Fund for freedom and flexibility.

The important thing to take away from this is, again, there is no one "right" approach for everybody. But don't go into this without any preparation or forethought at all.

It's better to think about this now, in a relative state of calm. That allows you to go out on your own terms, with a plan and savings in place… versus the alternative: you get laid off or fired, your choices taken away, and you find yourself scrambling, starting from a place of panic.

Go check out the Escape Plan in the companion guide (download free at **permissiontokickass.com/guide)** and figure out your next moves to get your business going.

Chapter 7: Know Your Numbers

Recently, I was on a Zoom coaching call with a would-be freelancer who had a long history in the field she wanted to freelance in. It was just a matter of connecting the dots to get the "Lemonade Stand" version of her business together, which would give her the courage to leave the day job.

As part of the preparation, I asked how much money she thought she'd need to earn to be okay.

"I'll be fine. All I need to make is $3,000 per month," she said.

"At the risk of making you gasp and clutch your pearls… You might want to aim for $6,000." I said.

"Why is that?"

"First of all, $6,000 is totally doable." I told her. "Also, if you want to take home $3,000 each month, you're going to have to earn about double that in revenue." Her eyes got big as saucers.

"Think about it—taxes are going to eat 20-30% of what you bring in, and then there are operating expenses for your business. Expenses are going to be small to start since you're a freelancer, but you'll have them. And without charging appropriately, that will all come out of the money you need for rent and bills."

I have this kind of conversation a lot, and I think it's a byproduct of what I call "the employee filter." For most of us that spent a significant portion of our life employed by others, we never had to think about the expense of running a business. I'm going to encourage you to start thinking about it now.

For instance, how much money does your current employer spend on you? Maybe they offer a health insurance plan or a matching 401(k) program. No? What about vacation and sick leave? Those are things to factor into your revenue goals when you're your own boss. The point isn't to start a business and barely make enough to feed yourself. That's not winning.

Why would you put all this work into building something that has you eating ramen noodles and worrying about whether you can pay the bills? Aim high, not low.

In short, you're in business to profit. And to have a profitable business that works FOR you instead of working you into the ground, you need to know your numbers. Setting prices shouldn't be a guessing game, but that's how many new entrepreneurs treat it. They pick a number out of thin air and wonder why they struggle.

You're not going to make that mistake, which is why you're going to figure out as much as you can in advance, including costs, taxes, and the minimum you need to personally make each month. From that data, we're going to set your prices in a way that makes you profitable.

Choose your rates based on what you want to make versus what you think people can afford. The beauty of this approach is you get to decide whether you're a Lamborghini, a Lexus, or a reasonably priced used minivan. You know where that number came from, and it's not negotiable. It's simply how you run your business.

Where to Start?

In my first stab at freelancing, I approached price setting by asking, "What are other people charging? What sounds reasonable? And what's the minimum I can make here and survive?" As I'm sure you can guess, my quotes were pretty freaking low, usually just a few hundred dollars a project.

In retrospect, I'm not all that surprised that my first attempt was a failure—I had no idea of how much time it would take me to find and close business, and I had no idea what my work was worth.

I use the word "worth" on purpose because this is less about price than value.

What's valuable to us? That depends on what we believe is valuable. Money is made up. You can't go out in the backyard and pick money off a tree. It exists because we have agreed it does as a society, just like we've agreed certain products cost certain amounts.

There are people who'd pay $1,000 for shoes, whereas I'd rather spend $1,000 on a spa day. Shoes aren't worth that much to me, but relaxation is. So, when you start thinking about what you charge in terms of the value you deliver, I think it becomes a lot easier to say bigger numbers out loud, with confidence.

Setting prices is where I see many freelancers unintentionally shoot themselves in the foot before they ever get their business off the ground. And it's precisely because they start by thinking, "This is the minimum I need to make the bills and that seems pretty doable." So, they go for something that feels "realistic," yet it's never going to work from a profit standpoint.

Here's how focusing on just covering the basics is setting you up to fail:

1. It's aiming too low

Like I said, you get to decide whether you're a minivan or a luxury car. Each option is going to attract different kinds of buyers with different kinds of budgets. When I was picking a number based on what I thought "sounded reasonable" (and take your pick of empty descriptors here— "affordable" and "competitive" fit in there too) … I wasn't playing to win. That thinking led me to undercharging, which was why even when I was getting work, I stayed basically broke.

2. It's ignoring growth

When you're focused on earning the bare minimum, you're subconsciously setting yourself up to aim for a low bar and be happy when you hit it. What is the likelihood that you will hit double, quadruple, 10x the minimum?

Not very likely at all because you're setting yourself up to where hitting the low bar is your reward. Once you get it and start thinking, "I've hit that, and great, I can breathe now," you're already letting up on the gas and losing some forward momentum. In other words, you're not very likely to be motivated to do EVEN MORE once you hit your goal because you're thinking of everything extra as gravy.

To put this insight into perspective, I encouraged the client I mentioned at the start of this chapter to create three different income goals. We kept her $3,000 goal because saying a bigger number terrified her, as did the idea of committing to a bigger number and not hitting it. But that was no longer the REAL number she was aiming for. That number was $6,000, which she would need to have a healthy and profitable business that gives her freedom AND pays the bills. Then we created a stretch goal of $8,000 (which is more than possible in her business model) that would give her extra money for savings and extra runway.

Here's the thing: if she's aiming for $6,000 or $8,000 from the start, she's much more likely to hit one of them than if she was aiming for $3,000. If she hits that upper number, what do you think that would do for her confidence and motivation to keep growing and building? How many more $3,000 months do you think she'll be willing to accept once she's proven to herself she can make over 260% more? And how quickly do you think she will get demoralized if she aims for AND hits the low number?

3. It's not actually covering the basics

What you need to survive and what you need to bring in are two different numbers, and that's because you now have business bills AND personal bills. When you think about what to charge, remember that you've got to take care of all the expenses an employer would be taking care of for you. Factor in the overhead for your business, such as health insurance, retirement savings, supplies, technology, work-associated travel, and continuing education (because what you know now will not necessarily be relevant in the future).

And don't forget about taxes. The tax man cometh, and he doesn't give a shit whether your rent is paid. The good news is, if you do wind up owing taxes, they usually ignore you if you get on a payment plan. But the IRS will eventually want its cut, so it's best to get in the habit of holding a certain amount in reserve so you can pay the big ass bill at the end of the year. Realistically speaking, about half of what you bring in (after taxes, expenses, and business savings) is yours to keep for your personal lifestyle and bills. So, if you want to bring home $5,000 a month, you want to aim for your business to bring in $10,000.

I teach my coaching clients to run two sets of calculations. The first is a simple formula, which I learned from Kevin Rogers, and it's the easiest way I know to calculate what to charge. The second exercise is an eye-opener because it shows you what you NEED to make. Once you do this exercise, you can turn away clients who try to lowball you or negotiate you below your minimum.

Go check out the Profit Framework EXERCISE in the companion guide (download for free at **permissiontokickass.com/guide)**.

Deciding What to Charge

The companion guide has some blank space for you to calculate these numbers, along with prompts to help ensure you're thinking through all your bills and target goals. Now let's dig into your numbers:

Exercise 1: The Simple Pricing Framework for Knowing What to Charge

First, pick a target monthly revenue. To keep the math super easy, let's use $20,000 as an example. Next, decide how many days a month you want to work. Monday through Friday, four weeks per month? Okay, that's 20 days. Now divide $20,000 by 20 days, and you get $1,000 a day. That's what you need to make per working day to hit your goal.

That may or may not seem like a big number, but now you can estimate how many days it'll take you to do a project, then throw together a price quote super quickly. The beauty of this kind of estimate is that if you estimate three days (or $3,000) for a project and you get it done in two? You just made a $1,000 profit, AND you can get started on your next project on day three. If you did that a few times in a row and kept stacking your projects, you could wind up working less than 20 days a month and still hitting your target.

After completing your first set of numbers with the Profit Framework, the numbers might seem wildly, uncomfortably high. You might think, "Wow, I don't think I can charge that much!" That makes so much sense if you're accustomed to thinking about your price in hourly amounts.

I see you, my friend—that's why I also want you to do this next exercise. I call it my Oh HELL No Number exercise, and it's a game changer because it shows you what you need to charge for your work, minimum. When you do this one, you'll be able to set prices more confidently (and walk away from any deal that doesn't pay you what you need to make to hit your goals).

Follow along in your companion guide (download free at **permissiontokickass.com/guide**) and complete the Oh HELL No Number EXERCISE.

This one is eye-opening. Most of my coaching clients have a visceral reaction to this exercise because it often shows them they were charging less than HALF of what they needed to survive. In fact, most find they were losing money with their pricing when compared to their old income from their job.

What you come up with for your Oh HELL No Number tells you what to charge at a bare minimum and makes it easier for you to pass on a project when you know it won't pay the money you need to be profitable. This number takes into consideration your rent or mortgage, utilities, cell phone, gas, food, and all the basics like health insurance, savings, etc. Then it layers in your aspirational goals—what do you like spending on? Vacations? Cars? Fancy dinners out?

Exercise 2: The Oh HELL No Number: Why You Have to Charge More Than What Might Feel Comfortable

Remember, you are leaving a lifestyle that is not working for you so that you can create a lifestyle that DOES work for you. Don't set your new lifestyle up to be all about rice and beans, scrimping and saving, always being home, and never being able to go out because you can't afford it. In your new monthly calculation, you need fun money. You need money that you get to burn. You need savings money. You need vacation money. Whatever your particular goal, you must add that to your monthly target. And then, once you add all that up into one monthly figure, do the same thing you did with the profit framework above—divide the monthly figure by the number of days you want to work per month.

Say you figure that with rent, basics, and all the fun lifestyle stuff you want—travel, eating out, hefty donations to charity, a new seasonal wardrobe—and you come up with a monthly figure of $15,000 in expenses. If you work four weeks a month Monday through Friday, divide $15k by 20 to get $750. That's the minimum you need to make per day to have a solid, profitable business that supports your lifestyle.

With this math, it's easy to see that any project that works out to $749 a day or less is not worth your time. That doesn't mean it's not a great project. It doesn't mean the client is a jerk or that no one would do that work for that amount. It simply means this is not the right project for you because it's not in alignment with your financial targets.

The great thing about both exercises—the Simple Pricing Framework and the Oh HELL No Number—is they essentially break it down into a day rate. I do it that way for a reason, versus hourly. First, hourly is a lose-lose proposition for you and your clients. It's applying employee thinking to an entrepreneurial problem and putting you squarely back in the trading-time-for-dollars trap you were in with your job.

Plus, getting the least number of hours from you is in their best interest. Getting as many dollars as possible for the least amount of work is in your best interest. Can you see how that's already putting you and your client at cross purposes?

I have a day rate (it's one I use to do behind-the-scenes calculations, not a number that's published anywhere), and I don't take any projects that will earn me less than that day rate. This may seem like something you have to ease into, like only experienced freelancers get to charge a day rate. But I'm going to challenge you to start here and grow.

Think about the work that goes into finding a new client, onboarding them, signing all the contracts, collecting the payments, and then doing a project that pays you only two hours. Is that worth all the time you invested in finding that client? This is time spent on your business that's unpaid. It's not as if you can bill your client to cover your electricity or the time you spend prospecting for other clients. Plus, taking a less-than-you're-worth gig causes you to miss out on a better opportunity because you're too busy with other work.

You probably spent at least four or five hours getting that two-hour project, so you're technically losing money. If I spend ten hours to land a day project, I'm still coming in a little bit behind, but my return is much better. And because I'm delivering value to that client, the odds are that they will come back to me, or they will refer someone to me. But if you set the bar low and go after two-hour projects just to get the money coming in… I've got news. You might think you are proving the business model but doing this math will show you how you're actually working against yourself. Plus, you're spending a lot more than you give yourself credit for because you're spending your time on unprofitable projects.

And time is something that you cannot get back. It's your only non-renewable resource, so make sure that you're spending it wisely.
These numbers may all seem super high, and they really should feel that way. This might make you uncomfortable. But I encourage you to avoid assuming other people think about money like you do. Don't project your money issues onto others. What you think of as expensive, others might think of as cheap (and vice versa).

There are people who make what you're thinking of charging… while they're sleeping. Some people are making this while they're showering, while they are masturbating, while they're breathing, and while they're staring blankly at a wall. There are people out there making the kind of money you want to make, so there's no real reason you can't do it, too. The only difference is whether you believe you can.

Your success largely depends on knowing these numbers for yourself. And by the way, you don't need to share these numbers with your clients. They're purely internal calculations, meaning you use them to set your rates, but you don't have to explain or justify them. You don't ask for a cost breakdown of each ingredient when you go out for a fancy steak dinner, do you? The price is the price.

You should at least try to figure out your financials before you start looking for clients. You don't want the first time you think about money to be the first time you're talking to a prospective client—then you're already starting off on the wrong foot, trying to "win" business instead of trying to evaluate whether this project is interesting and profitable for you.

Get Your Head on Straight

It's tempting to compete on price when you first start your business. Many freelancers make this mistake because they start doing competitive research and see what other people charge. Then, they have one of two reactions: *Oh! That seems about right!* (but you're losing money when you run the numbers) or, *Oh, that's a lot, and they've been doing this a while! I don't think I can get paid that much.*

But how much would you charge if you've run the numbers and know what your desired lifestyle costs to maintain? I don't know about you, but I'm not going back to living off ramen noodles. I'm too old for that. I'm not going to live in a house with twenty roommates just to save money. That's not the lifestyle that I want to live. I've planned my income based on the lifestyle I want to live, the retirement I want to have, the savings I need to feel comfortable, and the fun I want to enjoy.

I'm not working my ass off to never have any fun.

When you think about the money you've got to earn, it will become easier to say those numbers and have those conversations when you know what number makes a project profitable. It's no longer a concern about, "Oh my god, that seems expensive. I wonder if they'll accept that number?"

They can't afford you if they can't accept that number. Go find people who CAN afford you.

That makes your job much simpler—find people who CAN afford you instead of chasing people who can't. Now that you know what you need to make, you won't have to waste time and energy on people who don't see your value. You just move on because you know what you need to make to pay your bills and live your life, and there's someone out there who can afford it.

I'm a big fan of saying, "Don't spend other people's money." You have no idea what they're looking for (be it a $10 movie or a $10k retreat), and you have no way of knowing what's in their wallet. The goal is to treat everybody as if they can drop that money when they know it's the right fit, no questions asked. They're out there. I roll in some pretty successful circles. There are people out there spending money the same way they breathe. Don't even worry about whether they can afford it.

You don't have access to their bank accounts, so you don't know what they can spend. Period.

In addition to what people can afford, you might also wonder if your pricing aligns with market rates. *Am I sabotaging myself because I'm setting a rate that is too high/too low?* That's a valid worry, but when you know what you need to make, that high price becomes a position of strength in negotiations. The good thing about that high-seeming number is that an interested prospective client simply comes back to you and says, "That's a little higher than what I anticipated paying."

We call that an opening—otherwise, they'd ghost and find a cheaper provider. When they come back and admit that your quote is higher than they expected, they're giving you an opening. That's another opportunity for a dialog. And then it becomes a conversation versus a confrontation. You might find some middle ground. That doesn't mean you need to cut your price and give them a discount to fit into what they can afford, but you may be able to trim things out of the proposal (and do less work) to fit what they are willing to pay.

And this is what we mean by "It's just business. It's not personal."

Their budget not meeting your quote (and vice versa) doesn't mean they think you're shitty. That is just them saying it's more than they had in mind to spend. They may be realistic; they may not. They may have no clue what it costs to get this done, which means you may have to educate them or decide they're not a good fit. They might even be embarrassed because they can't afford to pay what you quoted.

The good thing about this being a dialog is if they come back to you and propose X amount of money for Y amount of work, you can run these numbers to see if it makes sense and easily turn down any project that is not profitable for you. And that is critical. Stop thinking of this in terms of, "I've got to do whatever it takes to bring money in the door," and start thinking like a business owner who says, "I can't take this project because it's losing me money. There will be other clients, so time to start hustling."

You're a human being, not a machine. You won't fix an unprofitable business decision by working longer and harder—you will, however, burn out. Taking on any project that doesn't meet your daily rate is a losing proposition any way you slice it. And it's not smart business. That's why you need to know these numbers.

One last note on rates: whenever you quote someone or set a price, make sure to include an expiration date on your proposal. You could say something like, "Once I sell ten, the price goes up." You could also say, "This is my intro rate for six months, and then the price goes up." I can't tell you how many folks take a set-and-forget approach to their rates, then wonder why a few years in, they're struggling. Or they give a client a quote, and two years later, that client pops back up expecting you to honor your early-days rates.

Every year you should raise your rates. This will help you adjust to the increased cost of living and prevent people from coming back and demanding beginner level rates from you once you've gained experience. As you increase your rates, your lower paying clients are naturally going to drop off because they can no longer afford you—but then space opens up for you to find clients who pay you more to do less (and people who pay more tend to respect you more too, in general). Your business and revenue grow, and you don't have to work as hard? Sign me up.

Rates are not static. Numbers are not your enemy. Rerun these calculations at least once a year and get in the habit of charging more as you get better and better.

Taking Care of Business (Read: Busy Work)

For everyone reading this book, I expect that you're in the process of starting or growing your freelance business. That means your most likely first step into the business world is as a solopreneur. At this stage, you're wearing all the hats and juggling all the things—meaning you're doing every job from sales to accounting to creating. Right now, staying focused on the things that will set you up for success in the long run is essential. I want to start by going through the basic building blocks of a thriving freelance business.

Managing Your Money

As I mentioned in Chapter 3, the quickest way to get your business going is modeling a lemonade stand. Start with:

1. A product or service to offer
2. People who want to buy it
3. Payment processor (can be simple as PayPal or accepting cash)
4. Email address

We just went over pricing, so you have an idea of how to set your rates. You know not only what you're selling, but also roughly what you should charge for it. If you didn't already open a business bank account (we talked about that back in Chapter 3), now's the time to do it. And PayPal counts—it lets you invoice, track expenditures, and even get a business debit card. You can keep it simple with that or find a local bank branch that'll get you set up.

I highly recommend having a business checking and a business savings account—the former for your daily expenses, like supplies, internet, contractor fees, etc. The latter is for tax savings and any other unexpected business expenses that pop up along the way.

In the last chapter, I talked about the importance of Emergency and F.U. Funds. I think you should keep those separate from the business accounts. The reason is sometimes things are weird. Clients do chargebacks instead of asking for a refund, and algorithms mistakenly flag you as someone to watch for shady business shit. Your PayPal or business funds could get temporarily held or frozen while the bank investigates, so you want to make sure you're set up to have access to cash whenever you need it.

I should note, the funds freeze is not a common issue, but it's always better to be prepared. It's happened to me a time or two (in over a decade I've been doing this, so again, fairly rare). When it happened, I was really in a bind because all my money was tied up in the investigation. Before, I had this head trash around the complexity of managing multiple business accounts. Now I can't imagine putting all my eggs into one bank account.

About managing multiple bank accounts—it sounds more complicated than it is. Especially since these days, many banks offer different "subaccounts" for different saving and spending goals. I have one set up with different funds earmarked for my F.U. Fund, taxes, medical expenses, car expenses and maintenance, vacations (if I'm taking myself somewhere, I'm really treating myself to something special), and retirement. It's a little extra work to move money between accounts, but because I've allocated this money to different goals, I can't accidentally spend it by glancing at my main account and thinking I have more money than I really do.

You'll want to play around with your allocations and account setup until it makes sense for you. At a high level, any revenue I receive breaks down like this: 45% is my personal pay, which includes all my bills, groceries, fun money, and non-business savings. 20% goes to the tax savings account, and 20% stays in the main business account to pay for business operations. 10% goes to my F.U. Fund and 5% goes into my Profit First account (*Profit First* is another business book I highly recommend).

There's no reason to hold yourself back from starting a business to wait and take these financial steps. **The key is not to use the business license, bank account, and revenue allocations as an unintentional stalling tactic.** All combined, these things take a few hours to complete, and I did them on lunch breaks while still at the day job. If you want to have these things in place when you get started, set aside an afternoon or two to get it all done, preferably while someone else is still paying you. I don't want you to wait until day one of your new business to set all this up because then you're cutting into valuable money-making time.

Spending Your Way to Success

A word to the wise, especially when you're doing something freelance/creative like writing: you don't have to invest in a whole bunch of equipment, offices, branding, etc. just to get started. Debt and investing are great tools if you use them in a smart way, but if credit cards get you in trouble in your regular life, you probably don't want to travel down that road for your business until you're bringing in a steady profit. I'm a big fan of making the money you need to pay for future investments rather than blowing your wad up front and figuring out how to pay it all back on the fly.

I know one person who started a baking business. She's particularly gifted and lives in a state where cottage baker laws apply, meaning she can legally bake in her house. The catch is she's limited in where she can sell her goods and must tell people they're homemade. By knowing her area, she was able to start her business without having to spend a ton on kitchen equipment, baking space, fancy trailers, or licensing.

Every time she goes to a winery or a local festival, she earns another fan who brings a friend along to buy even more goods the next time. Her business has grown through word of mouth, and eventually, she was able to invest in a fancy trailer to take to her events.

I think that's the smart way to do it—slow and steady. You can technically go as fast as you want, but I like a little breathing room over going 80 miles an hour all the time. It's tempting to think that one flashy purchase or spendy piece of software can magically catapult you to success, but it doesn't happen that way. You'll still have to learn how to find clients, what you want to sell, what your price is, and how you'll get your product or service to your customers. Those are skills you need regardless of equipment or software.

Cash flow is the most important thing to consider as you're starting your business. You want to spend less than you bring in, reinvest extra into your business, and always be socking money away in your F.U. Fund.

Once you're profitable, it's fun and a-okay to invest in things for your business. I bought a new laser printer once because I knew sometimes my eyes start to cross when I've been looking at the computer too long, and I needed to print something out and go line by line so I wouldn't strain my eyes. Eventually, I got tired of wasting paper (and refilling ink) and upgraded to an e-ink tablet for doing line edits.

The point is to focus on the basics, on your lemonade stand. The further you go and the more you get to know your customers, the more you'll get a feel for what kinds of investments you can make that will exponentially grow your business—versus an expensive way to flush money down the drain. Spend wisely, especially with credit. Don't think you can borrow your way into a successful business unless you're already really good at managing debt and risk.

Earn what you want so you can reinvest in your business. Grow by setting goals, going out there, and making shit happen.

Hiring Good Help

At some point, wearing all the hats will become overwhelming and exhausting. When you hit that point, you'll want to bring on some help. One of your first hires (and you can contract this out versus hiring someone full-time)—is a good bookkeeper.

Especially if you're anything like me, and the idea of reconciling bank statements and categorizing receipts makes you want to run screaming into the night. A good tax professional can help you save money in the long run, and that's something that pays for itself. At a bare minimum, invest in good bookkeeping software and set aside an hour or two per month to review your expenses and income. The investment is worth it at the end of the year when you don't have to spend days digging through files and statements, trying to figure out what goes where.

The very next hire I made after the bookkeeper was a part-time virtual assistant (VA). I was getting so busy that I was in danger of dropping balls in a big way. If I didn't get help, I knew people would seriously doubt my capabilities as a trusted expert. It took me a while to find one I liked (Ashlee

Berghoff, founder of A Squared Online and author of the book *Eureka Profits*, in case you're curious).

I was up-front about needing someone who could anticipate things for me and proactively get things done. I knew if they were waiting for me to give them a to-do list, we'd fail before we even started. So, when I found her, I dropped a scary amount on an assistant who wound up becoming my business manager/operations manager/assistant all in one. She was able to take a lot of little time-sucking tasks off my plate so that I could work on the stuff I did best.

It was another scary risk that wound up paying for itself because I could grow much faster and have much more time on any given day. I was not wasting hours scheduling meetings or handling blog and podcast posts myself. All those quick tasks that were taking up so much of my day were still getting done—and all I had to do was make a video or train her how to do something and then get back to making money.

More on hiring (including where to start and what to look for) in Chapter 14.

Establishing a Presence Online

Let's get one thing out of the way: you don't need a website to get started. Having one will help in the long run, but it's not worth putting off your work or bringing in money just to have a fancy site built. There are people who operate online with just Etsy or Shopify stores. There are people who sell through Facebook Marketplace or freelance sites like Upwork, and they don't have a website at all.

Website envy is another form of head trash.
It's an invisible barrier between you and success, and it doesn't have to be there. You can totally build a business without a $10k website, even in the digital age, so stop letting that hold you back. My first website was an

absolute piece of garbage for probably six or seven years. I built it myself from a shitty, free WordPress template. I spent a whole lot of time and money on building it myself because at the time, I kept telling myself I couldn't afford to pay anyone to help me.

You'd think I could have scraped up the money at any time during those six years if I didn't have my head up my ass, but I was convinced it was too expensive, so I took forever and did it all myself. I still cringe when I think of how many hours I spent on that site and what I would have made if I'd been PAID for all those hours.

To boot, my site was ridiculously ugly, so I refused to send people the link because I was embarrassed. And yet I still managed to get clients, close deals, and make money. I'm sure that at some point, they Googled me and found my horrible website, but they still chose to work with me—which just goes to show you the website is not the thing that sells. YOU are.

Eventually, I got tired of hiding my shitty website and saved up enough money to pay someone to build a new one. Investing in my site inspired me to take it seriously and really get into branding and copy. Those things were a lot easier since, after years in business, I knew what I was good at and what people liked about working with me.

Bottom line, you don't need a website to start selling.

You can store samples in the cloud. You can send correspondence via email. I know that not having a site might send signals to the suspicious types—there are those who doubt anyone they can't cyber stalk. But rest assured, there are still plenty of people who deliberately minimize their online time. They still get plenty of business via other channels and connections. So, find your people where they're hanging out—Facebook, forums, groups, Reddit. Interact with them and get to know them without ever having built a website. Magic!

Recharging the Well

I know I'm hammering on this again, but it bears repeating: always pay yourself first. Especially when you get unexpected money—throw some toward debt (if you have any) and put a chunk of that into savings. And then reserve a little bit for yourself to go blow on something fun, because **you absolutely should reward yourself every time you have a win.** It's not silly—it's a reminder of why you're doing all this. When you consciously balance out the challenging times and give yourself something to look forward to—it's super powerful motivation.

A couple of years ago, I'd been working on a client promo for months, and they surprised me with an unexpected performance bonus. We're talking high four figures, a healthy sum of money. It was enough to pay off a Disney vacation I had put on layaway and been steadily paying toward. So, I paid off that trip, put some money into savings, and spent the rest taking a friend to Savannah, GA to see the sights. We got room service, took a riverboat trip, and had a ton of fun. I came back renewed and ready to work.

Don't be afraid to have fun with your money—so long as your bills are paid, and your savings are funded, the rest is yours to enjoy. And you can always make more, especially when you take time to have fun and recharge your creativity well. Remind yourself why you do this. Don't just focus on surviving the lean times. Celebrate the wins too.

Remember that nothing is static in business (or in life), and things will change whether you want them to or not. You've got to be deliberate about how far to swing that pendulum between the bad times and the good.

When you've hit rock bottom, there's only one way to go, and that's up. And when you're at your high points, you know that it won't last forever. That's why I urge you to enjoy those highs with gusto and abandon and do it without shame or self-consciousness.

There's always going to be lean months, and there's always going to be flush months. But without the lows, we can't learn to appreciate the highs.

Chapter 8: Punching Fear in the Face

Fear will pop up in new and interesting ways as you progress through this journey. I learned that firsthand with my first major client after I left the day job.

One of my "Accountability Buddies" from the Copy Chief community reached out privately to ask if I was interested in contracting with a high-level marketer they knew, a big influencer in the online business space.

He is a celebrity in the entrepreneur world, but I didn't know that when I first threw my hat in the ring. Of course, the more I dug in and learned about him, the more intimidated I got. The nerves set in when I realized just how well-known he was.

The vetting process was intense, too. I was up against other top copywriters who'd worked with big names, and we had to do things that made a lot of freelancers squirm… namely a writing test to prove our skills. If I had given in to my fear of whether or not I had the goods to work with a "big name," I would've missed out on one of the biggest opportunities of my life. So, I gave myself permission to punch that fear in the face and give it my all.

Worst case scenario, if I tried my hardest and didn't get the gig—I didn't have the gig before, so it's not like I was losing anything but time by trying.

I had a good feeling about that one, but it took months for everything to play out. I kept in touch with them and expressed my excitement after two great interviews and a writing test, but I wasn't about to put all my eggs in that basket. That meant going back to pounding the pavement—prospecting and talking to new potential clients. I wasn't sure which opportunities would pan out, and I knew if I kept taking action, something good would come of it.

Then it happened… I got the gig! Instantly a new fear set in: I couldn't start on the day they wanted and was terrified to tell them.

Well before I'd even planned to leave my job, my best friend and I had booked and planned out a Disney World vacation. We spent the entire previous year obsessing over every detail, and given the shitty laid-off-from-a-job-I-didn't-have experience (which happened about a week prior to me getting this gig, by the way), we were both pumped to go blow off steam and have fun. We'd saved all year to make it happen, and the tickets had already been purchased.

I was so afraid that I was blowing the opportunity by not canceling my vacation, but eventually, I worked up the gumption to say, "I'd love to, but I can't start that day. I'm going on a trip to Disney that I've been planning for a year. I can start when I get back though!"

A few years before, I probably would have canceled or postponed vacation just to show them how over-the-top excited I was to accept their offer. I really needed that vacation though, so I told them where my head was. Within minutes, they let me know I could start when I got back.

I took the trip and had a blast, then I returned and started my 90-day trial period. Then I went to work and did my damnedest. It was fascinating work and really challenged me, especially since I'd never really ghostwritten as a guru.

Before long, we were creeping up on 90 days, and a new fear popped up: suddenly, I was anxious and wondering whether I'd done a good enough job to continue.

I really wanted to keep working with them, but we hadn't discussed extending my contract beyond 90 days. Naturally, I got a little nervous. And when I say nervous, I mean it rapidly devolved into an anxiety spiral.

My go-to method when I'm feeling anxious? Take action, any action. I reached out to a few contacts on the team to lightly prod and see if anyone knew anything about my contract being extended. If I was out on my ass, I knew I needed to turn up the gas on prospecting for the next gig.

Someone must have said something to the guru because minutes after I started reaching out to my contacts, he called me. He assured me, "Hey, I just wanted to let you know your role here is fine. You're doing a great job, and I'm sorry we didn't tell you that sooner."

Phew!

Then he said something that's stuck with me to this day. "I get the sense you're an anxious person," he told me. "And I really don't want you to be anxious because you can't create from that space. But if you really need something to worry about because that's how you process, worry about sounding different from everything else in our people's inboxes."

I tell you that story because it was one of the biggest challenges of my professional career—and I had to overcome a lot of fears just to put myself out there and try.

That's why I wanted to dedicate an entire chapter to overcoming what I call "head trash." This chapter is about getting your mindset right for long-term entrepreneurial success. The fact is, the further I go on this business building journey, the more I see this playing out in every field and niche—the most successful entrepreneurs out there are constantly working on mindset and self-improvement. And that's what has REALLY helped them get as far as they have.

If that surprised you at all, or if you cringe a little at the idea of personal development, then buckle up, buttercup. We're going to learn some mindset skills—and trust me when I say these are skills you can learn, practice, and improve. Improving these skills will be a constant, lifelong effort… but it's worth it.

Let's get started…

Facing Your Fears Head On

So, you've made the choice to do something big and exciting… Maybe you're interviewing for a new job, starting your own business, or even working up the courage to start a new relationship or get out and date again. Congrats! That's super exciting!

Why does it seem so hard to DO the thing?

It all comes down to fear. Your brain is taking you through the paces, flashing panicked questions at you like strobing lights.

There's no way to really know what's going to happen!

What if I fail?

What if I let everyone down?

What if I can't pay the bills and wind up homeless on the street, surrounded by feral cats?

Your brain is funny that way… you have this great idea, and it gets you all excited at the possibilities. Then when you make the choice to bring this idea to life, your brain basically hijacks you, and paralyzes you. The weird thing is that's its job. In fact, it's totally normal. In addition to keeping your body running, your brain's job is to protect you from situations where you might be in mortal danger.

Odds are you've already experienced this phenomenon… think of the times you've been creeped out while walking alone at night. Or when you felt a sudden urge to take a different road home and later read that there was an accident on your typical route. Your subconscious brain picks up on subtle signals and flips the switch on the ol' fight-or-flight response. So, while you may not know exactly what it was that spooked you, something in your "gut" was guiding you out of harm's way.

Okay. Cool—let's not die today. Thanks, brain!

But then there's this completely different situation where you're taking a risk that's really NOT about life or death. Like when you're deciding to leave a job or start a business… and the likelihood of imminent death is significantly lower than, say, alligator wrestling. Now that you've made this exciting decision, why does it suddenly seem like the scariest possible thing you could do?

There's this great quote I heard from Will Smith (of Men in Black and the "Oscar slap" fame):

"Fear can only exist when there's an unknown."

Before he became notorious for the Oscars incident, he did this phenomenal speech about fear. In it, he was talking about a time when he decided to go skydiving, and noticed he had an interesting reaction (I'm paraphrasing below):

In the moment, with friends: Okay, I'm in. Hell yeah, let's do this skydiving thing! Flying baby, yeah!

At home later, alone: WHAT WAS I THINKING? WHY WOULD I JUMP OUT OF A PERFECTLY GOOD PLANE?

Granted, jumping out of a plane does come with a little life-or-death risk. But so does life! You're risking your life every time you...

- text while walking down the street
- put your car in gear and hit the road
- eat delicious greasy food from an interesting looking food truck

I know things just got morbid REAL fast but stick with me—there's a point, I promise. Here's the mindset I try to have: death is simply the end result of living. It's the one thing that we all have in common. We're born, and we die… it's what we choose to do in between those two dates that makes all the difference.

To put it in perspective, do you really want to live your life in fear? I know I don't, especially when there are so many risks worth taking that make life worth living… love. Family. Success. Adventure. Freedom. No one dreams about sitting passively and letting life just happen to them, but that tends to be exactly what happens when you let fear make your choices for you.

The point I'm trying to make here is this: some things are worth the risk.

That's why Will Smith's speech hit me so hard. He talked about how the best things in life are on the other side of fear. Because we sit, we think, we imagine all kinds of worst-case scenarios, and we get all worked up. But all this fear, we feel it WAY before we do the thing.

Have you ever noticed how when we're at our most fearful (aside from actual life-and-death situations), we're not *actually* in danger? I know when I'm scared it usually looks something like this: I'm in bed terrified, my mind racing with all the possible things that can go wrong. Lying down, perfectly safe in my own bed. <u>I'm literally not in danger at all.</u> Nothing is happening, yet I'm in borderline panic attack mode just from the THOUGHT of what I am going to do.

All that said, it's one thing to realize it's there… and it's another thing entirely to convince yourself to calm the fuck down. It's not as if you can run to the mirror, look yourself in the eye, and yell at yourself to pull it together and STOP IT RIGHT NOW. Yelling doesn't really work on kids, pets, coworkers, or freaked-out psyches.

Fear has a way of shutting down rational thought, so the key is not to try and stop it, but instead simply to recognize when it's happening. When you can identify the feeling holding you hostage, you're well on your way to breaking its hold on you.

Remember: fear only exists when there is an unknown.

When you are getting ready to do something new, different, challenging, and risky, fear pops up and tries to derail you by leading you down an anxiety spiral. Before you know it, you're feeling hopeless. Paralyzed. Resigned to believing your current path is the only way forward.

But here's the thing about anxiety… it lies. It builds the unknown thing up until it's as big and intimidating as Mount Everest when it's really an ant hill you could sidestep (or wash away entirely).

I've been stuck on Mt. Fear before, and thankfully I started recognizing my patterns. I'd get sucked into this vortex of anxiety and worry and fear. Leaving my job? Great, you're going to wind up homeless and starving to death. Splitting with a romantic partner? Great, you're going to wind up homeless and starving to death, then eaten by feral cats.

Ever notice how that pendulum seems to swing in only one direction? My dear, sweet reader, if you take away only one thing from our time together, it should be this… you have more options than staying where you are OR DEATH.

That's because you're really making the choice between staying where you are... or trying something different.

And once you make your choice, the RESULTS of that decision aren't likely to be "OR DEATH" either. Let's be real—unless your new direction is tightrope walking between two skyscrapers with no safety net, the most likely outcomes are either: you do better than you thought, or you don't do as well as you thought.

So, forgive your brain for doing its job. It's just trying to protect you. But trust me when I say you won't starve to death… you are resourceful and capable, and you'll figure something out long before it comes to "OR DEATH." Because guess what? To date, you've survived 100% of the scary situations life has thrown at you. And I like those odds.

You've got this.

When Your Brain is a Bastard

Success isn't an accident.

It doesn't just happen to you if you hope hard enough or if you hit the lotto. Just look up "lotto curse" if you think that a windfall automagically solves all your problems.

But finding success is an incredibly uncomfortable process for a lot of people, and I'm including myself in that statement. Regardless of how hard it is, it's worth the effort. Mindset work is how successful people find solutions. It's how they get their behaviors and actions in alignment with their goals. It's how they get closer to their dreams that much more quickly.

And here's something interesting: most of the successful business owners I know aren't wasting precious time complaining or being hyper-focused on everything that's going wrong. Take a page from their playbook, and if you notice any of the following qualities in yourself, time to get to work!

Fixed Mindset

In her book, *Mindset: The New Psychology of Success*, Carol Dweck discusses two kinds of mindsets: fixed and growth. People with a fixed mindset are often looking for someone to blame. Whatever's happening is not their fault, and they tend to be comfortable as victims of their circumstances.

You might hear folks with a fixed mindset say something like, "I have the worst luck. No matter how hard I work, nothing ever goes my way. I'm killing myself here, but it never winds up working out. If everything keeps going wrong, it must be a sign that I'm not good enough to do this. Why even try?"

Then you have your folks with a growth mindset. These are people looking for what's good in any situation. They find the silver lining even in instances where nothing looks salvageable.

People with a growth mindset tend to say, "I haven't always had the best luck, but everything seems to work out—often even better than I expected. Sometimes I get a better result from 'failing' and having to find a new way than I could have if everything worked out the way I planned. No matter what happens to me, I find a way forward. I'm going to give it my best shot and see how it goes!"

See the difference?

Look, if you fall into the "fixed mindset" category, I'm sending you all my love and support. That was me, too, once upon a time. I only picked up *Mindset* because one day I was griping to my mentor about something, and he suggested it as a good read. He was right—it was a good read, and it showed me how my thinking impacted my decision making (and therefore my outcomes).

No shame in starting where you start. The key is to not stay there.

We are all victims of circumstances. Everyone around you is dealing with some sort of trauma, ranging from head trash to serious life-or-death escapes. And the big difference between the folks who survive and those who thrive is mindset. We can't control what happens to us, what's happening in the economy, or even what our customers, clients, and employees do. What we CAN control is how we behave and how we react.

Fixed mindset is one of the most challenging ones to crack—because it's solidly based in fear and looks for reasons to justify why you're feeling the way you are. Then those negative thought patterns burn neural pathways into your brain and become your default mode of thinking.

The downside is, while it's true that a fixed mindset is only trying to protect you, and it certainly doesn't make you a bad person… it's also making your thought processes rigid and inflexible. It's closing you down to even considering alternative possibilities if the one you wanted to work fails. Ever heard about something bending until it breaks? There's a reason earthquake-prone areas have houses with moving foundations and buildings with flexible supports—the more rigid and resistant the structure, the quicker the building shakes itself to pieces.

Open your mind to the part you play in your own circumstances and consider whether you have more power than you give yourself credit for.

To survive (and thrive) the ups and downs of life as a business owner, you'll want to find reasons to keep going. Decide you can figure it out, no matter what "it" is, and look for solutions versus shutting down and lamenting your situation. Growth mindset is the way to go if you want to have a successful business (not to mention being a lot less stressed and a lot more happy).

Self-Sabotage

People who self-sabotage usually wind up getting the dream gig—and then repeatedly blowing deadlines or making rookie mistakes until the client gets pissed and cuts them off.

What makes a perfectly sane person get all the way to the finish line and stop just shy of crossing it?

In a word? Fear, our old frenemy. Often self-sabotage feels like something overwhelming and out of your control, but when you stand back and look at it objectively, you can spot places where you could have made different choices. That's the key to all of this—because any kind of success you find in business (and in life) is going to involve the ability to look at yourself both critically AND compassionately. You've got to be able to evaluate, without judgment, where you may be making missteps and where you may be on the right path.

Hello growth mindset, my old friend…

Withhold judgment of yourself when you're looking at mistakes you've made. Remember that you're doing everything you're doing to get better. You don't need to suffer and torment yourself for falling short of perfection. Newsflash: none of us human beings on planet Earth are perfect—and trying to be is a recipe for crazy making. You can't take mistakes as a sign that you're a bad person or a failure. You've got to be able to detach from the outcomes because…

Reminder: failure is an event, not your identity.

And contrary to popular societal narratives, failure is critical to success. It's one of the fastest ways to find your way forward. Embrace failure, fail hard, and fail fast. You can even fail spectacularly if you're feeling sassy. Then get back up and try again.

Impostor Syndrome

People suffering from impostor syndrome often feel like they're not enough, as if they're not worthy and are constantly being evaluated and judged. They may feel like they're frauds, and that if anyone ever finds out they don't know enough, their career will be over.

I often see these folks apologizing in advance for some perceived slight or imperfection, as if they need to qualify why they're good enough to do the work. This sounds a lot like, "Hi, I'm new to this copywriting thing and I've never done it before, but I'm really interested in your project and think I can do a good job. I'll be the hardest worker you've ever met. Will you hire me?"

When I get messages like this (which is more often than I can count), first, I send a lot of love out into the universe. I can FEEL the insecurity and the fear coming through that email. Often, we're so afraid in the moment that leading with our shortcomings makes some sort of weird sense. But ask yourself, does that intro really inspire confidence?

The thing is: everyone starts at zero. Even the folks born into business empire families still must learn the skills to run that business, or they wind up going broke from mismanagement.

If you're brand new, don't apologize for it. Keep going until you get someone to take a chance on you. Learn everything you can, improve, and don't make the same mistake twice if you can help it. Rinse and repeat, one client or customer at a time, and be on a mission to learn as much as possible from each project and encounter.

There are hundreds, if not thousands, of people doing what you want to do and doing it successfully. That's good news because it means this thing you're trying to do is MORE than doable. But it's also bad news because there are lots of talented folks out there doing the same thing… so it's not enough to be new, and eager, and a hard worker. You've got to stand out from the crowd.

And the easiest way I know to stand out? Be 100% yourself.

Like making Star Wars references? Do it. Can't go a day without making a ranty video? Do it. Be YOU because people like doing business with people they like. And even if you're brand new, there's always someone out there who's willing to meet you where you're at.

Maybe their budget is small, and they can only afford someone just starting out. Maybe they love giving newbies a chance, or they're looking for someone raw and coachable that they can train and work with long-term. Don't assume everyone wants someone with boatloads of experience. There's someone out there who could use your help, exactly as you are right now.

Posturing and Projecting

There's an aspect of impostor syndrome where, instead of outing themselves as inexperienced, the person overcompensates and starts to posture. Think of posturing as puffery, and as bluster and bravado. It's people talking a good game and bragging about who they are because they don't believe in their own worth deep down.

They've got a fear of being found out as a fraud, and they think if they can convince everyone around them they're successful, that they'll eventually BECOME successful.

Here's the thing: anyone who's been in business for more than a few years can spot this behavior right away. People who are insecure enough to posture usually push buttons because they think dominance and cockiness are how they prove their expertise.

They'll jump in and talk over people, constantly throwing around proof that they know what they're talking about—even though nobody asked. This is impostor syndrome mixed in with a fixed mindset, which results in the posturer looking like a stubborn know-it-all who's difficult to work with versus a valued partner who commands top dollar.

I think the worst part of this kind of outlook is that it's based entirely on faulty logic. Posturing is trying to prove you have expertise—and most experts know enough to understand they DON'T know it all. In fact, most experts I've met are perfectly comfortable telling a paying client, "Oh, that's a great question. I don't have an answer, but I'll do some digging and get back to you." That was my biggest personal aha moment, and one that helped me break free from using posturing and impostor syndrome as crutches:

Experts don't know everything. They don't pretend to either. They have the ability to FIND answers, and their clients respect (and pay them well) for that.

You don't need to talk 90 miles a minute to prove you're an expert. One of the best ways I know to look really, really smart, while also positioning yourself as an expert, is to ask thoughtful questions that get people to think and listen.

That's how you lead them to new ideas and different choices. As you're asking them questions they didn't even know to ask, they're thinking critically and are more receptive to answers versus having someone talk at (and over) them or someone who's constantly trying to prove them wrong.

One client of mine had his heart set on a massive, multimillion-dollar affiliate launch. Just one of those promotions usually involved hundreds of emails sent to hundreds of thousands of people. So, my first question was, "How many people do you have on your email list?" The list was small, and he didn't have relationships with the kinds of influencers he needed to promote his product the way he wanted.

If I didn't ask the right questions to find that out, I might've just postured and run my mouth about how I could help them do this big launch, only to sign a contract, take a payment, and find out it wasn't possible. Or at least, it wouldn't be possible without a bunch of extra work to reach out to influencers and build up his list of email subscribers.

If you read that and think, "Man, I bet that client would have been pissed," you're right. That's why an open mind and smart questions are much more important than proving you know it all.

Retrain Your Brain

Let's talk about something I find fascinating—the Baader-Meinhof phenomenon. That's the thing where as soon as you buy a yellow car (because you love how it stands out), you start seeing yellow cars everywhere.

It's not that everyone suddenly decided yellow was "in." The manufacturers didn't make more yellow this year than any other. But because you have a yellow car, your brain now sees them, whereas before (when it didn't matter much to you) you didn't really notice them.

It's one of the many ways your brain protects you from information overwhelm—by filtering out things it deems as unnecessary or irrelevant. So, it stands to reason that you can train your brain to look for things you might not consciously be aware of right now—like all the good things you've got going for you.

Don't get me wrong—in setting your sights on more positive stuff, that doesn't mean the bad stuff suddenly disappears. You won't decide today to think more positively and magically wake up tomorrow a changed human who never has another negative thought. But by consciously deciding to practice it (and to be gentle with yourself when you fall short), it eventually becomes a default thought pattern that takes up less of your brainpower on any given day.

Anything can become a habit with enough practice—including looking for the positive.

And this ties in with our overall happiness, too. We all go through shitty seasons. I'm not advising you to become optimistic to the point of delusion. But if you're looking for reasons your life sucks, you're training your brain to look for more of the same. When you do that, your brain will quite literally ignore everything else, including the awesome stuff. Put more simply:

What you focus on, you find.

You tell yourself that life sucks, the world is hard and cruel, and your brain will look for evidence to prove you right. You tell yourself that the world isn't always fair, but you have plenty to celebrate, and surely more good stuff is on its way? Your brain will start to look for that good stuff, even if it's silly TikTok videos of goofy animals or a coffee date with friends where you share lots of laughs.

Looking for the positive doesn't mean there aren't sucky moments. It doesn't mean there will never be moments of depression, loneliness, or awfulness. You're still going to notice when you didn't quite nail that last project. You're going to have moments that feel like a gut punch and like you let someone down, making you wonder if you can even do this at all.

The difference is, when you consciously refocus your attention on what you've got going for you versus what you lack, you gain invaluable perspective.

You have hope. You understand that things may suck for now, but for now is not forever.
This takes practice—it's not a flip you can switch, so again, I want to remind you to be gentle with yourself. Treat yourself like you would a best friend, or a child you adore, or a treasured parental figure. If they came to you, beating themselves up because they felt like colossal failures, odds are you'd hug them and help them see how awesome they are.

You deserve the same faith and support from yourself.

All that said, it's one thing to talk about training your brain, and it's quite another to do the damn thing. That's why I spent so much time harping on the fact that it's a process, not a magic button. Start with noticing. That's all. Just notice that a negative thought popped up and tried to tell you, "Here are all the reasons I suck." Just by noticing it and giving that emotion a name, like "That's just my fear talking," you've already broken the thought pattern and short-circuited the spiral. Eventually, you can try adding in a little private thought to yourself of, "I don't have to think this right now."

It's your brain—you absolutely have a say in what you want to think at any given time! That little 3-pound lump of meat doesn't get to hijack you just because the hormones went haywire!

I would never let someone walk into my house and tell me I'm a piece of garbage, yet all too often we let our brains rail on us as if we're the worst human being on the planet. You wouldn't let someone talk to your best friend, or niece, or parent, or someone you care about like that. Don't let YOU talk to you like that. Shut it, brain. Stop being a jerk.

I want to prepare you for the reality of this practice—when you start noticing your negative thoughts, a couple of things might happen:

1) You might realize you have way more negative thoughts than you were aware of, and that it almost runs like constant café chatter in the background.

2) You might not even recognize it until you've been ruminating on the bad shit for a while and suddenly you think, "Oh, right. Negative thoughts. I don't have to think this."

Resist the urge to immediately pile on yourself for having too many negative thoughts or for not noticing them quickly enough. This is a skill you develop with practice, and you won't be good at it immediately. Especially considering your lifetime of conditioning toward the negative.

When you get a little better at noticing those negative thoughts, you'll free up brain space to treat those thoughts with a little curiosity. Ask yourself, "Is this true, or is it fear/anxiety talking? What makes this true? What makes this false? Why is this popping up right now? What am I really worried about?" The key is to detach from emotion and judgment as much as possible. This is where journaling really comes in handy—you get to write down all the questions and really think about the answers.

Let's practice: say a potential client you were really excited about wound up hiring someone else.

Your brain might jump to the conclusion that you did something wrong—maybe you turned in a quote that was too high, or you didn't ask the right questions, or your samples weren't strong enough. Your brain might pile on with, "You messed up, big time! They know you're a fraud because of how badly you fucked that up, and they're getting ready to tell EVERYONE."

Stop.

Notice that thought and how quickly it went from zero to jerk.

Now detach from self-judgment and get curious. "What if my application was great, my samples were strong, and they loved me? What might have happened? Could there be a reason it makes sense that I did everything right and still didn't get it?"

You might start getting answers from somewhere inside yourself like, *Yes, it's true they hired someone else. Maybe that person has the exact experience they needed, and I was their number one pick until I wasn't. Maybe I didn't hear back because they decided not to go forward with that project after all. I won't think about that now because I've got all these other things going for me. Maybe this just wasn't the right opportunity for me. Now I have more time available to look for something new that could be even better for me.*

Do you see the reframe in action? Yes, it's true that you weren't hired. But in this scenario, you're detached from judgment, and not using this experience as justification to beat yourself up. More importantly, you're not stuck spiraling on one lost opportunity so long that you miss all the others that will come along in short order.

It's important to keep your perspective of yourself balanced with a healthy dose of reality. You're never the worst person there is at what you do, and there's almost always someone better than you at any skill set. That's life. It's rare that you're going to be the absolute number one best at something out there.

My advice: stop trying to be the best. You can create a freaking FANTASTIC life without being the best or even anywhere close to it.

Think about how many people are in the world. How hard would you have to work to be the best of eight billion? And think of the astronomical odds of being the best. The Steven Hawking of something. The Serena Williams of something. How much work did they put in to be the best? Do you even want to work that hard?

Confession time: I don't want to work that hard.

I'm lazy. I want to be good enough to do stuff, and I want to be always working on being better. But I won't be upset with myself if I'm not the best at everything I try. The reality is that there will always be people ahead of me that do a way better job than I ever could. No matter how hard I work, odds are I'll never catch up to those people.

This is good news! Because for every person ahead of me, there are countless behind me thinking the same thing about me. They believe they'll always be playing catch up to ME, and are striving to be like me because that feels much more attainable than being like people who are more advanced than me.

Perspective, my friend.

Most of us are somewhere in the middle part of the bell curve. Maybe you're toward the top of the middle. I like to think I'm toward the top of the middle (ego!). But that's the reality—you're not the worst, and you're not the best, and that's okay. You can always be good enough as you are AND simultaneously work on being better.

And that's the key to happiness in a nutshell: accepting that this is where you are right now and knowing that you're a good person trying to do better.

Two tools have really helped me in this practice: gratitudes and acknowledgments. I keep a notebook for these two things, and I like to start the morning with gratitude and end the day with acknowledgment. For gratitude, I consciously look for the blessing, advantage, or good fortune in my life. It can be little things we take for granted… like "I woke up this morning. My knees ache, and they move my body reliably. I have awesome friends." The things I'm grateful for could also be big, like "I'm grateful that guy who hit the ice patch on the highway didn't hit me. I also just landed a big project, woo!"

But acknowledgment (a trick I picked up from my life coach Brian McCarthy) has been even more impactful for me—because it's all about looking at what you tried to do and giving yourself credit for even the tiniest of forward steps. "I laced up my shoes and walked to the end of the block before deciding it was too cold out. I acknowledge myself for getting up and moving my body, even if I didn't go as far as I intended to." It's almost a mini celebration of forward momentum, even if it's small.

Maybe your first acknowledgment can be that you noticed a negative thought—because that's a big win in my book.

Separating Your Thoughts from Your Feels

Now, let's talk about what happens when you DON'T notice the negative thought.

First, let me be blunt: you're not the most objective judge of your talent and skills, for better or for worse. Your perception of your capabilities could be wildly skewed depending on how you're feeling any given day.

Case in point: about eight months after leaving the toxic day job, I found myself juggling a bad breakup, packing up for a cross-country move, and worrying about my contract renewal with the big-name marketer… all at the same time.

I was barely sleeping, and when I did nod off, I'd wake up at 3 am, fully alert. Ever have those nights where you wake up in the middle of a thought, which you then follow down the rabbit hole into a full-blown anxiety spiral? Yeah, that was me for several months.

I was wound so tightly that I was in serious danger of snapping. In a moment of desperation, I reached out to a friend who'd been in a similar bad breakup situation. I asked how she had kept herself going when it felt like the world was collapsing around her ears. She introduced me to the concept of cognitive behavioral therapy, which, at its core, is about separating thoughts from feelings.

I know we're getting a little deep into brain stuff here, and if any of this speaks to you, I highly encourage you to do some additional reading and talk to a therapist. What follows is my VERY high-level understanding of how all this works, based on my own years of therapy:

When powerful, body-hijacking feelings arise, they're an almost instantaneous response to a thought that just popped into your head.

This thought-feeling train often blows by so quickly that it's hard to distinguish between the two. But it's almost always thought first, feelings next. So, separating them helped me to practice noticing when a thought pops into my head and observe how I feel immediately after.

I don't know about you, but I'm an "intense feels" kinda person. When I get caught up, I feel it in my body—hearing a well-written piece of music can make me happy to the point I'm shivering with goosebumps. Or if I'm feeling sad and overwhelmed, I often want to collapse into a puddle on the floor and sob until I'm all cried out.

Once those feelings settle in my body, it's easy for the brain to justify and indulge in them… which often kickstarts a spiral.

By that, I mean if I don't notice a negative thought and deliberately refocus my attention, the feelings will jump in and gleefully drag me down the emo rabbit hole. And once it gets to that point?

The only way out is through.

The shitty thing about being a human in business is that eventually, you're going to encounter a situation that inspires strong negative feelings. And you can't compartmentalize and avoid feeling them—at least not for long.

Fighting them is like standing on the beach and trying to hold back the ocean with your arms. Eventually, a wave will hit you just right and knock you on your ass. Basically, if you bury the feelings instead of processing them, they will pop up and demand to be dealt with, usually at the worst possible time.

So, what does it mean to process feelings versus burying them? Processing means finding a way to let the feelings pass through your body, instead of telling yourself, "Nope! I'm not going to feel that." You're a human being, baby doll. You're going to feel feelings, whether you want to or not. Instead of trying to stop the ocean with your arms, sit down and let the waves carry you back to shore.

Don't fight it—FEEL it. That's how you neutralize it enough to get back to center.

Now, everyone's way of processing looks a little different. For some people, it's going to be finding a way to laugh at the mistakes that they made. For others, it's going to be more physical, like taking a kickboxing class or going to one of those warehouses where you can pay to smash a bunch of things with a sledgehammer.

If you've got to break things, or run until your lungs feel like they'll burst, or sing loud rock music with the window down and drive around for hours… do it. If you've got to make jokes and say, "This was goofy, and I don't understand how I did this …" do it.

Embrace whatever method you've developed to process the emotions and get them out of your body so they're no longer controlling you.

Once you've let it pass through your body and you're back in a state of relative calm, you can share your struggles with trusted friends and colleagues. Ideally, these people are good enough friends or mentors to say, "Yeah, but you also have this going for you, and you've also accomplished this thing, and don't you remember that time when you figured out a problem that was almost identical to this one, but you're feeling overwhelmed now and can't remember that?"

That's what I call looking in the "loving mirror." A loving mirror is someone who gives a damn about you and can reflect the truth of your awesomeness back at you when you're feeling like crap.

I have several of these people in my life, and they show me who I really am on days when my faith is low. They remind me of all I'm capable of achieving (and all I have already achieved!) and help short-circuit the anxiety spirals and negative self-talk.

Now, sometimes those folks aren't available. After all, they're individuals with lives and responsibilities, and worries of their own. When I can't tap into that support network, I step up and become my own loving mirror. I do that with the help of something I call the Kickass Confidence File (an overview of how to set up your own is in your companion guide, which you can download free at permissiontokickass.com/guide).

I've trained myself, over the years, to grab a screenshot of every compliment and kind word that people send me, and I dump all those screenshots into a folder so I can read them when I'm feeling low.

This file has one purpose, and one purpose alone: to remind you that you're awesome.

It's my 24/7 on-demand personal cheerleader whenever I have a down day.

Look, your brain will either do what you tell it to do, or what society tells it to do (and society loves picking apart good people, almost for sport). Whatever you think on a deep, subconscious level, will have you either working toward or against your own success—and perhaps not even realizing that you're self-sabotaging. If all you ever tell yourself is that you're horrible, you're going to start to act in horrible ways. Essentially, whatever you believe yourself to be, you will be right.

So why wouldn't you choose to be right about yourself being a great person, full of potential, and capable of all kinds of incredible things?

If you've been looking for your own personal 24/7 cheerleader, I'll show you how to create this with the Kickass Confidence File exercise in your companion guide. Visit **permissiontokickass.com/guide** to download for free.

Find the Fear, Physically

Have you ever noticed how when you're feeling something strong, your body reacts strongly too? If not, try to slow down next time you have a powerful emotional reaction—the feeling will appear somewhere in your body as a physical sensation. Be on the lookout for tension in the shoulders, a fluttering in the gut, etc., and then observe what thoughts are happening while that sensation is present.

As an example, when I'm feeling anxious, I feel tension between the shoulder blades and a weight on my chest. My neck gets tight and crunchy. That's where I keep the anxiety of, *Oh no! I'm trying something new. I really hope it works. I want this for myself, but I don't know if I'm doing the right thing. I don't know if people will like it, and I don't know if there's a market for what I'm offering.*

Then, because I'm no stranger to those sensations or anxious feelings, I notice them and do what I can to process them. I'll put on a yoga video or do some shoulder/neck rolls to dispel the tension. And I'll remind myself that I have felt this exact feeling in my body before and survived. You can learn how to examine your thoughts with a certain level of detachment, but it takes practice.

It's not that successful people have learned how NOT to feel—rather they feel it, honor it, respect it, process it, and then move on... because they've chosen not to let their emotions control their actions.

And make no mistake: going out of your way to avoid all emotions is still allowing yourself to be controlled by them. To be truly free from being at the mercy of your most powerful emotions, you've got to learn how to let them flow through you and let them go.

Looking back, I can't believe I spent so much time freaking out over so many things. Why? Because I can't even remember what it was that freaked me out in the first place. Once I got over the worst of it, I completely forgot the details. I did NOT forget how those feelings show up in my body however, and now whenever that tightness in my neck or the tension between my shoulder blades pops up, I can look at that fear as a sign that something good is coming.

If you want different results, you've got to be willing to do things differently, even if it's scary. I believe in you, and I want to invite you to borrow my faith in you until your brain gets on board.

SECTION III: Into the Unknown

Now we get to tackle the fun part: running the business!

I'm not saying that sarcastically, either. Being good at business is a whole different skillset from being good at your craft. I know that was true for me—I'm a pretty good writer (or should be by now, with as long as I've been doing this). Regardless of my skill with words, I still had to learn how to run a business.

For me, it breaks down into six main categories:

1. Prospecting

2. Client Management and Admin

3. Creative Work

4. Problem-Solving

5. Sharpening the Saw

6. Leveling Up

You may even discover you have some natural talents in some (or all!) of the above categories. It's worth trying your hand at each of these to see what you enjoy. At a minimum, it's critical to understand how each of these components functions within your business so that you can better delegate (or find software solutions for) tasks you don't enjoy.

Odds are that any challenge you encounter while growing your business will fall into one of these six categories. You may want to keep this section handy for future reference! It's all about helping you get up to speed on the skillset of being a business owner, so you can get paid to do what you love—on your terms.

Chapter 9: Prospecting

Prospecting looks a little different to everyone, and the big things to remember are:

1) You can find clients and customers almost anywhere, and...

2) Just about every kind of outreach strategy in existence works. It's simply a matter of finding one or two methods you like that work for you.

I enjoy meeting people at events, and often I close business right then and there. That's not bragging so much as owning my natural strength, which is building relationships face-to-face.

I'm so good at talking about business in person that I once landed a deal from a date!

Here's how it went down: I went out with a dude who was the co-founder of a tech startup. This was back when I lived in Silicon Valley, which is startup central. We had a great rapport and ended up closing down the restaurant, talking about anything and everything.

We got along great. Except, I wasn't feeling it romantically. I don't think he was feeling it either—but we had a connection and we were both very passionate about business.

The next day, I was surprised to get a call from him since I expected to be in the "friend zone." He wasn't calling about setting up another date—he needed help with a press release for his startup and wanted to know if that was something I did.

I wasn't even actively looking for work, but because I raved about what I did, he recognized a need for my services. You never know where work is going to come from, and if you have the freedom to be able to go out and meet people, do it. It can even happen on a date. He and I are still friends to this day, by the way.

When I first started my freelance copy career, I read a book that amped up the idea of cold calling people to drum up business. I spent a lot of time at the library, looking up local businesses and making lists of people I could call to ask if they needed a copywriter.

I found no traction with that tactic. I was supremely uncomfortable on the phone, and it showed in the way I talked to people. It got to the point where I would actively put off making those calls for weeks at a time—great way to build a business, right? It wasn't long after I recognized my resistance that I also realized cold calling was making me hate this whole freelance life I was building.

I went back into research mode. *Is there another way to meet prospective clients, aside from cold calling?* I discovered direct mail, which turned me down the path of direct response marketing, which introduced me to marketing communities online. I learned a ton from those communities, which ultimately led me to the marketing leaders who wound up mentoring me and collaborating with me on business deals.

All of this came from trying something, then stepping back and asking, "Is this for me? No, I don't like this (or it's not working the way I thought it would), so what else can I try?" Or "Alright I'm going to stick with this thing because it seems to be working."

The main point of all this is to keep trying tactics until you find what works for you.

Start With People You Know

Remember your pre-prospecting list, from back in Chapter 5? Time to get that out. We're giving it a new name—the Band of Badasses List—because these people will be your secret goldmine. The full exercise is in your companion guide, so make sure to download it free at **permissiontokickass.com/guide** after you read this section.

Odds are if you want to work in a creative (or really any) industry, then you already know way more people in that industry than you give yourself credit for. There are old college acquaintances, friends of friends, and former colleagues you met through work. If you set aside some quiet time to go through your LinkedIn connections, social media friends, and email and phone contacts list, you'll probably find someone you know that either works in a field close to what you're looking for, or knows someone who does.

When I first started thinking about having a freelance business, I realized I wanted to be a copywriter working somewhere in marketing. That's an important distinction because there are lots of different types of writers out there—ghostwriters, case study writers, resume specialists, etc. So, while I'm looking for marketing contacts, another writer might be looking for authors and agents (ghostwriters), and yet another might be looking for career coaches and executives (resume writers).

Obviously, the criteria will be different for artists, musicians, and other creatives—but the idea is to write down anyone who might be able to hire you (or who might know someone who could hire you). If you don't know who could use your product or service, that's something to stop and think about right now.

Artists might want to write down gallery managers or interior decorators or folks high up in hotel chains who bulk buy art. Musicians might want to connect with wedding planners, booking agents, and corporate offices that bring in outside entertainment for events. Whatever it is you do, you can probably find people in related businesses who can connect you to people who might need your services.

Make a list of everyone you think might have a need for your work.

Since I wanted to work as a copywriter, I made a list of people that I knew who worked in marketing. I have three degrees from three different universities, so there were plenty of alumni and old classmates I could reach out to. I also had a lot of LinkedIn connections I've built up over the years. When I finished with the first draft of my list, I was shocked to see I had over a hundred people I could reach out to. And that was from going through old contacts (versus the weeks I spent in the library compiling names of strangers I'd later refuse to call).

Once you've got your list together, it's time to start reaching out. Make it a point to reach out to a handful of people every day, or at minimum a couple of times a week. Don't beat yourself up if you haven't been the best at staying in touch. Odds are, they didn't either! People have changed roles, they've moved companies, and they've moved states. You have no idea what people are doing these days until you check in on them.

It's not about earning extra points for reaching out first. You're not competing for the "busiest life" award, nor do you have to apologize for focusing on your own thing. Sometimes you fall out of touch and that's all there is to it—no need to feel guilt or shame for that. In fact, having news to share (like starting a business) gives you a great reason to reach out and rekindle some of those old relationships. People love getting good news!

That's how I did it when I went freelance. I reached out to the people I knew with a version of the email below:

"Hey NAME,

Your name popped up in my head the other day. I smiled and thought about [MEMORY WE SHARE]. How are you? Hope all is well!

I know it's been a while—on my end, I just left my job to start a business. I'm now doing X, so if you know anybody who could use a little help with X kinds of projects, I'm available. I have [this specific kind of experience] and I'd love to help.

SIGN OFF

P.S. Even if you don't know anyone, I'd love to reconnect and hear how you've been doing. Have a great day!"

This strategy may seem overly simplistic. But just doing this (and ZERO other advertising), I brought in five figures in the first month after I left the toxic day job. I don't think I even made it through a quarter of the list before I was booked solid.

Now at first, you may or may not get much of a response. The same is true of any method of client attraction you try... some will work, some won't. Sometimes you'll see a quick response, and sometimes it'll feel like nothing is working until suddenly, one day, something shifts, and you get a bunch of interest at once. Keep going regardless of what's happening. It's about showing up every day and doing things, whether you're seeing results.

All you can do is reach out and try to connect. At first, you're not going to know if it's any good or if it's working, but you have to take action anyway. Let them pick up the other end of the line and determine how much they want to engage. Some people may assume you want something from them and are only loosely using the "Hey thought about you" line to make an ask.

That's okay. Let them think what they want. Next!

Put yourself out there. Share your thoughts and teach people what you know so they know to reach out when they need your help. Most of all, be consistent... because the people who show up day after day and keep doing the work, they're the ones who wake up one day to find that traffic has increased to their site or that one person stumbled across their article and shared it with a hundred thousand followers, and suddenly it's viral.

Now it's time to go to your Band of Badasses List in your companion work book (download free at **permissiontokickass.com/guide**) and start prospecting! This might be the only time I want you to put this book down and send emails. Go send at least ten, then come back. I'll be here waiting for you.

What About the Competition?

If you've been working in a field for some time, some of your contacts might be clients from one of your old jobs (or even your current job). If that's the case, pay special attention to the details of any non-compete agreements you might have signed. I'm not a lawyer (and it's always worth an hour of a lawyer's time to get advice specific to your situation), but in my experience, I've found non-competes very hard to enforce.

The reason is simple: if this is your field of expertise, they can't prevent you from making a living doing the thing you know best.

Most companies that want you to sign a non-compete mainly want to prevent their clients, intellectual property, and company secrets from being stolen. That's completely understandable in my book—I don't want anyone stealing that stuff from me! So come at it from a place of integrity—don't try to take clients with you or screw people over, no matter how frustrated you might be with your old job.

You don't have to tell your boss that you have side projects (unless policy dictates you must disclose such info), but I would avoid working directly with the company's clients while you are still working for the company. Once I've left a company, I don't have a problem reaching out to people I used to work with and seeing if they have a need.

That's where I think the line is. And here are some questions to help you find where YOUR line is:

Are you working with your company's clients while you're still on the job?

Is there a chance you will cost the company business by doing this? Or is it genuine networking?

I prefer to stay above board in my dealings, which means my approach was more networking than poaching. I wasn't asking anyone to leave the company and come follow me.

Here's the thing: there is more than enough business for everybody. And I don't believe people have to forsake one person to work with another. They can work with multiple people or businesses if they choose! Some of the clients I've worked with had a full-time writing team. Yet when there were projects needing specialized expertise, or when the team was overloaded and backed up with existing projects, they'd outsource to freelancers like me.

This doesn't have to be an either/or situation.

Don't Be a Dick

By now, you've been prospecting a bit, and someone wants to schedule a call to talk about potentially hiring you. Woohoo! Time to celebrate!

This is also time to get serious about sales, which, contrary to popular belief, is not about being a pushy asshole who doesn't understand the word "No."

I've seen many new entrepreneurs get to that hard-earned sales call and shoot themselves in the foot. It almost always boils down to one of two things; 1) talking more than they listen, or 2) trying to show off how much they know. This kind of posturing usually stems from insecurity and impostor syndrome, which we talked about back in Chapter 8.

So how do you prevent yourself from either talking too much or showing off? The key is to approach your sales calls like a first date. You're there to make a good impression, learn more about them and whether you can help them, and ask thoughtful questions that convey your expertise.

With sales calls, your main job is to allow your prospects to talk their problems out with you. A prospective client wants to talk about themselves, their business, and their challenges. They want to know you give a damn about more than just what they can pay you or how they can raise YOUR status in the world.

Be a sounding board. Listen to understand rather than respond. And when you DO respond to what they tell you, don't throw around big jargony words—that's just another form of showing off. Talk to them like a human being. That's what gives them confidence in your ability to help them—because you listened and understood versus pressuring them to buy.

Remember, a sales call with a prospective client is NOT a job interview.

There's no smarmy middle manager trying to trip you up or pressuring you to prove yourself worthy. Sales calls with prospects are about connecting, and about learning enough to tell whether you might be able to work well together.

The reason is simple—you don't want to ~~get into bed~~ do business with a sociopath, a narcissist, or someone who hates your style and thinks your approach is stupid. You want to make sure this is a good fit, that you get along, they have a problem you can solve, and that you both agree on how best to work together.

At some point you may meet a charismatic coach who tells you The Way™ is asserting your authority. In almost every industry, there's some douche bro loudly leading a cult of assholery that preaches smugness, one-upmanship, and "negging." Barf.

In the marketing and copywriting world, there's a school of thought that encourages newbies to get business by reaching out to prospective clients with a free critique. If you're a videographer, you're critiquing their videos. If you're a designer, you're critiquing their site. If you're a writer, you're critiquing their emails or sales pages.

There's nothing wrong with this angle, by the way… but it's all in the approach. Coming across as a dick can derail the whole thing.

How much would you want to work with someone who provides unsolicited feedback on your stuff, knows nothing about you or your business (or your struggles and hard work to date), and who criticizes what you're doing as if you're a clueless schmuck? I get how tempting it is to flaunt your knowledge by showing people they're doing everything all wrong, and you've got the RIGHT way. But I sure as hell don't enjoy having my work picked apart. Do you? By a total stranger? As your first contact? I didn't think so.

If you want me to give you my hard-earned money, I'd advise you not to shit all over my work in our very first conversation. You can assume the same is true of most prospective clients. If you MUST critique, do it in a way that connects—point out what they're doing well FIRST, then suggest a tweak or improvement. For every negative, there must be at least one positive, if not two.

One last note on sales conversations: don't go into any given conversation with a goal to "land" something. That kind of thinking leads you to turn off your listening ears and focus on closing above helping. Be a human and connect. Ask questions and let them talk out their problems with you. Resist the urge to over-explain. Don't feel like you must overcompensate, justify, or prove yourself. Listen and respond. Lead them through the conversation and see where it goes. Create an offer that solves their problem and price it according to the value you deliver. Don't pressure them into anything.

Do this enough times, and even when a prospective client's answer is no, it becomes a lot easier to trust that a "Yes!" is just around the corner.

Converting Strangers into Prospects

I once got a lead for a consultation when I hired someone to clean my house, and their email system sent me a dozen emails in the span of a couple of days.

I wrote back to say, "Hey, I'm happy with my service. Appreciate you! I have a suggestion if you're open to it. I'm an email marketing expert, and this was a bit overwhelming on the receiving end. You could get a lot of mileage by sending out just the first three emails." Turns out he'd been having a lot of trouble trying to figure out his email marketing. We didn't end up working together, but we had a great call before deciding not to move forward.

Aside from everyday opportunities like this that pop up, there are online gig platforms like Upwork, Fiverr, and others where you can get your feet wet. Other people have had luck in Facebook groups where their ideal client hangs out.

What's most important is finding where YOUR ideal client (the people you sell your product or service to, from your lemonade stand) hangs out. Put yourself in that arena and get as close to them as possible. That's how you start conversations with people who might hire you.

If you don't know many folks, then it's time to expand your circle. The best way to do that is getting involved in business owner communities because, for the most part, those folks understand that investing money leads to making money. Plus, they might know people who could use your product or service.

Start getting involved in your local Chamber of Commerce. Save up the money to pay for a membership, or just show up to a mixer. Find local Meetup groups if you can't afford the Chamber of Commerce. Start to meet and network with other entrepreneurs and business owners. See if you can join a professional online community—for me, that was my community of copywriters, Copy Chief. For you, that might be a different professional group. And it may take trying several groups to find the right blend of good vibes and prospective clients.

I'm a member of many groups, and more than once, I've seen this scenario play itself out: an entrepreneur posted that she was pulling her hair out trying to figure out some tech stuff. The next day, another business owner in the group got on a call with her and walked her through exactly how to resolve the tech issue. That business owner normally charged $500 an hour for her consulting time, but she knew this problem was easy to solve and just wanted to be helpful.

This kind of thing is happening around you all the time, in many different groups. If it's not happening in the groups you're hanging out in, you might want to ask yourself why you're hanging out there. Especially since people often ask for referrals in their networking groups… which could lead to a connection that leads to your next gig.

Something to note here is that generosity needs to flow. You can't be all about giving and not receiving; neither can you be about only receiving and never giving. That stops the flow. To sound slightly Zen master-y: you've got to be able to both give AND receive. That means if you have a solution, you offer to help others get unstuck (which leads them to see you as a hero) versus keeping it close to your chest until someone pays you.

I can hear it now: but Angie, doesn't that mean I'll be giving all my best stuff away and NOT getting paid?

Yes and no.

Yes, because sharing freely is a great way to give someone a preview of what it's like to work with you. And you shouldn't give someone shitty, subpar advice, or half-assed solutions, just because they haven't yet paid you. You don't want them thinking, "This person MIGHT know what they're doing, but I have questions, and I'm not getting answers. I guess I'll only find out if I pay them, which kinda sucks."

No, because sharing what you know doesn't mean you're opening the tap on your brain and letting everyone fill up their cups. You don't have to give all your knowledge away to anyone, anywhere, at any time, just because they asked. That's a recipe for stress and burnout—the freebie seekers will happily take up all your time if you let them, preventing you from making a living and leaving you wondering why you ever started down this road.

It's a fine line to walk, and it requires you to develop some discernment skills. And trust me, it gets easier to distinguish a legit prospect from a tire kicker or a freebie seeker over time. But here's the main reason I'm such a big advocate for sharing what you know:

I believe in generosity as a business model. And being generous does NOT mean I have to give everything away.

I decide who I'll help, how much I'll help them, and when I'll provide said help.

My rule is this: I'll do it if it takes me less than five minutes (like making an introduction, sharing a resource, or recording a quick video with some top-of-mind thoughts). This doesn't cost me much in the way of time or money, but it could very well change someone's life and business for the better. Pretty big outcome for such a low commitment of my energy, right? If that was the ONE resource or intro they needed to help their business take off, they will remember that.

How this connects to outreach…

As you meet more and more people, you should be adding them to your Band of Badasses List and reaching out on occasion to connect, see where you can help, and drum up business. And don't just focus on creating relationships with prospects—clients are an excellent source of repeat business, and they're usually much easier to sell the second time!

Stay top of mind with your clients by making it a practice to reach out to them every few months to see how they're doing. And provide value first: always be human and connect with them about their life and business before you ask for more work. If they're thinking of any upcoming projects you can help with, guess who's now top of mind?

Staying in touch is time intensive, true. But it's work that others won't do, so you'll stand out while making your clients feel valued and special. Closing business can be THAT simple if you let it be.

Now let's talk about figuring out who has money to spend to hire someone like you. Short of asking (and yes, there is a professional way to do this that's totally expected and welcomed), the easiest way I know to find people who invest in business is to find events and masterminds people pay to attend.

That was the biggest eye-opener for me—realizing that if someone paid to be in a room, they value their development and growth enough to invest in it. That means they are much more likely to have a budget allocated for projects they can hire out to contractors.

That also means if you want to move beyond fighting for scraps in free online groups, you must be willing to pay to get in the room too. Note: I'm not saying you will never succeed unless you join a paid network group. I'm telling you that you must understand the VALUE of those groups and be willing to invest in the right one.

If you don't see the value of investing in your own business, how do you expect to convince someone else to invest in theirs by hiring you?

And I know networking can be soul sucking on a couple of different levels, especially if you identify as an introvert. But this is where you've got to stretch out of your comfort zone. If you truly want to stay an introvert for the rest of your life, then make peace with being a behind-the-scenes day job drone doing what people tell you to do.

If you're an introvert, I get that I'm asking you to do something uncomfortable. I identify as an ambivert, and I have moments of extreme extroverted-ness when I'm riding high on the energy of people. And then I have weeks at a time when I'm in a very "Don't talk to me. I need to be alone" kind of headspace. Or I'll be at a conference or some other such intense, high-energy situation, and afterward, I need a week or two to recover. I call it being "peopled out."

I know some introverts who create a character they can step into when it's time to be "on." They become this alter ego when it's time to go out, meet people, and do business. It's okay to pretend to be someone else for a little while (by someone else I mean a different aspect of your personality—one that's confident and good with people and closes business) and then come back to your cocoon and rest.

To own a business, you have to be a people person (to an extent). Part of being a good businessperson is building relationships. Come out of the shell enough to create and strengthen relationships with people, and retreat to it when you're peopled out. I don't care how many cold calls you make or ads you run—you won't get where you're going nearly as fast as you can just talking to someone face to face, asking what they're struggling with, and figuring out how you can help them.

Specialist or Generalist?

Depending on where (or whether) you hang out online, you may have seen this debate raging in entrepreneur groups.

- Should you be a specialist who commands high fees for that rare and valuable knowledge (AKA inch wide and a mile deep)?

- Or should you be a generalist who has a broad depth of knowledge and can solve a myriad of problems (AKA mile wide and an inch deep)?

The specialist has a smaller pool of clients, but they also have way less competition. The generalist has a bigger pool, but a lot of others in the same space are looking for the same kind of work. Neither choice is good or bad, and you could conceivably bounce back and forth between both throughout the entirety of your career. It's up to you to decide which feels more appealing to you. I know both specialists and generalists who are making a damn fine living.

Starting as a specialist is a good idea if you've worked in a certain field for a long time. For example, I know a writer who was in corporate branding for almost 30 years. When she decided to become a copywriter, she thought she had to start over from scratch. I helped her see that she could apply all that wonderful branding expertise to her writing business and help folks who really needed to improve their branding. She's someone with enough background expertise to come into freelancing as a specialist.

Side rant: I see this happen often, where people who have years and years of experience from their job somehow dismiss that expertise and treat themselves as total newbies when it comes to freelancing and starting a business.

While it's true that learning how to build a successful business is a new skillset that has its own learning curve… if you've been working for 20+ years, odds are you don't need to come all the way down from whatever mountain you're on and start at the bottom of Freelance Mountain.

There's a bridge from your mountain to Freelance Mountain, and it's made up of all the wonderful transferable skills and expertise you've spent decades acquiring. All that to say: I rarely meet someone outside their teens or early twenties who's TRULY starting from scratch. Give yourself a little more credit, my friend!

If you ARE brand new, I highly recommend trying out the generalist track first. Think of this as being "test mode." I want you to feel free to take any interesting-sounding gigs that come to you because it will teach you who you want to work with (and who you don't want to work with). That will help you with prospecting, as you can quickly tell who's a good fit. You'll also be able to recognize what you're truly interested in doing, rather than having to take on every project under the sun because you need the money.

Especially when you're first starting, your first primary goal is to get clients and prove the model. That may mean taking on projects you wind up hating as soon as you get started. Sometimes you won't know if something is for you until you say yes and work your way through it. Even if you hate the work, fulfill what you promised (or give them a refund to walk away free and clear), because you're a pro… and then add that industry or niche to your "never again" list.

That happened to me once—I quoted $1,500 to rewrite a medical equipment site—30+ pages of similar-sounding copy with strategic keywords. I had to fight to convince myself to sit down at the computer every day and eke out those words. It was agony, but I'm a pro, so I delivered what I promised and ensured it was my very best work. Then when I was finished, I decided I wasn't really into wholesale manufacturing. That was my first (and last) foray into medical equipment, yet I've still had a decent career as a writer.

For every job you take on as a generalist, keep notes on which types of projects you enjoyed and why. What kinds of clients were those? It can take freelancers years to figure these things out, but it doesn't have to if you're keeping track from the start. And remember, for now is not forever. If you get bored you can always try something else.

You do not have to keep doing work you don't like, and you do not have to work with people you don't like.

This isn't your job, it's your business—and finding work you like to do (that supports the life you want to live) is the whole point of this book! This applies whether you're a generalist or specialist.

If you're leaving an industry because you hate it and have no desire to keep doing that work, don't make that industry the foundation of your freelance work—become a generalist instead. And if you don't have decades of experience, have no idea what you want to specialize in, or if you're leaving one field and want to try something else on for size—start as a generalist.

You'll be able to use every project and client interaction as another data point to help you get clearer on what kind of work you do (and don't) like doing.

Chapter 10: Business Realities

I once wrote the sales page for a crowdfunding campaign. The project was to raise money for an '80s-themed accessory for computer tablets. It was a cool gig, and I thought the product was great, so I was excited to help get this funding.

The product had a lot going for it; support from big-name brands, coast-to-coast publicity, and a famous artist doing exclusive art for the launch. I turned in the first drafts of nostalgia-filled copy to take people back to the good old days of E.T. and the Rubik's Cube. I figured tapping into those core memories would really drive folks to want this product for themselves, if for nothing else than a smile. Then I added specs and perks because I wanted to communicate that it was both functional AND awesome.

Shortly after I sent the first draft, the client replied, "You sound like a carnival barker." I was more than a little crabby. *Umm, excuse me?* I sound like a direct response copywriter who wrote a persuasive sales page because I thought we wanted this project to get funded. My bad.

It turned out that he (an engineer, for context) wanted the message to be simple. He insisted we present it plainly, in "just the facts" style. Here's what it is and what it does—take it or leave it. By then, I had a few years of writing experience and a few wins under my belt. I vehemently disagreed with the "take it or leave it" strategy. I wanted to inspire people to reconnect with their childhoods, to like, share, and buy for their family and friends.

I was so convinced that my instincts were right that I refused to write the Plain Jane version, and we decided to part ways. I found out later his campaign failed by more than $50k. That part was validation, but the bigger message here is that in the real world, even amazing opportunities can go sideways in ways you don't expect.

These things happen, and it's okay to trust your gut and walk away when something doesn't feel quite right. The important thing is to reflect on what contributed to things not working. That will help you figure out your own early warning system and start to set rules of engagement for how you prefer to work.

In the end, much like dating, it's about figuring out what is and isn't okay with you. And to do that, you'll have to go through some tricky situations with a mindset of "What can I learn from this that will help me do better next time?"

Sometimes you may have to learn a lesson a time or two before it really sinks in. Case in point: a few months later, I was thinking about how to drum up business. I knew a lot of people sent Christmas cards to clients over the holidays, so to be different, I got the bright idea to send my previous clients Valentine's Day cards.

I figured it was a cute way to let them know I appreciated them, was thinking of them, and was available to help with more projects if needed. The strategy worked—within a week, I had a $1,500 project, more than 10x what it cost me to send the cards. But I also got a response from the engineer…

He wanted to know if it was my coy way of asking him out on a date.

That was just about the furthest thing from my mind when I sent the card. He wasn't a bad guy, but we weren't on the same page energetically. That was when I learned I probably shouldn't send Valentine's Day cards to people with whom I didn't have the best working relationship.

The Business-Body Connection

If you're solely responsible for your business, then every day that you're sick is a day that you can't work. Folks who deal with chronic illnesses already understand what I'm saying here—your work will be impacted by how you feel on any given day. So instead of forcing yourself to work through the discomfort and potentially produce sub-par work, take care of your mind and body so you feel as good as possible when it's time to get down to business.

Pay attention to your body—odds are your intuition is already trying to tell you what you need to feel and be at your best. For instance, when my body tells me I need to nap, I lie down for half an hour and then get up to try again. Maybe a nap will help because you didn't sleep well last night or (like me) you really like naps.

However, suddenly needing a lot of naps is something to pay attention to—it could be an early warning that you're coming down with a cold or that depression or anxiety could be lurking underneath the surface. And in that case, you want to get some extra rest. Load up on vitamins, water, and sleep to flush it out of your system.

It's better to reduce your work capacity to a few hours a day (if not taking a few days off entirely) so you can fully recover. The alternative is forcing yourself to work through the discomfort, succumbing, and being out of commission even longer. I've known people who pushed themselves and worked really long days and said, "Nah, it's just fatigue from working too much," only to find out later they had a serious illness. One of my friends was trying to work through viral meningitis and wound up in the hospital for three weeks.

Pay attention to your health. Make sure that you are getting regular checkups. If you can't afford a doctor, some apps let you talk to a doctor, tell them what your symptoms are, and sometimes even get a prescription. I don't want to make any medical recommendations because I'm not a medical professional, but check with your physician regularly, and take care of yourself. There's that old saying—an ounce of prevention is worth a pound of cure.

Another thing you can do for your health is get out in the fresh air. Nature does wonders for your body and your spirit. If you're into meditating, do that. If you like long walks, do that. Spend some time in the quiet outdoors, getting in touch with your inner creative person. And make sure you're getting sufficient exercise so you can go to sleep at night. Also, get adequate nutrition instead of relying solely on sugar and caffeine for energy.

All these things work together to give you a balanced routine that has you feeling your best. I don't get sick often—partly because of genetics, but mostly because I prioritize my health.

It's also important to limit your screen time. Seriously, resist the temptation to check your phone or computer around the clock. All that input is putting a major drain on your brain capacity, even if it feels like you're simply absorbing and not thinking. Your brain is still processing all that info, and just like sitting in an idling car—it's using up a lot of juice.

One counter-intuitive trick to limit screen time is to schedule time off and set up limits on your phone. In the morning, Focus Mode automatically kicks in on my phone, preventing me from checking Slack, email, or social media. My laptop shuts off at a particular time of the day—when I leave this office at five o'clock, I'm done with work.

Because I'm a writer, there's a very real possibility that I'll come up with an idea while I'm out and about, trying to recharge. For this reason, I carry around a notebook where I can write things down. I do NOT open my laptop back up and get myself sucked back into working for a few more hours.

I need that mental space to recharge the well because that ensures I have ideas when I need them later. If I keep drawing and drawing without replenishing, I'll be in the danger zone. My "idea well" will literally run dry, and odds are it'll happen just when I need it most. You've got to separate yourself from work and create space so that you have time to recover and recharge.

Feed your mind, too. I encourage you to read as much as possible. If you're not a reader, listen to audiobooks or podcasts. Check out fiction, nonfiction, art, and music. Pick up a new hobby or learn a new dance. While improving your skills at something else, you may get an unexpected idea for your business that winds up taking you to the next level. Self-education is important, and it doesn't have to be all business all the time to be valuable.

Finally, think about your workload. I hate to break it to you, but part of knowing where the "too much work" line is, is crossing it. Early on, you'll overload yourself because you haven't yet developed the context for understanding how much you can handle. So, you're going to take on too much work, and because you're a pro who honors your commitments, you'll figure out how to make it work, then adjust your availability and expectations for the next gig.

When I was first starting out, I assumed working with five to ten clients at a time was how I'd hit my income goal. I was very, very wrong. I had no idea how much work that would be, let alone how I'd juggle it all. Some freelancers can handle that much and more, but they have systems and contractors in place to support them. It didn't work for me, but that's only something I could learn by trying it out for myself.

Balance your health and self-care with delivering what you've promised the clients.

That might mean occasionally, you have to work long hours or sacrifice some free time. Just make sure that doesn't become your daily routine—it should be infrequent, if at all. Otherwise, you're on the fast track to burnout, and there's no guarantee you will bounce back.

Take care of yourself because you're the one best suited to know what you need.

Be Available for What You Want

I wonder if you've noticed this: whenever it's time for a change, the first thing to pop up for me is either resentment or stress. I'll be easily frustrated by ordinary situations, leading to procrastination and even more stress and resentment. That kicks off some anxiety about whether what I'm doing is right for me, and if I should really be doing something else.

Don't get me wrong—sometimes a stressful period is just a stressful period, and it too shall pass. But if none of the usual tools are working for me—things like taking walks, meditating, journaling, playing music, and doing other things that bring me back to a place of fun and joy—then it's usually a sign that it's time for a change.

Change is a challenge to step up. A call to adventure. A new stage of growth. We were NOT designed to be born in misery, live a miserable life, and die a miserable death.

There's an old Buddhist saying that goes something like this: pain is inevitable, but suffering is optional. In essence, you can choose to stay where you are, bear the brunt of increasing pain and stress, and suffer as a result… or you can choose a different path.

If you look back on your life, what was it that finally forced you to make changes for the better? I'm willing to bet it wasn't that things were going swimmingly, with a lot of peace, stability, and comfort… until you got bored and decided to blow it all up to make things more interesting.

Most of us are content to stay exactly where we are so long as there's a certain level of comfort. Once it gets uncomfortable or impossible, we think about doing something different, something new and scary. So now I challenge you to pay attention to your discomfort, stress, anxiety, and resentment. Are you being called to do something better?

Within every challenge is buried a seed of opportunity to do something great if only you have the courage to answer the call.

It might seem kind of woo, but I almost feel like it's the universe checking to see how badly you want it. Consider it a test of your resolve and determination, even a test of your faith. And I'm not talking about praying or anything religious or churchy. I'm talking about faith in yourself and the belief that you can do better and were meant for more than this.

But the fact remains: opportunities don't just fall in your lap, especially if people around you don't even know you're open to them. When I was stuck in that toxic job and ready to leave, my boss (who's an amazing human) did everything in his power to try and get me to stay. He always left the door open for me to change my mind.

It got to a point where when I was struggling those first few critical months, I seriously considered swallowing my pride and asking for my job back. The funny thing is—and this is only something I could see with the blessing of hindsight—if I had lost faith and gone back, I wouldn't have had the opportunity to interview for the writing team I ran for four years. Not to mention, I would have been laid off with the rest of the team, but I digress.

If I'd gone back to my old job, I would have been busy and distracted when a career-making opportunity came up.

A friend put me up for the gig where I would ultimately run the writing team for a big-name marketing guru. That friend wouldn't have known that I was available because I would've had a full-time job. Then all the opportunities I've had because of working with that marketing leader never would have materialized. I don't even know if I'd be sitting here, writing this book.

All this was possible because I made a conscious decision to walk away and free up that time and that mental space for something new and better to come along.

I love how this semi-woo topic of creating space ties into the very practical financial idea of opportunity costs, which should factor into every decision you make. If I had said, "Yes, I'm staying in this day job," I'd have really been saying, "No, I'm not available for this massive opportunity to work with a marketing leader." When you say yes to something, you say no to at least a dozen other opportunities. Something to think about.

Another thing to consider: I have yet to encounter a situation where someone said, "Enough, I deserve better. I'm going to find better. I'm walking away," and found themselves in a worse situation because of it. It doesn't mean that it never happens, but it doesn't happen as often as you might think (or as often as your brain wants you to believe).

This is partly due to you doing the work of learning where your limits are. You're discovering and setting new boundaries around what helps you do your best work. You're moving forward, looking for something that fits this bigger, better box that you're creating for yourself. That doesn't mean there won't be struggles or setbacks. But know that those who "make it" are often simply the most persistent and don't let setbacks deter them from their goals (at least not for very long).

On a related note, when you've decided to do something new and put yourself out there, you may encounter some pressure and resistance. Some of it may be from clients and colleagues, and some of it may be from your own internal struggles. The cool thing about being in business for yourself is if you try something new and you don't like it, or it's more stressful than you thought it'd be and not worth your time, it's totally okay to pivot and try a new direction.

You are not obligated to keep doing a thing that no longer works for you.

I don't know about you, but I started a business so I could do work I like with people I like, so it doesn't make sense to stay stuck in situations where I'm miserable and stressed. You can always walk away but knowing that fact doesn't necessarily ease anxiety. Still, you've got more options than "stay and be miserable" or "death."

As long as you're alive, whatever choices you make can be unmade.

Self-Management for Client Management

Sometimes, a gig seems like a great opportunity and winds up being a bad fit. The good news is you're far from alone—we all experience this. It's part of the process. No matter how good you get at vetting people and setting boundaries, it's highly unlikely you'll ever get to a point where all your clients are awesome and no one stresses you out.

You're working with people. People are imperfect and irrational, so you might as well get used to it. I encourage you to accept that shortcoming—of being a human in business and therefore being susceptible to human whims—as part of the journey. Failure is also part of the work. You could have all the information you need to make an educated decision and do everything technically "right" yet still have something fail for reasons beyond your control.

All you can do is use the information you've got in front of you to make the best decision that you possibly can. And that's life in a nutshell.

And it stands to reason that if that's true for you—that you're making the best decision you can with the information you've got—it's also true for the human beings you work with. That's why when it comes to client management, the key thing to remember is to **assume positive intent with every single interaction**.

It's an unfortunate byproduct of today's society that we're quick to anger and quick to judge. We assume the person that cut us off in traffic is deliberately trying to make us angry, but if we unintentionally cut someone off because we were distracted, and it was an accident. There's a term for this pattern of thought, and it's called the Correspondence Bias, or sometimes the Attribution Effect.

Don't beat yourself up for what your brain does—this is just how it's wired. The key is to recognize this default pattern. Most of the time, someone's behavior, even if it makes no sense to you, can be explained reasonably by the circumstances in their life. Because you're not in that person's head, you have zero insight into what's happening in their life that might make this make sense.

And while it's true that there are legit assholes out there, that's more a product of who they are and what they're dealing with in their life than who YOU are. In other words, I don't believe for a second that someone singled out Angie Colee on the road and thought, *There she is. I'm going to cut her off. I'm going to fuck up Angie's day.*

It's not about me.

Let's translate this into a business context with a quick thought exercise. I'm going to put you in the shoes of a busy executive or someone who has the power to hire you as a freelancer. This is an experience I know well, having been both hirer and hire-ee.

Picture it: you're a freelancer who is excited about working with me. You spent several hours digging up info on me, figuring out how you might be able to help me, and crafting the perfect email. You fire it off, excited to hear back from me.

Crickets.

Anxiety kicks in. You might start to wonder if you made a mistake or said something out of turn that offended me. Maybe you send a follow-up or simply give up on me after a few days and move on to the next prospect.

Here's what's happening on my side of the fence: from the moment I sit down and boot up the laptop, I've got dozens, if not a hundred, emails to catch up on from last night and this morning. I've got people pinging me on Slack that urgently need my attention on their projects. And I've got three big promos in various stages of development as I write this page, each of which means there are a bunch of different people waiting on me for different things. And that is all within the first five minutes of sitting down.

Weeks (or months) later, when I have a few hours to spare, I am seized by the compulsion to catch up on email. I find your email buried under a ton of stuff that, at the time, was more urgent. I remember seeing that subject line and making a mental note to respond, but then it was out of sight, out of mind, and I never did.

Nothing personal, just the reality of business. If someone ignores your email, try not to assume that they're having trouble paying you or that they hate you and don't want to talk to you. Don't jump to the conclusion that you did something wrong or that they're upset. These things aren't necessarily true.

Eight or nine times out of ten, when you're having trouble getting a hold of someone, shit just blew up, or they forgot. If you try giving people grace (the same grace that you would hope for if time slipped away from you and you forgot), you'll often find that you attract a better caliber of client who will give you the same level of respect.

I saw a post recently in a copywriter group from a guy who wrote a page-long rant about trying to recoup $80. Think about that for a second. I'm at the point in my career where I charge $500+ for an hour for consulting. If I put hours of my time into writing an angry, ranty post, chasing a client down, and venting to my friends... that adds up to a massive opportunity cost.

Even if I limited my venting to one hour, that would still be like setting $500 on fire. All the time you spend being angry is time you can't spend making money. I can't charge anyone for that wasted time. So basically, I spent $500 of my own money on an hour of bitching. I'd rather go find a non-shitty client who will treat me well and move on.

Let's do another thought exercise. Imagine you're the guy upset over the $80 you were stiffed, and you fired off an angry scorched earth email—the kind of email that really shows them your rage. Now imagine the client had a family emergency that prevented them from responding in a timely manner. By the time the client gets to their messages, they've not only got the bill, but a series of steadily more angry emails and escalating behavior.

I don't know about you, but if I had something personal happen and came back to that, I'd be thinking, "Well, now I don't want to pay this guy at all. I just had a death in the family, and I'm trying to settle my business after being away for a week. And I've got five angry emails about why I didn't pay you fucking $80?" Ouch.

Grace, understanding, and kindness are the foundations for lasting professional relationships.

If you're constantly assuming that people are out to get you, you will attract clients who will take advantage of you. That's just the nature of things because what you focus on is what you get more of (we covered this in Chapter 8 with mindset and the Baader-Meinhof phenomenon).

Assume positive intent. Assume they have every intention of paying and getting back to you, they know what's going on, and that you may have to be gently persistent (without being a nag) in reaching out to them until you get a response.

While we're on the topic of giving people grace, don't expect clients to remember how you work. Clients have busy lives, and even when you repeatedly tell them your policies, people will get distracted and forget. Yes, even if you put it in your contract—how often do you look up a contract you've signed to ensure you're clear on the terms before asking a question?

I once had a client who repeatedly asked me for meetings on Mondays. However, at the time, my Mondays were filled with back-to-back calls, and I had no room to squeeze anything else in—not unless I wanted my brain to leak out of my ears.

Every time he said, "Hey, does Monday at X time work for you?" I didn't get pissy and say, "Hey, look douchebag. I told you a million times that Mondays don't work for me!" I simply repeated, "Monday's out. We can do it on a different day, or you can catch me up later."

Client management can be a lot, much like dealing with a curious kid. When a child asks a million questions, you don't scream at them—you'd traumatize them! You patiently repeat yourself over and over again. Very calmly, very coolly, not making any assumptions, just reminding them: *This is how I operate. Hey, I'm happy to talk to you more if there's something that's unclear or you don't understand, but this is how I operate, this is how things work with me.*

Be easy to work with. That counts for a lot in business because businesspeople work with people they enjoy working with. So don't be a diva. Don't think that just because you've had some success people owe you something. Be nice, be pleasant to work with, and people will treat you incredibly well.

Do no harm but take no shit.

Most hurt feelings and frustration (in both life and business) come from miscommunication. And most miscommunications between vendors and clients happen because you're not on the same page regarding expectations. The best thing you can do for yourself and your business (not to mention your sanity) is to get good at setting clear expectations.

Think about how you operate, and then communicate that to your clients. How should they contact you, and when can they expect a response? What do you need from them, and when can you get them something to look at? Start with what you need and err on the side of over-communicating. That's how you become the adult in the room, who leads folks to a solution they feel good about.

When you lead, any reasonable client will follow.

Sorry introverts—this is the part where you must interact with people! Just because you've landed the gig doesn't mean you can disappear into your bubble and create. Even if you explain your process to them in advance, when they don't hear from you for a while, they'll forget that you gave them the heads up and start wondering what happened.

I see too many freelancers with a process something along the lines of "We'll talk, I'll get all this information from you, and then I'm going to disappear for two weeks and be in creation mode." My mentor Kevin Rogers advises to think of it like dating. Say you hit it off. You were going hot and heavy, and everybody felt good when the relationship first started. And then, when there's radio silence for a couple of weeks, the worry and overthinking start to set in.

Client management is a daily, ongoing part of your business that you will have to become accustomed to. Clients want to know that things are on track. They want to know they can reach you if they have questions.

And that's a two-way street as well. You're going to start to feel very insecure in this relationship if you reach out to them and they're not getting back to you in a timely manner. Imagine if you sent an invoice and got radio silence—that's about how they feel when you take their money and go incommunicado.

And once again, be gentle with yourself. I've been in the game for years now and I still have to practice consistent communication. It's a skill you can develop, so make sure to get plenty of practice.

Last thing on self-management—don't fall into the trap of thinking there's one logical way to do things and that everyone knows your way is The Thing.

Your method is one among billions, literally. And even when you are 1,000% sure your solution works for every problem, everywhere, in every situation—and you have the evidence to back it up—that still doesn't mean that it's the BEST solution and that nothing out there will work better.

That means, from time to time, you will encounter a client who doesn't understand the solution you're proposing or the strategy you're recommending. They'll challenge you or openly disagree with you and resist doing it. That's okay because their solution may work just as well as yours!

In situations like that where a client has hired me for my expertise, but they disagree with my recommendation, I usually tell them the pros and cons of the decision they're making… and then I let them make their own choice because it's their business to run. I know I won't always be right (even though I have a decent batting average).

All anyone can do is make the best decision they can with the information they have.

Chapter 11: Client Relations: the Good, the Bad, and the Ugly

If there IS such a thing as a "battle" in business, it's not you against your clients or colleagues—it's you fighting your own ego, inertia, laziness, apathy, and fear.

But there is one fight that comes up often in the course of growing a business, and that's picking your battles when it comes to client pushback.

Allow me to share a simple perspective shift that will instantly help you become better at peopling:

You and me versus the problem.

As soon as it devolves into "Me versus you," you're in trouble. No matter who "wins" in that situation, someone will be unhappy. The relationship may or may not survive that kind of direct challenge.

My friend Chris Orzechowski always said something when we were working together: "I'd rather be rich than right."

That's pure gold right there—it means that when it came to client disagreements, we would err on the side of preserving the working relationship rather than letting ego run the show. It does no one any good if I get to say I was right, but we lose the client as a result.

Not everything is worth fighting for, which is why you've got to pick your battles.

That said, it can be hard to de-escalate when you're in the thick of it. When I have an opinion contrary to what my clients want, I divide it into three possible outcomes:

1) If the impact is negligible, I let the client have their way. Think punctuation rules like the Oxford comma or whether to use pink or orange in the new logo. Those choices will not significantly impact sales or the larger business picture, so they're not hills I'm prepared to die on.

2) If the impact is potentially negative (or the choice has any ethical implications), I advise them on what I think is the best course and then let their decision influence where I go next. If they disregard my advice and get a negative outcome, I'm watching to see if they try to shift blame, or if they own their piece, use it as a learning experience, and vow to do better next time. And if they deliberately do something deceptive, I'm out. They're fired. I can't control them, but I can control me. I won't work with people who put self-interest above the wellbeing of their customers. And since I always warn clients of the potential consequences of any given action, ignorance is not something they can claim.

3) If the impact is potentially positive in a big way, I'll advise on what I think is the best course and again defer to their call. If I feel very strongly about what I'm suggesting, I may propose a head-to-head test of their idea against mine, or I may bring it up two to three times until it's obvious they won't go with my idea.

At the end of the day, it's the client's money and their risk to take. They make the choices, for better or worse. And they ignore their paid experts at their peril. You cannot force anyone to do anything they don't want to do, so pick your battles wisely.

And if you're struggling over whether this is a battle worth fighting, that's exactly what your network is for. Whenever you're feeling strong feelings about something or you're unsure about something, that's the perfect opportunity to reach out and reconnect with other humans in business. Odds are they can help you recognize the difference between something that FEELS important and something that IS important.

Setting Boundaries

Early in my career, a client emailed me with a request for edits at 3 am. When 8 am rolled around, the follow-up arrived—he was angry that I hadn't made the edits yet.

I'd been asleep!

At first, I was upset. Did he expect me to be available 24/7 and still do good work? But when I had a chance to calm down, I looked back over the course of our working relationship and started to see a pattern of little concessions on my part. I gave the client my personal cell and invited him to text me (which he subsequently did—at all hours). I'd replied to late night emails within minutes. I'd taken phone calls after dinner.

I let this happen because I had been desperate for that job and came to it with the mindset of "anything to make the client happy." But notice how no matter what I did, he still wasn't happy. He had all the power because he had the money I needed… and he knew it.

The lesson: there are non-obvious ways that you might be giving away your power, communicating that you are desperate and willing to do just about anything for money.

Even if you never say a word about your personal situation, desperation has a way of bleeding through. It comes out in the way you write, the conversations you have, the compromises you make, and even the way you structure your deals. Boundaries and knowing your rules of engagement (plus having enough savings to confidently walk) are how you stop desperation in its tracks.

If you don't let assholes walk all over you, they'll find someone else to annoy with their unreasonable expectations.

Respect isn't something you have to earn. It's the bare minimum we can give each other, human to human. I'm not *asking* for your respect—I'm simply refusing to stick around if you choose not to give it. I don't care whether you're paying me or not.

This is why it's so important to set boundaries. Counter to popular belief, setting boundaries (and getting people to respect them) has nothing to do with forcing others to follow your rules. You're not laying down the law. You are communicating what you need to someone versus threatening them with consequences—there's a BIG difference.

To do this effectively requires you to know what you need, though.

When you don't know what you need, you send off subtle "I don't have boundaries" signals—that's true both in your business and your personal life. And trust me when I say the people who intend to take advantage of you can practically smell it.

That's why I keep hammering on every experience, for better or worse, being "good data." After years of my own data gathering, I realized that I couldn't get a whole lot done if I was answering emails and Slack pings all day. I also discovered that my work suffers if I'm constantly task switching, so I started limiting meetings to certain days to give me enough time for deep focus work.

Here's how that sounds when setting boundaries with clients: "I've disabled notifications on my laptop and phone, but you're welcome to email or ping as often as you need. I'll get back to you as soon as I am back online, usually within a business day." Or "Click this link to grab any available spot on my calendar for our chat."

Notice how I'm not screeching about THE RULES. I'm not telling folks I've blocked off focus days because having too many calls distracts me from work. Doesn't that feel rational and level-headed, even though I gave zero explanation and justification?

Since I instituted this policy, not once have I heard someone say, "You disable pings and refuse to answer emails the instant I send them?! You want to eliminate distractions and do the work I'm paying you to do?! HOW DARE YOU?!" If someone did say that, the next step would be discussing how and when to end the working arrangement since I'm clearly not a good fit for their needs.

In Chapter 8, I wrote about how you can't create from a place of anxiety. I pose an addendum to that assertion: *you can't think straight when you're stuck in a bad situation.*

Strong emotions, overwhelm, and stress will skew the way you see your reality, which can lead to you drowning in a stream of bad clients. I recommend something radical here: be ruthless about cutting clients who stress you out and make you miserable. They're a trap because bad clients attract and recommend more of the same. You'll feel overworked and underpaid, not to mention unappreciated. And when all your clients treat you this way, your confidence will take a hit, further eroding your boundaries and confidence.

I've fallen into that trap a few different times 'cause I'm a hard-headed so-and-so. Apparently, I have to learn certain lessons several times before they stick. Please be a faster learner than me on this—but please also be gentle with yourself. Like me, you may have to bang your head against the wall a couple of times before it really sinks in.

Case in point, not too long after I let go of the 3 am emailer, I took on another client under an impossible deadline. That deadline, by the way? One I proposed. *I set the impossible deadline, not him.* That was his first hint that he could push me.

He kept asking me to do more and more. I kept letting him add to my plate without adjusting the timelines or pushing back with a simple, cheerful, "Hey, that's great. We can add that on, and it's going to cost this much. I can get it to you in two weeks. Let me know how you want to proceed."

I didn't take control of that situation. I let him walk all over me, and I got increasingly frustrated (as I was getting less and less sleep trying to deliver everything I'd promised). Something in me finally snapped, and I called a mentor.

This mentor was a loving mirror and told me what I didn't want to (but needed to) hear: fire the client.

Yes, finish the project, be a professional, and deliver my best work. But he told me in no uncertain terms that I had to stop working and living like a doormat. My clients needed me to be the adult in the room and set boundaries. I couldn't do that when I was so much less concerned with my own wellbeing than I was with doing anything and everything to keep the client from leaving me.

I took my mentor's advice to heart. The next time the client tried to add something, I said, "I can't make that work with my schedule right now. If you really need this done, I can introduce you to other writers." That's one of the easiest ways I know to gently turn down a client you're not interested in working with.

Suppose you don't ever want them to contact you again. In that case, you have to be even more direct and say, "Hey, I am moving my business in a different direction. I am not the best fit for this kind of project anymore. I'm happy to refer you to someone else," and leave it at that. You don't owe anyone an explanation or reason why. "No" is a complete sentence.

Caveat on referrals: if you hate working with this person and think they'd make your colleagues as miserable as they made you think carefully before making that introduction. Since referrals are an important part of business, the quality of the people you connect reflects on you. If you encounter that situation and you really don't feel comfortable connecting this nightmare client to any of your colleagues, it's okay to say, "I'm sorry, I can't help with that."

I know that might seem harsh, especially if you're just starting and don't feel like you have many options. It's hard to turn away work when someone's waving cash in your face, but it's critical that you learn how to do it. Letting go of what's holding you back is the only way to make space for a better fit client to come along.

Go fill out the Doing Your Best Work exercise in your companion guide (download free at **permissiontokickass.com/guide**) to determine which boundaries to incorporate with your clients. It's important to think about this when you're in a place of calm because when emotions are high, or you're in a reactive state, trying to figure out and enforce rules can easily cross the line into trying to control other people.

Remember: you're not laying down the law—you're simply telling them what you need to do a great job. Trust that if you hold people accountable to your reasonable expectations, the good clients will stay (and the trash will take itself out).

When to Stay and When to Walk Away

Make this your mantra:

No one project, no one client.

Learn it, live it, and love it. It's deceptively simple, but this idea makes your business practically invincible. Think about it—when you were an employee, that one job mattered a LOT. If they got upset with you or business got bad, they'd take away your job and pay.

So why would you go through all the risk of quitting to start your own thing, only to behave just like you did when you were an employee?

No one client or project is the key to your success, even if it feels like the biggest opportunity in the world and like you'll die if you blow this chance. You don't have a business if your whole business depends on one client or project. You have a self-created job. That client could fire you just as easily as a boss could.

That's not to say we don't all START there. But the goal should be to build up your savings and create several revenue streams so that you don't have to depend on any one thing.

That said, it's one thing to know that, eventually, you'll need to walk away from a client. It's another thing entirely to know WHEN and WHY to walk away. Below I've shared three common "upset client" scenarios and how to handle them like a total pro.

Fire ASAP: Rude, Abusive, and Disrespectful Clients

Say a job goes wrong (and sometimes they just do, with no fault to either party) or things get personal in all the wrong ways.

If a client turns abusive and starts lobbing emotional grenades like, "You are really awful at this," or "I can't believe that we paid you money," or even "I'm going to leave you bad reviews online and make sure the world knows you SUCK," the relationship is over. That is not someone who will reason with you or listen to any input, no matter how well rationalized.

Here's the thing: they will treat you how you allow yourself to be treated. So don't let anybody treat you like shit.

They may refuse to hear you out or decide not to work with you. But someone who insults or verbally abuses you and constantly fights you on your work hasn't earned the right to keep doing business with you. If they're toxic, walk away.

You're not a mat they can wipe their dirty boots on and stomp all over. They can talk to you respectfully, or they can leave. You get to set that rule for yourself, whether you feel like you messed up or not. We all have bad days, but that doesn't give anyone the right to abuse you or lash out.

And I cannot stress that enough. This is not what business is. Successful people, by and large (aside from sociopaths), are not assholes to each other because they realize this all depends on good relationships.

If a project goes sideways or the work doesn't turn out the way you thought it would… they might be disappointed or upset. But if they're mean and nasty, cut them loose. If you can afford to return their money, then issue a refund and cut ties. In my experience, it's not worth the emotional exhaustion of fighting them to keep the money when you can refund them. Say, "I'm sorry it didn't work out," and walk away with your head held high and your hands clean.

Resist the urge to join an upset client in mudslinging. There's an old saying, "Don't wrestle in the mud with pigs. You both get dirty, and the pig likes it." Take a deep breath, meditate, go for a run, vent to a friend… whatever you need to do to bring yourself back to baseline and disengage from the intensity of the emotions. Eventually, those toxic people will flame out, develop a reputation for being difficult to work with, and ultimately burn the wrong people.

At some point, the person with a bone to pick looks like an unhinged lunatic if they can't let it go and move on. By taking the high road when publicly attacked (versus taking every opportunity to explode, throw a temper tantrum, and smear shit), you're subtly reinforcing the message that you're someone good to work with.

Healthy, balanced adults take criticism, use what they can, ignore what they can't, and move the fuck on.

They get over it because they've got more important things to worry about than inflicting maximum pain on someone else. Criticism and disagreements are not life-enders. Sometimes two people just can't find a way to work together and must find a way to move on. It doesn't make either person a BAD person. It simply makes us human.

So, if they threaten to damage your reputation, just blow them a kiss and wish them the best of luck. Then take that high road right on out of Crazy Town. Remember—acting on your anger may get you some short-term satisfaction, but the long-term impact could be incredibly detrimental to your reputation and business growth.

Don't let today's temper tantrum impact tomorrow's earning potential.

Ride it Out: Clients Who Listen, Communicate, and Try

Because it's worth repeating: you'll eventually let someone down, whether it's yourself or a client. The good news is that disappointing a client doesn't have to become a dumpster fire or a mud-wrestling match. A decent client who's been around the block a time or two has developed some emotional resilience and is much more likely to say something like, "This is not working, and I'm disappointed."

While that line stings when you're on the receiving end, I challenge you to see it as an opening. Someone who communicates frustration with you gives you a golden opportunity to connect on a human level and find a solution. They're being honest and respectful about how they feel, giving you a chance to say, "Let's dig into this together. Can you get me some more information? Let's walk through what happened. Maybe we'll spot an obvious fix if we take a second look."

As a rule, when there are strong feelings (especially if clients are stressed or unhappy), it's best to get on a call as soon as possible. People can come up with creative ways to get even more upset when left to their own devices, so to prevent them (or you!) from getting even more worked up, it's best to get in front of it—sooner rather than later.

I encourage you to proactively step up and identify problems and work to solve them. That's how you turn around a situation where you're on shaky ground, feeling like you've just blown things up. Even if you're in a sticky situation where you know you messed up, sometimes the client isn't upset so much as concerned. Or they're disappointed but willing to give you a chance to fix things. Those are the ones to keep a good relationship with.

Above all, don't take a disappointed client or a butting of heads as a sure sign that you're a failure, this project is doomed, or you have no idea what you're doing. Failure shows us where we have a chance to improve and do better. Embrace it because even though you are for-sure going to fail, you are smart enough and resourceful enough to fix it.

You've also got an incredible network ready to help whenever you call, because you're actively building relationships. So, when a disappointed client gives you that chance to make it right… instead of getting defensive, angry, or hurt, step up and do your best to turn it around.

When you do that, guess who looks like a hero now? Not only did you come in and behave like an absolute pro from start to finish, but you also took your lumps and said, "You know what? That was a mistake. I don't know what went wrong, but I'm going to do my best to fix it because I care."

Let Go: Clients Who Fall Off the Face of the Earth

This last situation is probably the most gut-wrenching and anxiety-inducing. In both dating and business, you can be ghosted by people who seemed to be very much into it before disappearing. And, of course, it's much easier to deal with it before things get serious—if they ghost before you get started, then you don't have to waste much time or energy on their project. But if you've done your best work, they seem excited about it—and then crickets? I feel that anxiety in my soul, my friend.

But remember that humans gonna human. A lack of response doesn't necessarily mean they hate you.

Sometimes it might be because things in their business blew up, and they had to go into crisis management mode. Maybe a key employee quit, or they lost a big account and are trying to figure out how to cover payroll. Or maybe they had something to happen at home, in their personal life… and that thing has all their attention and focus. If their spouse was in a major car accident, or they lost their house in a fire (these things happen!), they are understandably moving your work to lower on their priority list.

But without the context, it can feel like a door's been slammed in your face. When they don't answer your emails or calls, it's hard to convince yourself that it's not your fault. So, remember to assume positive intent—that they were every bit as excited about your work as they made it seem.

Follow up at least two to three times and give it a good faith effort to get in touch. But if they don't respond, do your best to let it go and keep moving forward. Understand that it's their choice not to communicate with you, and you can't control that. What you can control is what you do next, for better or worse.

Being ghosted isn't a reflection on you, even if they disappeared because they didn't want to work with you. Their behavior is theirs to own, and your behavior is yours. If you're willing to try and they're not, you can't control them, only you. Accept it, learn what you can from it, and look for opportunities to do better.

Is there something in your process you could improve? Something in your delivery that might have come across in a weird way?

Please don't misunderstand me here: I'm not asking you to look for reasons to beat yourself up. There's no need to dig until you find all the ways you screwed up. When you look for opportunities to improve, you might find something, and you might find out you did everything "right," and it still fell apart. Just remember to take what serves you and let go of the rest—find what improvements you can make, if any, and use them to get ready for the next big thing when it comes along.

Sometimes the client screws up and doesn't want to take responsibility. That's the kind of situation where empathy really makes a difference and can have people coming back to work with you for years. Humans aren't always gracious about mistakes they make (especially if pointed out by someone else). They may get defensive, try to toss it back onto you and make it seem like the mistake was your fault when it wasn't.

I challenge you to be the bigger person and the adult in the room in this situation.

I can't say I've always been the perfect example of someone taking the high road. I had one job that was a bad fit, so I self-sabotaged and was a horrible communicator. I was very resistant to getting on the phone and tried to handle everything via email.

I couldn't articulate what I needed from her to make the edits she wanted. Plus, she came to the table already having an idea of what the promotion should look like. She shared a launch plan doc and told me to use that as a template—and I did, against my better judgment, without asking nearly as many questions as I normally would.

That was a point in time where I didn't fully trust my own expertise and assumed she knew better than I did. Instead of challenging her or suggesting another way, I did as she asked because that's what she was paying me to do, right?

Eventually, I got over myself, swallowed my pride, and got on the phone with her. We got the promotion to a place where we were both satisfied. She did the launch and got one sale. Deemed it an abject failure.

That hurt, but she wasn't wrong—the project and the launch had been a failure, both in how I handled myself and in how we missed the targets we set.

I took it hard, because my ego thought I was better than one measly sale. I wallowed in my disappointment, but eventually, I realized one sale is a positive sign—and there might be hope for turning it around if we dug into the data to see what happened. The numbers would show us if there were any disconnects that we could fix.

I offered to do that for her, but she never spoke to me again. That was probably one of my hardest lessons—it really hurt knowing in my heart that I could find a solution, but that my client was too disappointed to want to try again.

You can't control them, only you. And sometimes, knowing you did what you could is the only win.

Chapter 12: Execution

There's this trite thing that always pops up whenever you search for "how to start a business online." You may have come across this one too—it sounds something like, "You can make money from anywhere in the world with a laptop and an internet connection, even at the beach!"

Personally, I don't want to be working on the beach. If I'm at the beach, I want my business to be making money without my input, not a single fucking laptop in sight. That's the end game for me. And funnily enough, at a high level, I think that's the thing we're all working toward—a life of freedom and flexibility, without the money worries. To create that requires intentionally creating the space and the freedom to think about how to grow your business.

This is what it means to work ON your business versus hiring yourself as an employee who's stuck working IN the business.

It's one thing for me to tell you all this, but once that money starts flowing, logic has a way of flying right out the window. It's hard to say no when someone's waving money in your face. Becoming a business owner requires stepping back and looking at the bigger picture. That's hard to do when you're stuck inside, constantly churning out work.

When I started freelancing, I believed all I had to do was hustle harder. If the money wasn't flowing, hustle harder. If there weren't enough clients, hustle harder. And while some amount of hustle is critical to your success, so is smartly allocating your energy and brainpower.

I had no target, which is part of the reason I struggled so hard to find consistent work. My only goal was "find clients"—I gave zero thought to who my best clients were, where my interests and strengths lie, and what kind of work I wanted to do. Any client was a good client in my mind, and that belief led to a lot of frustration and wheel spinning.

Over time I figured out that the key to smart, sustainable business growth is a balance of short-term goals (like getting that money, honey) and long-term goals (like becoming a bestselling author or hiring a staff and expanding). Without both, you're always hustling for the next client, never sure where you're going. That's not a strategy so much as a hamster wheel.

Knowing Where You're Going

Let's start with the big picture because in any successful plan, your short-term goals should be steps along the path to your ultimate end goal. With a long-term vision in the back of your mind, you'll be better able to assess whether any given client, project, or strategy will likely get you closer to or further from your targets.

So, what's your endgame with this business?

I want you to do more than just think about it—journal about it. Put it on paper. Take it seriously. Getting it out of your head is the first step toward making it a reality, so write it down. Be as specific as you possibly can.

Here are some ideas you can riff on:

Do you want to work six months and take the next six months off?

Do you want a four-day work week? How about a four-hour work week?

Do you want to travel full-time while working with clients (that's what I'm doing as I write this book)?

What about making a million dollars?

Or is your goal more to make enough to get by? What is "enough to get by" anyway? Have you slapped a number on that?

This isn't an exercise in daydreaming or fantasizing, by the way. Any kind of lifestyle you can imagine is totally possible—but you must be willing to articulate exactly what you want (and no, "best life" doesn't count because it's not nearly specific enough).

Setting a clear vision is the only way you'll be able to figure out how to get from where you are to where you want to be.

It's just that most people are too afraid to say what they want out loud, or they never really think about what they want to begin with. How the hell are you going to get there if you're not confident enough to tell the universe where you're going, my friend?

Next, let's talk about revenue streams. It's smart to avoid putting all your eggs in one basket. By that, I mean we don't want to create a business that depends solely on doing client work as your only source of income.

When you only have one source of income—clients—it's much more tempting to take on shitty ones because they've got money, and you've only got a single source of revenue.

The cool thing about working with clients is you start to notice patterns after a while. You may find yourself following the same steps, asking the same questions, or using the same solutions with multiple clients. That's not lazy—it's brilliant!

Not only is it smart to work efficiently (especially if it WORKS for your clients), but it also means you've created your own method or system.

You could potentially develop that into a book, course, or workshop that you can sell in addition to your services. You could bring on others and train them to do what you do and grow an agency. This is how you start to build a business that can survive without you—by deliberately choosing to bring in multiple sources of revenue.

And that's the beauty of this. It's super easy to become a freelancer in the age of the internet. This is a low-cost, low overhead way to start a business. The double-edged sword is that your business depends on you to show up every day, making YOU a potential point of failure.

In showing up every day to do the work, you develop systems and efficiencies you can leverage into additional sales, turn into a different business model, or outsource some tasks—thereby freeing yourself up more to find even more opportunities.

This is a little more advanced and won't be something you need immediately. However, I do want to plant that seed—eventually, you will want to move beyond freelancing and trading dollars for hours because, eventually, you'll run out of hours.

Now let's talk short-term goals—if your long-term goals are the destination, then short-term goals are the roadmap to get you there. Each one should ideally get you closer to that end vision, which is why we set the big life goals first. Then we backtrack from that vision to where we are now and figure out how to get there, step by step.

Depending on where you are, your next step could be consciously stopping the "any client is a good client" line of thinking and getting clear on who you like working with. It could look like outlining a book or creating your first product. You're the best one to decide your next step, so if you're unsure, start brainstorming!

Doing the Creative Work

As a creative person, when you were first daydreaming about starting your business, I bet it looked like being able to create all day, every day. And yes, now that you're your own boss, you get to decide what your day looks like and how you spend your time. However, there are a few things to consider.

The first is, just because you have 40 working hours available, that doesn't mean you'll spend all that time doing creative work every week.

A 40-hour work week doesn't mean you sit your ass at a desk for eight hours a day and create—it didn't mean that at the day job, and it certainly doesn't mean that when you're on your own.

The reality is, there will be a mix of creative work, admin work, prospecting for leads, and continuing to learn. While these activities are critical to your success, that's not time spent making you money. Prospecting and creating are. The basic rule of thumb is that freelancers spend about 30% of their workday doing the creative work they're getting paid to do.[4]

The reason is simple: you can't bill your current client for the time you spent doing administrative work or prospecting for more clients. That all needs to be baked into not only your pricing, but how you're spending your time on a daily, weekly, and monthly basis.

If you are pricing based on billing 40 hours, the reality is you're working 60-80 hours (if not more) to pull in 40 hours' worth of work. This is why I advise most freelancers I work with to immediately triple what they

---

[4] "How Freelancers Spend Time." Clockify. 2021. https://clockify.me/how-freelancers-spend-time

charge—because even though that 3x rate feels high, it's necessary to cover all the time you spend running your business.

So, while it's only 30% of your time, this creative time is your bread and butter. You'll want to ensure you're not only blocking out enough time to do it well, but also fiercely guarding that time.

This isn't always easy. I once lived in the same town as one of my best friends, who was a stay-at-home mom. I adore stay-at-home parents—if that's you, I think you have one of the hardest jobs around. But this friend and I constantly butted heads because most of the time, when she wanted to go out and do something—go to the gym, have a long lunch, get our nails done—she was calling right in the middle of my creation time. I'd have to tell her, "I can't, I have to work," to which she'd usually respond, "You can work any time, let's go!"

Yeah, but I didn't want to work all night because I took off most of the day goofing off and having fun with my friends.

My compromise was one or two days a week, I'd go with her to the gym or take a long lunch (after all, I built my business so I could have the freedom to do what I want when I want). The rest of the time, we hung out in the evening after I closed my laptop for the day.

When it comes to creating your schedule, I recommend starting with a day at a time. How many hours do you want to work per day? To keep the math easy, let's go with eight since most of us were conditioned to expect that with the day job.

What time of day do you do your best creative work? Is it morning, midday, evening… late nights? It's important to know when you do your best work because you're going to block off your creative time accordingly—I do mean literally blocking those times off in your calendar and not letting anyone else steal that time from you.

243

Note: most creatives I know have a good two to four hours a day of creation time before they're mentally tapped out. Please don't go into this thinking that you'll be able (or even want) to create for six to eight hours straight. That's a brain drain and a half, and a recipe for burnout.

Now that your creative time is blocked out, think about what else you need to do in a day. When are you going to prospect? When are you having calls with clients or prospective clients? When are you doing your admin work?

Slot those in wherever they fit. I have a two-hour creative burst in the morning with coffee, I spend my afternoons making calls and doing other admin work, and usually, after a brief power nap, I've got another creative hour or two I can squeeze in around dinner time.

When we're talking about blocking off your calendar, I'm not saying you need to have every day scheduled down to the minute—I know I rebel against that kind of planning and never manage to stick to it. But I do have creative time carved out daily (because that's a muscle that needs daily exercise), and I also have themed days.

Tuesdays and Thursdays are about coaching and consulting calls. Wednesdays are podcast recording days. Monday and Friday are days to catch up or do whatever (even play hooky). I have those days marked as "unavailable" for calls in my schedule.

It's taken me years to arrive at this schedule, so you may have to play with it a bit. But now I know, at minimum, I need to create from about 9 am to 11 am, and then the rest of the day I can do whatever—admin, prospecting, learning, taking calls. The important thing to remember here is that there's no one to stop you from spending all your time watching Netflix versus doing the work.

There's no boss to write you up if you repeatedly blow deadlines, no coworkers bitching about you slacking off. You're the boss, so maybe you won't get "fired" from your company for goofing off, but eventually, if you procrastinate enough, your clients may get the sense you're not invested in the project and decide to part ways. Or you might wind up screwing around all day and working all night, and then suddenly, you're stuck in a cycle of exhaustion.

Don't do that to yourself. There's a time and place for Netflix, and it's not when you need to be doing the work.

We covered avoiding the work with binge watching, so now we need to talk about overloading yourself. It can be really tempting to say yes to everyone who wants to pay you, but you've got to be realistic about what you have time to deliver.

You are allowed to take on as many projects as your heart desires. But if you're burning the candle at both ends, you're not producing your best work, which can come back to bite you. My method for preventing overload and overwhelm? I learned to start telling new clients, "Absolutely. If you get me your deposit by tomorrow, I can start on that in three weeks." Obviously, it doesn't have to be three weeks, but it should reflect a future date you can start, once you've fulfilled your commitments.

You are not required to start right away just because someone asked you to.

If you were working a job and a bunch of projects came in with competing priorities, some would naturally slide because you can't possibly do everything at the same time. Working for yourself will be similar in that regard—you can take on all the projects if you want but be realistic about the time you're giving yourself to get it all done. Then add 20% more time just to cover your bases.

One last piece of the creation puzzle—self-care. This looks like something different for everyone, depending on where your interests lie. At a high level, self-care means taking time off, away from the computer and the pinging of the phone, to do something you like doing.

For me, trips to Disney World and lunch by the water are self-care. So, what does that look like for you? Are you spending time with friends and family? What are your creative hobbies outside your freelance skills?

I love singing, and while I've occasionally been paid to do it, I mostly do it for fun. It's something creative that makes me feel alive. Even if you read, go to a concert, tend to the garden, or cook an epic meal, disconnecting from the computer and the work to do something else for a while will help stimulate your brain and refresh your creativity, which helps you do better work.

At a minimum, you should be eating well, sleeping well, and getting some regular movement in. The better you care for your mind and body, the more stamina you'll have to keep your business going.

You've got to take care of the WHOLE you to make this business work for the long term.

Business Budgeting

Once you've gotten into a groove (that is, you've figured out who you like to work with, what work you like doing, how to charge for that work, and how to keep a consistent flow of revenue coming in), it's time to figure out your business budgeting. You'll have things the business needs, and ideally, you're not pulling from your personal pay to support the business—that's not sustainable long-term.

I'm touching on this at a super high level, as I am not the world's foremost financial expert (we've established that). If you want to go deeper, I highly recommend Jess and the team over at The Bottom Line CPA. They're phenomenal at helping with all things business finance.

That said, I divide business finances into three main budget categories:

1) Operating expenses: these are the day-to-day expenditures that help you keep the lights on. We're talking electricity, internet, software subscriptions, insurance, your VA, etc.

2) Taxes and other long-term savings: since you're now on the hook for paying your own taxes, you'll want to have some cash set aside. You'll also want to consider having a separate business F.U. Fund so that a dry spell doesn't force you to dip into your personal savings for business operations. I recommend the same rule here, which is to set aside six (or nine or twelve) months of operating expenses, enough to help you stay afloat and keep staff on board (if applicable) if your revenue takes a hit.

3) Investments: in the next chapter, we will cover what I call "sharpening the saw." That's all the additional training and support you'll want to invest in to stay at the top of your game. This category could include training courses, coaching, travel for conferences, and hiring consultants or advisors for specific projects. It can also include investments in equipment, like if you wanted to get a new computer, camera, vehicle, etc., for your business.

How it breaks down for me: I've allocated 40% of my total monthly revenue to the business, and 60% goes to me personally as my pay. That 40% business "chunk" pays for all three of the categories above—operations, investments, and various business savings accounts. The 60% personal "chunk" of the revenue covers all my personal bills, including housing, entertainment, food, savings, and individual taxes.

See why setting your prices should factor in more than "what feels good?"

Your numbers and allocations may look very different from mine, and that's okay. That's why I'm not going to belabor the point here, especially when there are many excellent finance books and other resources (like Jess) available to help you find solutions relevant to you.

If you know what you need to make to live comfortably and finance your business and life goals, you'll be much more discerning about which gigs you put yourself up for. And you'll get a lot pickier with people who approach you with potential projects. It's all about finding the right fit, the right exchange of value.

Cash flow is your key to freedom.

With more money comes more freedom. But also, more money brings more problems and new and interesting challenges you could never have foreseen. This is why we save and plan.

Raising Your Prices

We've covered basic budgeting; now let's talk about the foundation of long-term growth—raising your prices. That's what will buy you the freedom to bring on help and think up additional revenue streams so your business can grow to meet your personal goals.

I'm not talking about aiming for multi-millions if you are perfectly fine with a solid six-figure business. But now that you know your overall goal, we've got to buy back some of your time so you can figure out how to get there. You do that by having a strong F.U. Fund and by raising your prices semi-regularly.

A consultant I follow talks about regularly shedding the bottom 20% of your business (kind of like you'd exfoliate dry skin). The reason is simple: it gives you space for bigger, better-paying clients to enter the arena.

And this has held true for me—the more they pay you, the more they tend to trust you and leave you to work your magic. In my experience, the folks paying the least almost always wanted the most from me—and they felt entitled to a lot more of my time and energy than I wanted to give.

By creating space for better paying clients, you get more income for less time commitment. At the same time, you're getting better (read: more efficient) at what you do. So, you spend less time achieving the same results, and then raise your rates? Profit!

Now, there's a caveat: it can be hard to let go of those first few clients, especially if they were with you from the start.

I get it, and it's only natural to feel loyalty toward someone who gave you your first real shot at being a legit professional creative. But remember that you're always going to be growing and evolving. What you're doing for now is not what you'll do forever. As your interests change and your skills sharpen, you'll naturally outgrow or sometimes pivot entirely away from your early-stage clients.

It's normal for people to drop off as their interests (and their budgets) diverge from you and your goals. Knowing that you're aiming to drop the bottom 20% gives you the freedom to stop offering a service you resent providing but that you have been obligated to do because you needed the money.

Great news! There are probably people in your network who would love to take on that project for you! You can connect your client to someone you know who can pick up the project. This way, you leave the client in a great position and reinforce your status as a well-connected expert.

And just because I'm talking growth doesn't mean you need to ramp up your spending.

You can't overspend your way to a successful business, especially if debt gets you into trouble in your daily life. I highly recommend reading the book *Profit First* by Mike Michalowicz if you want an eye-opening take on the financial mistakes businesses make (and how to set yourself up in a way that puts a natural cap on your expenses).

I get that regularly upping rates and deliberately losing clients might be mildly terrifying. But think of it this way: when you're totally comfortable with your rates, you're also not really daring yourself to step up to higher level work and clients. Ouch.

If you only feel comfortable charging $25 an hour, I'm going to lovingly challenge you—put a cap on that and commit to doing it for no longer than six months. Once the six months are up, double it. Don't explain or rationalize—just put your new rate into effect on your next quote for a new prospective client. I think you'll be surprised how many people accept without question or haggling.

Then double it again after six months or a year. Whoa! Scary, huh? But what if they were willing to pay you $100 an hour, yet you only charged them $25 because you were afraid they would reject you? You'd be leaving money on the table, all because of a fear that's not even accurate.

Challenge yourself to throw a higher quote out there just to see what happens. If you scare people away, it could just be that they're someone you don't want to work with. It doesn't mean that NO ONE out there can afford you. And the great news is once you get a yes to a ridiculously high price, that's your new "level," there's no turning back and accepting what you took when you were first starting out.

Once I got paid $10,000 a month to write, I became a $10,000 a month writer. But first, I had to name that price and believe I could deliver the value.

One last note on raising prices: if you can't seem to get beyond a certain income threshold or can't get clients to meet certain quotes, it's likely because there's a disconnect somewhere. It's not that they don't think you're worth it… they just don't understand the value.

From the client's perspective, there's always a risk in entering an agreement to have a freelancer take over something for you. They're trusting you with their baby, so you have to ensure you're delivering. Sometimes that means charging what feels like a lot of money… but then again, raising your rates also forces you to step up your game.

Trust yourself to take smart risks and to find clients who pay you well and respect you. In turn, being paid well and respected will inspire you to do your best work, leading to referrals to more amazing clients and… well, you see how it goes.

Chapter 13: When It Feels Like You Don't Know What You're Doing

At one point in my journey, I had a major opportunity pop up:

I was invited to attend a three-day private mastermind meeting with some really big names in the online business space.

For years, I'd told myself that success was just around the corner, and all I needed to do was get to that next level. And in the business world, you couldn't get much higher than being at this mastermind.

"This is it," I thought to myself. "I've made it! I'm in the room where it happens—it's smooth sailing from here!"

Day one came, and I felt like I was back in high school—nervous but excited for the next step. Me being me, I wanted to get it RIGHT and make a great impression from the start. I arrived half an hour early to scope out the room, shoving my massively overpacked "prepared for anything" bag out of the way so people wouldn't trip. I looked around to find my name tent, which was set up next to someone widely acknowledged as a celebrity in online business.

I eagerly unpacked my laptop and took out my notebook—might as well have both on hand, right? Doesn't hurt to be prepared!

I got myself situated at the meeting, and I waited…

And waited…

And waited…

Maybe five minutes prior to the start, people started strolling in, making their way to the back for coffee and snacks. They clustered in groups, talking to their business buddies, not one of them noticing my hyper-preparedness and readiness to BRING IT.

Looking back at myself, I cringe a little—sometimes I took that whole "never get a second chance to make a first impression" bit of advice a tad too seriously. I know now that my over-the-top preparation for this meeting was me seeking validation. I desperately wanted to fit in with what I perceived to be the Made It™ circle of success.

The meeting kicked off about 15 minutes late after the staff finally managed to wrangle everyone to their seats. I sat with my pen at the ready, waiting for my mind to be blown with the magic I was about to witness. I would finally get access to the SECRET, the piece I was missing that would skyrocket me to success!

My mind was blown alright, but not in the way I'd imagined.

It turns out the secret is that there is no secret.

I had convinced myself that I was missing something, something important that was preventing me from the kind of success I'd always wanted. If only I could get into that room, I could figure out the missing piece!

The missing piece was me, thinking I didn't have enough information or skills to hit ambitious goals. It was me not showing up for myself and acting on what I'd already learned.

Over the next three days, we'd dive deep into each other's businesses, and I was shocked at what my peek behind the curtain revealed…

The bigwigs were struggling with the exact same issues as me, only on a different scale.

They were…

- paranoid that their next big offer would be the one to tank the whole company, the one that finally exposed them as a fraud.

- navigating big life changes like losing a partner or caring for sick and aging family members while trying to keep their businesses running.

- struggling with difficult clients and challenging teammates, desperately trying to figure out what they were doing wrong.

I say all that to say this:

No matter how far you go or how much success and wealth you accumulate—you're never really going to know for certain that the next move is the right one. All you can do is follow your gut and try as hard as you can.

Welcome to the table, my friend.

Happily Never After?

Life is 80/20.

This is commonly known as the Pareto Principle, and you've probably seen me reference those numbers a couple of times.

Essentially, 80% of your results come from 20% of your efforts. I find that rule applies broadly to life, too. If you're doing alright 80% of the time and struggling 20% of the time, you're better off than most people in the world.

Applying the Pareto Principle here, you're building your own business because you want to work on your terms. You don't want to have to go into a day job and report to The Man every day, swallowing your pride 'cause you need that paycheck. Unfortunately, building a business doesn't include magical transport to the land of no problems.

Even when you design your business well, iron out all the kinks, and figure out what you need to earn to get to where you're satisfied, things won't always be rosy. You will have days when you're unhappy with your clients and don't want to get up and do the work. Here comes the perspective shift: if 80% of the time you're happy with your business and 20% of the time you're not, <u>you're doing great</u>.

Don't set yourself up for future disappointment by thinking you'll be 100% happy 100% of the time.

That's just not realistic. For most employees, those numbers will be reversed, where the majority of their daily reality is that they're unhappy, upset, or looking for a way out. Create something that allows you to be satisfied (or even happy!) most of the time, and you're way ahead of the curve.

If you're not actively practicing being happy and satisfied with where you are (while also trying to improve—they aren't mutually exclusive), then I've got bad news: the Happiness Fairy isn't coming. She's not waiting in the wings for you to check all the boxes so she can sprinkle happy dust on you.

Real, true happiness and satisfaction comes from *within*, not outside of you.

You'll never experience that magical happiness if you're putting off your dreams until someday when you suddenly have all your shit together. I can tell you from experience that you never feel "ready." Things don't come together into some flashing sign from the universe that indicates now is the time to act. You just decide to do the thing and figure it out. So, there's not much of a point in putting things off.

You might as well start working on that mindset shift today—because it's totally possible to have happiness and joy in your life right now, exactly where you are.

Whenever someone tells me it's impossible, I point them toward Viktor Frankl's *Man's Search for Meaning*. Highly recommend it—in a nutshell, the book talks about finding meaning and little moments of joy in a concentration camp, where you'd think there would be absolutely none to be had. And that's a decision—to not let circumstances you can't control dictate your outlook or your actions. He said:

> "Everything can be taken from a man but one thing: the last of the human freedoms—to choose one's attitude in any given set of circumstances, to choose one's own way."

In other words, no one can MAKE you do something you don't want to do. <u>Not even with a gun to the head.</u>

For me, I get a great deal of joy and satisfaction from the work I do. And I don't plan on allowing anyone to take that away from me. It may take a backseat from time to time—hell, in the middle of writing this book, I was unceremoniously dumped. For four to five months, I felt pretty low, but I clung to any tiny bits of laughter and joy I experienced along the way. Those moments kept me going through the grief and reminded me of who I ultimately wanted to be, the person I wanted to find my way back to.

Until the day you die, every day is a chance to try again. Practice setting the finish line a couple of feet ahead of you, crossing over it, being happy for a little while, and then setting new goals with new finish lines.

Keep moving forward to the best of your ability because even when you accomplish everything on your to-do list and achieve your goals, what will you do next? Sit on your ass for all eternity? That's going to get boring real fucking fast.

I mean, once you've achieved your goals, celebrate however you want to. Take a wildly indulgent vacation to a foreign country. Stay at home on the couch in your sweatpants, watching Netflix for three weeks, not taking calls, and refusing to shower. I'm not saying that's what I've done, but it may or may not be true based on my own reality. Celebrate however you celebrate; you'll get no judgment from me.

But after the excitement winds down, you'll want to set a new goal. Otherwise, you'll get bored doing the same ol', same ol'. Your dreams, goals, and definitions of success will always change as you grow and evolve. Stop trying to plan it all out right now. Stop trying to figure out what the ultimate endgame finish line looks like.

The finish line is just a few feet in front of you. Cross that and then find the next one.

You might just find that you can be happy right here and now (versus someday when all the stars are aligned).

I remember having a breakthrough with my coach, Brian McCarthy, one random Thursday. I was spiraling (a regular occurrence for me on those calls), and he was helping me figure out what was causing my anxiety to kick into overdrive.

"I feel like I'm behind. I have these huge revenue goals, and it doesn't seem like I'm getting any closer to them. It's really stressing me out," I told him.

"Tell me more," he said. "What is the goal, and why doesn't it feel like you're getting close?"

"I'd love to have a million-dollar business. I don't have any particular attachment to that number, but it'd be nice just to say I did it—I figured that out. I clawed my way out of living paycheck to paycheck and built something with stable, predictable revenue."

"That's an awesome goal! And what will that stable, predictable revenue help you achieve? Why is it so important to hit that goal?"

"I want to be able to travel and see the sights and eat great food without worrying about the cost. I'd love to be able to spoil the hell out of the people I love, take them on vacations, and help them out financially if needed. I want to do that for them for supporting me and these crazy dreams."

"I love that for you," he said. "Help me understand something. Where are you right now?"

At the time, I was in southern California and had just returned from a trip to Disneyland with my two best friends. I told him as much.

"Does that not qualify as traveling, seeing the sights, eating great food, and, let me check my notes… spoiling people you love?"

I was grateful we were on the phone instead of on a Zoom call. I'm pretty sure I turned 20 different shades of red when it dawned on me… I was working my ass off, beating myself up, trying to hit a goal so I could live a certain lifestyle.

A lifestyle I was already living. The only thing missing was the million-dollar revenue/no money worries piece.

This is why it's critical to think about what life looks like once you've hit your goals—otherwise, you might spend so much time focusing on the number that you miss how close you already are. And it's okay if you only have a vague picture of where you want to be or if that picture changes along the way.

You'll learn how you work best as you get more experience. You'll get ideas about how you prefer to live and what brings you balance and personal satisfaction. Your bliss may look completely different from mine, and that's normal—travel is part of who I am, but it's deeply stressful for others and not worth the hassle. A lot of the joy comes from experimenting and figuring it out for yourself.

It's important to know what you're working for, and to find ways you can incorporate parts of that now instead of waiting until "someday."

When Shit Goes Wrong

Uncomfortable truth slap: you're going to fail.

The only true failure is giving up and never giving it a real shot.

If you are learning from every failure and adjusting, improving, and iterating, you will eventually get to where you want to go. Or you'll find something even better than you imagined for yourself.

And this is important—the more you succeed, the less individual failures will matter. With more experience, you'll get better and better at learning from mistakes and missteps. That doesn't mean they won't sting or you'll never be embarrassed or stressed again. But as we talked about in Chapter 8, you can learn how to control your emotional reactions and avoid reacting out of fear, shame, and anger.

One of my favorite tactics for this is treating yourself like you would treat your best friend (or someone else in your life you care very deeply for).

When you've experienced a setback, being gentle with yourself is critical. You're a human being doing your best, and you deserve the same grace you give to others.

Imagine if, instead of happening to you, the shitty situation you're in was happening to someone you really care about. You wouldn't bullshit them and try to convince them everything is sunshine and roses when it's not. But you're also not going to kick them when they're down and tell them they're the biggest piece of crap ever to walk the earth. If you speak to someone you care about that way, you can kiss that relationship goodbye 'cause you just set it on fire.

And yet we think it's okay to talk to *ourselves* like that?

Treat yourself like someone you care about. Acknowledge where you're coming up short. Challenge yourself to do better, but don't beat yourself up when you mess up because that's just being a human. Welcome to being human. We all fall short sometimes.

Everybody fails. Your gurus have failed. If you dig back in their history, they've all probably shared their stories about a desperate point in their life that spurred them to make a massive change. I have shared my personal story about living out of my car with my diabetic cat. I checked into the most horrible no-tell motel that ever existed just to have a place to shower. But that experience led me to where I am now and taught me just how much I'm capable of—and how far I'm willing to go to make my dreams a reality.

If you want to learn from failure, know this: you can't lie to yourself. Being dishonest about your situation is the biggest disservice you could do yourself. You might be able to convince everyone around you that you're in a different place, but to get yourself out, you have to start with where you're at. And if you're in a bad spot, you can't build your escape plan on a fantasy.

You might be wondering who on earth would lie to themselves, but it happens all the time—when we refuse to look at bank statements for fear of what we'll see or we refuse to step on the scale for similar reasons. We convince ourselves that we're safe if we don't acknowledge the truth. But the longer we ignore it, the more stuck we get, and the harder it is to break free and move forward.

Do what you can to get back to center. Take the emotional sting out of it and look at your situation as objectively as possible. That might mean taking a walk, going out with friends, or doing a hardcore kickboxing workout. Whatever you need to do to feel the feelings and start to process them, do that, and come back to look at the failure again when the emotions aren't so raw.

That will allow you to reflect on the situation and be honest with yourself. *What happened? Was it me? Was it outside circumstances? Is this something I can prevent in the future, or is this a one-off occurrence that I never could have foreseen?*

Honest, objective evaluation will help you identify the root cause of the problem, even if this time it's you. And because you're not under the influence of extreme emotions, it gets a lot easier to admit, "Okay, that was my mistake. I made the wrong call, and next time I'll choose something different."

That is how you fail your way forward.

Creators Create

Since you know you'll have to face your fear at some point to get to the thing you want the most, you might as well arm yourself. I can't imagine any scenario where someone would walk into an MMA cage and challenge a champion without ever taking a martial arts lesson in their life, thinking, "Let's see what I can do!"

What you can do is prepare for a beatdown because you didn't do any other preparation.

Get yourself ready for your next move to the extent you are able. If you want to start a freelance writing career, then write as much as you can, whether it's paid or not. So many would-be writers ask me how to become a writer and scoff when I ask them how much they write.

"I haven't had a paying client yet," they tell me.

"It doesn't matter," I tell them. "Writers write because it's who they are, not because they'll only pick up a pen or sit at a keyboard once the check clears. If you're not writing for clients, what are you writing for YOU?" That usually takes the snark out of the sails quickly.

The point is, write. Create. Take every project you can. Invest in a mentor or a coach to help you level up that much faster. Pitch articles. Write for your own blog. Give yourself goals and deadlines, then hit them—even if you're the only one who knows you did. Get as much writing experience as you can beforehand—because the last thing you want is to figure out you can't deliver after you've already cashed and spent your client's check.

The same goes for any medium you create in. Bakers bake. Painters paint. Dancers dance.

Arm yourself as best you can and know that there are going to be battles and fights that you can't possibly predict in the future. There will be projects you love and projects you can't stand. Your path will probably change direction a few times before you land where you want, and even after you've landed, you may find yourself itching for a new challenge after a while.

You'll discover things you didn't even know you wanted. I never knew that I wanted to be a copywriter. It's not a career I learned about in school, or that I trained professionally for. I never even knew this field existed until I got laid off and picked up a copy of *The Well-Fed Writer*. I read that book in an afternoon and thought, *I could probably do that.*

I did that for over a decade, and now you are reading a book I wrote. I didn't plan any of this, yet here we are… purely because I kept taking action and working on my craft.

Be Willing to Walk Away

Even if it means that you have to scramble and hustle for money, you must be willing to walk away from a project or client—especially if there's disrespect happening.

When you do that, you buy back something infinitely more valuable, and it technically didn't cost you a single cent. I'm talking about your mental space, brainpower, and peace of mind. You don't have to feel resentment toward that client. You don't have to feel stressed about delivering this thing under pressure. You don't have to worry about not getting paid well (while at the same time turning down work from paying clients who might stress you a hell of a lot less while valuing you and your work more).

You are buying back your power when you're willing to walk away. And to me, that's priceless.

Back in Chapter 2, I mentioned getting a $2,500 sales letter gig from a referral after attending a seminar. However, I left out one critical detail—I felt incredibly anxious when I took on that project. Looking back, it's probably because I really needed the money—after all, I'd just totaled my car. As a result, every time that client tightened the deadline or added more things on, I kept adding things to the plate without adding fees or extra time. It never even occurred to me to push back on the price. I needed the money that badly.

Before long, that $2,500 sales letter (that I wrote and delivered within a week, by the way, which is insane) had ballooned into a sales letter, three press releases, and edits to six email sequences—and I'd thrown all that extra stuff in for free. The sales letter itself was already a crazy amount of work and a ridiculously tight deadline. That could easily have been two to three months of work and quadruple the price I charged.

I did all that because of insecurity. I was paranoid that he'd take his money and run if I didn't do everything he asked, and I'd be screwed.

And he knew the truth about me. He may not have known on a conscious level that, *This writer is insecure, so I'm going to push and see how far I can go.* But every time I caved, he knew he could just ask me for more, and I would do it to keep his business. It took me a lot of time and processing to realize that that's not the way to do business (at least not if you want your business to thrive).

What I want you to take away from this story is that HE didn't do this to ME.

I did it to myself.

No is always one possible answer, but often we let fear convince us it's not. I didn't think "No" was available to me. And once he realized I wouldn't say no, it became easier for him to push and squeeze every last drop out of that working relationship.

I don't blame him—it's a smart business move to try and get maximum value out of minimal expenditure. I can gripe all day long about how he should have known he was pushing too far, but the reality is, the buck stops with me. I was too afraid to say no, and too afraid to walk and go find another client, and so I suffered. I chose to stay, even though it felt like I had no other options at the time.

I get that saying no is hard, especially when someone's paying you a lot of money. But you increase your value and respect in others' eyes when you use it wisely. No is your trump card. You can play it whenever you want to end a situation that no longer serves you. The client doesn't have to like that you turned them down, nor do they need to agree with your point of view for you to say no. You have already earned the right to say it by merit of being a human with free will.

People will always push to see what they can get—it's human nature. There are folks who are self-aware enough to know what they're doing, and others who have no clue that they're pushing too hard until they get pushback. Remember to assume positive intent—that they fall into that latter camp of someone who doesn't realize they're being pushy. And when something comes up that makes you bristle or feel resentful, remember our old pal, "No" and act accordingly, with kindness.

"I can't do that, but here's what I CAN do" is always an option. So is walking away.

Chapter 14: Staying Sharp and Starting to Grow

Things will work much more smoothly for you if you keep your blade nice and sharp. Trust me—I once volunteered for a wildlife rescue and learned firsthand the importance of that cutting edge.

One day they had me do a marathon veggie-chopping session to batch prep food for all the rescue animals. Unfortunately, the knife blade was so dull that when I finally removed my gloves after hours of chopping, I had huge blisters from the extra effort.

I didn't realize the extent of the damage until that moment because my fingers had gone numb from the force I had to use to get the knife all the way through the veggies. If I'd had a sharpener, not only could I have done all that chopping in about half the time, but I could have spared myself a lot of pain too.

In life and in business, this concept of staying sharp is important. Its origins lie in an old quote attributed to Abraham Lincoln:

"Give me six hours to chop down a tree and I will spend four hours sharpening the ax."

Like everything we've discussed so far, getting up to speed with new technology and new industry best practices is a balance. The tools you use will make or break you, but that doesn't mean you have to be first in line at the Apple store. Everyone in business has plenty of opportunity, whether you're a technophobe verging on luddite or the leading expert in The Next Big Thing.

When I first started my business, I had a Palm Pilot (a hand-held digital to-do list and organizer) to help me keep things straight. Right around that time, the first-generation iPhones came out, revolutionizing how we tracked and managed things. Now technology is developing at the speed of light.

The good news is that the way humans engage and connect with one another hasn't changed in millennia. And it's unlikely to change no matter how sophisticated the digital landscape becomes.

By the same token, if you never work on learning new skills, you risk being left behind as tech and best practices evolve. I'd be creating double the work if I stuck to using that old Palm Pilot when I've got a smart phone on the table beside me that can do the same thing more efficiently.

As you progress, you'll want to explore new skills, strategies, tactics, and technologies. Don't get too hung up on how much time to carve out for this—it could be a scheduled half hour every morning, or however long it takes you to figure out how to make a screencap video.

The number of hours doesn't matter so long as you're making it part of your process in a way that works for you (and it's not interfering with your money-making work).

Dedicate a little bit of regularly scheduled time to improving your skills (not to mention your mental well-being and your health)… your future self will thank you.

Trying New Things

Let's start with the truth: not every new tech or trend is worth the time it takes to learn. Nor will it help you in the long term if you're constantly jumping from software to software or tactic to tactic.

You don't need to become an expert at EVERYTHING just to stay relevant, but you should be aware of what's happening in your industry and the advantages (and pitfalls) of the new options. Knowing how and where your potential clients and customers prefer to communicate is more important. Do they prefer text? Social media? Email? Wherever your people are, that's where you should be, which means there might be a new skill you need to learn.

One thing that helped me with tech overwhelm was recognizing that there's a difference between the core "thing" and the fads that come and go.

For instance, who remembers Vine? When it was still around, everybody said its 6-second videos would be the next big thing, especially after it was acquired by Twitter (now called "X") in 2012. There were people creating courses, talking about how essential Vine would be for marketing your business and how anyone who wasn't participating on the platform would be hurting.

By 2016 all new Vine uploads were halted, and in 2017 it was archived. Just like that, we were onto the next trend. Vine was the fad, the exciting new packaging around the core "thing," which was video. However, Vine was simply one of many video platforms, and it was still shuttered despite the growing popularity of video.

It just goes to show—if you're good at the "thing," you can always incorporate a new platform (especially as developers get better and better at intuitive apps and software). Just make sure it's where your people are hanging out before you dive in.

As I write this book, everyone in the field of copywriting is up in arms over Artificial Intelligence (AI). There are programs that can write articles and spin headlines faster than a copywriter can come up with them… plus it can test all those headlines (and declare a winner) without a human doing a thing. As a result, there are a lot of people that think that AI will replace copywriters.

Personally, I'm not scared a machine will take my place because:

1) **I've seen the garbage AI currently churns out**—and while it may improve in the future, right now I'm not all that impressed. The problem with AI generated copy is still going to be people for the foreseeable future. By that, I mean that folks who thought they'd save money by firing copywriters to "hire" AI are about to find out they suck at creating a strategic direction and giving feedback, two vital pieces of communication that AI needs as much as any copywriter does.

   They will spend hours clicking "regenerate" and getting frustrated when they don't get what they want or when AI spits out made-up sources and ineffective copy. At that point, the user will likely blame AI for not being all it was cracked up to be instead of looking at how they could learn how to use it better.

2) **There will always be a subset of people who prefer working with people** over working with machines, and…

3) **Machines don't come up with creative ideas.** The day they do is probably the day that we need to bow down to our robot overlords. But until the machines can come up with an emotion-based creative idea that really appeals to a human, on a human level, without any skepticism or uncanny valley weirdness… I'm not worried about AI replacing me.

Do I want to be aware of what's happening with AI? Absolutely, because I may partner with a business that has an AI functionality and I'd have to understand how I fit into their overall plan. But just because things are changing doesn't necessarily mean your industry is dying. It's evolving, as we all must also do.

It's critical to stay on that cutting edge, go to conferences, and connect with colleagues and peers to see what they're doing. LinkedIn and other professional groups are a great way to stay on top of what's happening because as soon as your peers see an article or presentation discussing potential industry disruptors, they're going to share it and start conversations.

Leverage that network to understand what's happening, what's changing, and where you may need to pivot. That's how you stay forward-focused without jumping from new thing to new thing.

Here's one last "secret" about staying sharp—there's nothing new under the sun. By that, I mean there's just as much value in exploring conventional wisdom and experts from previous generations as there is in learning all the new tech.

I recently reread Dale Carnegie's *How to Win Friends and Influence People*. That one stands the test of time—Carnegie had no idea that the internet and cell phones were coming. Yet every strategy he teaches in that book still applies to human beings today, because it's about how we connect and relate to each other.

Just because information is technically "old" doesn't mean it can't be just as useful as new tech. Learn and practice to keep a competitive edge in a constantly changing landscape. Don't sit idly by and let the future run right over you.

Finding the Fast Track

Until this point, we've been talking largely about self-education—things like books, conferences, and self-guided courses that require you to sift through everything, find the knowledge nuggets, and put them into play.

That's a valid way to learn, but it's also the slow path because it involves a lot of experimentation and hard lessons learned.

At one point I got frustrated with my own slow progress. I was growing, but my nature is to move fast. So, I started talking to friends and colleagues (noticing a theme in this book?) and discovered something that drastically shortcut my learning curve: coaching and masterminds.

First let's talk about coaching because that's usually a more personalized experience.

When you join a small group coaching program, the cool thing is you not only get to be in a room with smart business owners asking smart questions, you also don't have to flip through 16 books or do hours of Google searching to find a solution to a problem—you can just ask your peers.

You can also invest in 1:1 coaching where you work privately and exclusively on your business, but that tends to be a bit spendier than group programs. Both group and individual coaching will probably cost you a pretty penny if the coach is any good.

But remember the opportunity cost: if it took me ten hours to look through a bunch of books and courses to find an answer to my problem, and I charge $500 an hour to consult, then I just spent $5,000 finding that answer. Why not spend $5,000 on a six- or twelve-month coaching program, get answers to multiple questions in mere minutes, and save yourself a ton of time while getting ongoing personal support?

A word on finding a good coach: like dating, there's going to be trial and error involved. You may get lucky and find an amazing coach the first time you go looking—and you may have to try a few on for size before you find the right fit.

I once had a coach whose teaching style was fundamentally incompatible with my learning style. He was a "figure it out" kind of teacher who gave minimal info or direction. I'm an "I need to understand why" person who wants to dig deep into the thought process behind different approaches. We ultimately discontinued working together because neither of us was getting what we wanted. Doesn't make him a bad coach or me a bad student—it was a bad fit, period.

The best coaches are flexible and can adapt their teaching to different learning styles. They also teach you to trust your intuition and find your own solutions versus spoon feeding you answers (thereby training you to depend on them).

The next shortcut option is a mastermind.

Good news—usually, if you find a good coach, they either will have a mastermind or know of a good one and be able to make recommendations. Masterminds are a lot like coaching groups, except for two key differences:

1) Coaching tends to be a group of people in similar businesses trying to learn a particular skill or strategy from an expert.

2) Masterminds tend to be led or facilitated by an expert, but not focused on any one topic or tactic. The members could be very similar or from drastically different kinds of businesses, and the focus is on the members collaborating and supporting one another.

What I love about being in a room with people from different backgrounds and fields is all the inspiration I get to try something new. Often, ideas and strategies—with a little bit of tweaking—are transferable between businesses and industries. Talking to someone who spends all their time working in another field can provide a fresh, creative spark that really helps you stand out from what your competitors are doing.

Plus, if you want to be a respected, highly paid consultant—hey, being in the room with people who pay a lot of money to improve their businesses is a good sign. They already want to get better and are willing to pay to do so. And if you happen to be there with a skill they need, it may naturally lead to a working relationship.

For me, the best part of coaching groups and masterminds is how drastically it shortens my learning curve. Being in the room with so many smart people puts my problems into perspective and gets me unstuck. I get to hear answers to questions I didn't even know to ask simply by listening to what others are going through. I can pick up awesome ideas for certain efficiencies, client-getting strategies, or offer creation tactics to increase my revenue.

The key: surround yourself with like-minded people who are hell-bent on achieving a certain level of success.

As you look for networking and continuing education, make sure you're choosing the next level up. Challenge yourself to step into a room where you have space to grow, new fields to experience, and new information and expertise to add to your repertoire—versus hanging out with dreamers who never actually DO.

If you're not sure whether you're to join a coaching program or need guidance on which resource is best for you right now, check out the Finding the Right Resources Cheat Sheet. You'll find it in the companion guide, which you can download free at **permissiontokickass.com/guide.**

Asking For (and Getting) Help with Grace

Asking for help has been a lifelong struggle for me—I blame it on my Southern heritage with its not-so-subtle pressure to be "self-made" and avoid "bothering" people at all costs.

But here's the thing: we all got to where we are because someone helped us.

And personally, it is truly a pleasure to see someone who was struggling to resolve their issue and move on. I'm elated when someone I helped comes back and says, "Hey, thank you for your advice on that. I did that thing, and it fixed everything, and I'm great."

I want to consciously reframe "What if I need help?" to "What am I going to do WHEN I need help?"

This is exactly why you've been working hard to reach out to people in your industry, attend networking events and conferences, join communities, and build your pre-prospecting list. These people are all potential resources, advisors, clients, and connectors. And they want to see you succeed. Don't be so prideful that you can't ask for and accept help. Put another way:

Don't rob someone else of the joy of helping you.

By the same token, when you reach a certain level of success, it's critical to turn around and help the people that are coming up behind you. If the idea of helping people makes you worry about "giving away the farm," here's a simple framework I use to keep the help requests from taking up all my time, while still being helpful to people who reach out.

I use the five-minute rule: if someone's ask takes me less than five minutes, I'll just go ahead and help them. Most people love to be helpful, and so if you need me to listen to you ramble for five minutes and then spout some advice back at you, well, that was five whole minutes of my time that made a pretty big difference for you—so isn't that time well spent? If it takes longer than five minutes, we can find a different solution, whether it's a referral or a paid consultation. This simple practice has helped me grow an incredible network of people I'd move mountains for (and who would move mountains for me).
The weirdest part of all this is how the goodwill you put out into the world comes back around, often more quickly than you realize.

With a few successes under your belt, suddenly, you graduate from being the person asking the questions to having others ask you questions. This just happened to one of my students, who considered herself a total newbie to the field she's been working in for the last three years. She was shocked when someone reached out to her with questions, but I wasn't surprised at all.

To someone with only six months of experience, someone with three years of experience looks like an expert.

Tapping into your network is not just good for you mentally and spiritually… it's also good for your business growth. So don't sit in your corner and be a martyr for the cause, pretending you can do it all on your own.

Ideas don't come from isolation and sitting in your own stagnation.

If you're looking for a spark, new ideas, and fresh creativity, you've got to go out into the world and yes… occasionally ask for (and graciously receive) help.

Chapter 15: Leveling Up

I learned an important lesson when I was a volunteer answering the phones for a domestic violence crisis center hotline.

This mission is close to my heart because I've been in an abusive situation myself. I put my heart and soul into every call I answered, trying to make the callers feel safe and supported. And, of course, I loved giving back, but sometimes it really sucked that I couldn't do more. Part of me desperately wanted to be a superhero for the people I talked to. In retrospect, I think it was because fixing others' problems was a hell of a lot easier than facing my own.

But I couldn't swoop in and magically fix everything—I could only listen to their struggles, point them toward resources, and encourage them to take steps that felt right and realistic for them.

In fact, that was part of our training—recognizing that we can't make choices for other people because, at best, we'd be making those choices through our own filters and feelings. At worst, we could be missing vital context that might actually put that person in danger.

One day, I'd had a lot of emotionally heavy calls, and melted down at my inability to do anything but listen. It felt like the weight of the world was on my shoulders, and it was hard for me to see (let alone believe) that there was anything good left.

I reached out to a friend who had experience working on suicide hotlines. He seemed so well-adjusted, and it didn't seem like the heaviness of those calls hit him as hard, so I had to know his secret. I thought he might reply to my email with a few brief coping tactics—instead, he recorded an amazing 20-minute voice message for me. That audio changed my life, and I'm paraphrasing a small snippet below:

"No one expects you to be a superhero. You're not here to save the world single-handedly. You're not even here to save that person calling into the hotline, because this problem existed long before you were born and will be around long after you're gone. You didn't create this problem, and you can't save people. ***All you can do is get them one step closer to safety.****"*

He helped me see that those calls were not about waving a magic wand and fixing people's problems—it was about moving people one step closer to their goal (in this case, safety).

That's when I realized I didn't want power and control over other people's lives. Pretending I could make the right choices for others was a fantasy. Doing things for a person that they didn't ask you to do can lead to a whole host of issues, especially since we'll never have the full context and understanding that another human has.

We can get close through the practice of empathy, but in the end, we can only be in our OWN heads—and trying to be in someone else's will lead to heartache.

The same rule applies to business and life in general—you can only get your clients one step closer to solving the problem, but you can't fix others' lives (or businesses) for them.

When Doing Good Work Goes Wrong

I tell you my story so I can tell you this… there are two potential danger zones in client work (and we all get tempted from time to time, so be gentle if you see yourself below). Those are:

1) Going a little too deep into the work and becoming a "fixer"

2) Going a little too deep into the work and never taking time to rest

Situation one: becoming "The Fixer"

This happens when we insert ourselves into someone else's life or business in a way that's unhealthy. By that, I mean maybe you're working with an awesome client and notice they have this other problem over here you can fix, and find yourself thinking, *Oh it's no big deal for me to jump in and do that because they REALLY need it...*

Before long, you're working around the clock doing projects you assigned YOURSELF in the interest of being helpful.

I get it, and I'm going to challenge you: you can't live someone else's life for them, and you can't run their entire business for them—at least, not if you expect to also run YOUR life and business. Trying to control someone else's life is a recipe for crazy making—you're you and they're them.

Not only that, this behavior indicates that you don't trust them to make decisions for themselves. I use the word "behavior" with intent because it's a decision (even if unconscious and well-intentioned) to try and control someone else's actions.

It's their business. Some things can only be learned with context, which they might not ever gain until they make a choice you wouldn't. They have to make their own calls, even if it's not how you think things should be done.

Resist the urge to go so deep into other people's issues that you ignore (or avoid) your own challenges. Fix your own stuff first, and then help others figure out how to fix theirs. Let it go if they choose to do things differently than you would.

Situation two: never stopping to rest

Maybe you've heard this one: you can't feed others if your cupboard is bare.

That's what happened to me the day I melted down—I was trying to do too much, give too much, be too much. By trying to achieve the impossible and be a superhuman who saves everyone from a horrible situation, I was putting others (and myself) at risk.

There was no way I'd be able to continue to help people if I kept trying to do more than I could.

That was a sobering realization.

And a quick aside, in case prioritizing your own wellbeing somehow feels selfish: I did a brief stint as a firefighter in my late teens and early twenties. One of the first things they taught us in rookie training was to take care of number one.

That's not selfish—it's practical. Firefighters who aren't looking out for themselves are in danger of becoming additional victims, leaving the crew with fewer hands to help (and more people to rescue). So, take care of yourself—otherwise, you won't be available to assist others.

It's counter-intuitive, but you MUST deliberately step back and make time to fill your cupboard so you actually have something to give when the time comes. This means taking breaks and yes… even vacations! Otherwise, you won't have much left over for anyone or anything else.

You can't work on projects around the clock and expect to give your clients your absolute best.

This idea sounds radical compared to the Silicon Valley hustle-and-grind culture I came up in, where you're clearly not trying hard enough if you're not living in your car in the company parking lot, working 20-hour days.

That's not an exaggeration—I lived and worked in Silicon Valley for years. I know people who did this.

It's hard not to get sucked up in that culture when it's so pervasive in business.

Occasionally, I still struggle with the concept of charging more and working less—it feels like I'm not doing enough to "earn" what I'm charging. Especially in the context of my blue-collar upbringing, where the only way to make more was to work more.

The fact remains: you NEED to take time away from your business to be able to better work in the business.

With ALL that said, there is hope! We all go through these phases, especially folks with big hearts and world-changing missions. It does not make you less of a person to acknowledge your human-ness and accept that you can only do what you can and that doing what you can is enough.

Outgrowing Your Solopreneur Business

"I don't want to do this. You can't make me, screw you lady!"

That's what my brain said the first few times I sat down with TurboTax to reconcile my books. It was a very visceral response, not unlike the first time I tried steamed spinach and violently shuddered in my attempt not to hurl (it's a texture thing—don't come at me).

As you run your business, you'll start to notice that certain activities cause you stress (and sometimes even physical discomfort)… and yet they still must get done, even if the thought of doing it sends you into panic mode. Stress, and especially resistance, are signals from your body. When we talk about learning to trust your gut and your intuition, it starts with being aware of what's happening in your body.

If you break out in sweat, pick up your phone for the millionth time, or get slightly nauseated at the idea of doing a certain task… yeah, sometimes it's just procrastination or anxiety. But more often than we realize, it's the body trying to communicate just how draining this work is.

This is invaluable data because stress and resistance to certain tasks are clear signs of what to outsource and seek help with as you grow your business.

I want you to start noticing these things if you haven't already. Whenever you're putting off projects or feeling overwhelmed by the idea of doing a 15-minute task… write it down. Create a file or someplace where you can keep all these notes together. Over time you'll start to see patterns in the things you put off. They might be related to sales calls, calendaring, finances, or marketing.

Here's the thing though: try to document this stuff without adding a heaping helping of self-judgment. It's okay to not be great at everything, everywhere, all the time. We want you focused on doing the things you do best.

As you might have guessed from my story above, admin work and bookkeeping are not my strong suit. I constantly found myself resisting sitting down with the books, even though, as a responsible business owner, I know that financial awareness and literacy are essential to my success.

I don't avoid looking at financials entirely because that wouldn't be very smart of me. But I'm also not going to sit down every morning and reconcile expenses when I've got other things to do that bring in the money. After all, I started my business to write and coach, not figure out strategies for maximizing my tax deductions.

That's why as soon as I had some extra money to invest, one of my first hires was a bookkeeper. The next was a VA to help me get organized and streamlined. I've found that this is common with entrepreneurs—to bring in financial and administrative help as a first step toward expansion.

And here's the good news: no matter how much you hate doing something, someone out there fricking loves doing it. There are people out there who love balancing checkbooks and adore filing things and holding meetings. They love talking on the phone or creating and maintaining color-coded spreadsheets. They will gleefully do everything I won't. And that's a GOOD thing.

Because it also means there are people out there looking to outsource things they don't like to YOU and your business.

When I recognized that fact, my whole business changed. I used to assume that because I didn't like finances and filing, every other business owner out there also hated them. I thought everyone wanted to do the fun, creative stuff I loved doing, and I couldn't have been more wrong…

There are people out there that wouldn't write an email if you paid them because they have no idea where to even start. The idea of putting words down on paper (real or virtual) is paralyzing. They worry about whether they'll be clear, they don't know how to word things, and writing becomes a source of anxiety that stops them from growing their business.

Me? I'll write emails all day. I'm a writer. That's what I do. I'm good at it, and I happen to love it, so it makes sense for a person who struggles to write to bring in someone like me.

This is perhaps one of my favorite things about business: the freedom that comes when you admit that you don't have to do EVERYTHING in your business to have a successful one. Outsourcing doesn't mean you're lazy or that you're not brilliant. It means you're savvy and resourceful, someone who's determined to make the most of their time rather than wasting such a precious resource on something draining.

Okay Angie, I'm sold on hiring someone… but what? How? Can I even?

Yeah, I hear you—letting go of a piece of the business and learning how to hire someone you trust is a whole 'nother skill set, and entire books have been written on just this process alone. But it's something you can learn, and below is my quick and dirty primer on hiring.

For me, it breaks down into four steps:

1) Identify *specific* tasks you need help with.
2) Figure out how much you can afford to invest.
3) Find the right person.
4) Take 'em on a trial run.

Let's break those steps down even further…

Step One: Identify specific tasks you need help with

Something I see often in the entrepreneurs I work with (and I'm including myself in this observation) is the tendency to keep too much in our heads. By that, I mean we have the vision of what we want to accomplish in our minds, but the critical mistake we make is assuming everyone else can see it the same way we can.

That kind of assumption leads to all kinds of miscommunication and frustration. On the hiring front, it can lead you to believe you suck at business… especially if you hire several people who never seem to work out for one reason or another. Often that whole "not working out" thing stems from either a lack of specificity or a lack of communication.

Do you know which tasks you want this person to do? Can you show them how you want things done (if you're particular about them)? Or do you really not care about the process so long as the end goal is achieved? What IS the end goal, by the way? Is it a certain number of hours, a certain metric to hit?

I'm not asking those questions to overwhelm you or to make hiring sound hard. They're how I want you to think whenever you need to give someone direction. Can someone outside your head picture what "done" looks like in their mind? How will they know what "done" and "satisfactory" look like?

Let me put it another way: there's a big difference between "I need someone to help with creating consistent content" and "My goal is to publish one blog post, two social posts, and send three emails per week."

In the first scenario, YOU are the only one who knows what you really mean by "help with content." It's not clear and specific enough to be accurately interpreted by another person—they could take consistent content to mean one piece a month or one piece a day. In the second scenario, you've communicated the same goal with tangible details of what you mean.

If those tangibles are something you struggle with, here's a trick I use to get outside of my own head and get super clear: I add, "which means…" or "which looks like…" to the end of the goal statement. That will help you articulate how you're thinking about the goal and what completion looks like to you. When your tasks and goals are vague and undefined, they're open to interpretation. And if your interpretation is different from the person you hired, everyone will feel frustrated before long. Get as specific as possible— and know it's okay if the goals change or adjust, so long as you start somewhere specific.

Now that I've said that, I'm gonna say this: it's okay if you don't have all those questions answered. Often the first time you hire, you don't know what you don't know. The right person can help you figure out how to answer those questions.

Back in Chapter 7, I mentioned hiring my first VA. I didn't have much in the way of specific tasks I wanted to give her because I was so overwhelmed that even thinking about it caused panicky feelings. I solved this problem by directly calling it out in the ad I posted. Here's a paraphrased version of that post:

I am a copywriter and marketing consultant looking for a VA. I need someone who's got experience with distressed entrepreneurs. I'm overloaded and can't think about everything I need to get done without shutting down, and yet I know I'm in danger of dropping balls in a big way and letting clients down. The person I'm looking for knows how to guide an overwhelmed creative entrepreneur and pull things out of their head. I don't even know what to ask you to do at this point, so if you're coming into this waiting on me to come up with a list of tasks, we're gonna fail before we even start.

I received several inquiries from folks, as expected, and they ran the gamut. Some folks told me they were brand spanking new to VA work but would knock it out of the park for me. Some told me they loved cracking down on creative chaos. And some set up interviews with me and then flaked.

Eventually, I met Ashlee, who seemed to understand exactly what I needed. We started a trial run to see how well we worked together (more on that in Step Four). Once a week, we would meet, and she'd listen to me ramble about everything I needed to get done.

After our meeting, she'd make a list of tasks and assign herself the things she knew she could take off my plate. Then she'd give me the tasks only I could do and send me down the path. She'd also stay on top of me to ensure those tasks were getting done, giving me both the visibility and accountability I needed.

Step Two: Figure out *How much can I afford to invest in this person?*

Before you freak out, you have permission to start where you are. The budget is the budget, and most professional operators understand that you can't spend what you don't have. It also makes perfect sense that you'll want to keep your investments conservative while you're growing.

So, if you're starting with a low budget (think part-time hourly help versus full-time salaried role or consultant), there are plenty of places where you can hire a VA for relatively low hourly rates. There are bookkeepers with package deals to fit any kind of budget. Let one of those folks take on some of those administrative tasks so you're free to do the high-dollar work that brings money into your business.

Find the balance between what you can pay and what you need this person to do, because there's someone for everyone at every stage and every budget. Just be aware of what you're signing up for—when you're hiring at the lower end of the cost scale, those folks are typically at a more junior or beginner level and will need a lot more guidance, training, and feedback from you. Suppose you need an experienced, senior-level person to come in to immediately take things off your plate. In that case, that's a bigger investment since it comes with the added perk of them being able to make strategic calls with less hand-holding.

My first VA, Ashlee, was expensive and worth every penny because of her level of experience. I didn't want to take a chance on hiring someone brand new and then figuring out how to train them AND how to do my work simultaneously. I needed someone who could lead me through what I didn't know about management, automation, and planning. Her going rate at the time was $70 an hour and she effectively became my office manager.

Spendy? Yes. The good news is that I was upfront about what I could afford at the time, which was roughly ten hours a month. She gladly worked with me part-time to stay within my budget. Having a limited amount of time forced me to focus on where I could best use her skills, and she got a LOT done in those ten hours a month because she could do something in minutes where it would take me hours or even days to figure it out.

So, if you need someone to create graphics for you, maybe that's a graphic designer with high-end packages. Or maybe that's a local college student who would appreciate the experience. Both are acceptable options if you're being realistic about what you can afford to spend, what you expect for your investment, and how much time you're willing to commit to training and oversight. A college kid might not deliver award-winning, agency-level work, but they can still deliver good work that saves you a ton of time.

Step Three: Find the right person to work with you.

The best way I've found by far is reaching out to my network. When a lot of people vouch for someone publicly, that speaks volumes. My former VA is working with probably at least ten people I know simply because I hyped her up and sang her praises to my network.

However, even if a bunch of people recommend someone to you, it's still important to do your due diligence before signing them. You'll want to speak with a potential hire and make sure your personalities gel. Look for signs that they might not be on the same page with you about how to do the job, what the pay should be, when and how you'll communicate, etc.

Sometimes it takes a few conversations to know exactly what role you've got to fill and find the right person to do it well. That might mean that once you exhaust your network, you may need to post to a job board (or in an entrepreneur group, like I did when I found Ashlee).

That's where specifics are important because as you widen your candidate pool, you will get more candidates approaching you. Clearly defining your role and expectations will help you weed out people who aren't a great fit, allowing you to focus on finding the right fit.

When I made the post that helped me find Ashlee, I had lots of people reach out and excitedly tell me they didn't have the experience I wanted but couldn't wait to work with me. Because I'd set my expectations up front, I was able to quickly and tactfully let them know that I was grateful to them for taking the time and was sure they'd find a great client. But for all the reasons listed in the ad, someone brand new is not the right fit for me.

Don't be afraid to stick to your guns—you will meet many awesome people, and you will get along with them famously, but they won't be able to do what you need them to do. Likeability isn't enough to make for a good contractor or employee—they also need to be able to do what you asked them to do and to do it without creating extra work for you.

I made that mistake when I hired my first bookkeeper, a perfectly lovely person I liked and wanted to help out. Her business was growing, and my business was growing… what's not to love? Initially, I let her know that I'm a scatterbrained, unorganized, creative person, and I need people to stay on top of me and hold me accountable when they're waiting on me for something. Basically, I gave her permission to say, "No, Angie, I can't do this thing that you're paying me to do until you give me the things that I need, so please go do them."

Unfortunately, that was not the way this person operated. She was a lot more organized and on top of things than I was, so in her mind, it made sense to send me all the paperwork for the year in one packet, assuming that I'd check in throughout the year to see what needed to be done. That was a clear working style (not to mention a communication style) clash from the very beginning, and it stemmed from hiring someone I liked versus focusing on what I needed.

I knew it wasn't working about midway through year one, but I let it go another full year before getting frustrated enough to end things, again because I liked her and didn't want to disappoint or upset her. Always remember, though: you are the boss of your business, and you don't need more friends. You need people in your corner that can do the things you need them to do.

That brings me to quite possibly the most important step of your first (and any) hire:

Step Four: Take them on a trial run and evaluate how it's working.

When it came to tax time (this was many years ago), that bookkeeper asked me if I had filed quarterly reports and quarterly taxes, and I told her, "That is literally the thing that I am paying you to tell me I need to do. I asked you to stay on top of me for that."

In retrospect, I can see where I went wrong—I went straight from first date to marriage. I assumed from those first few conversations that we were on the same page, and I could let go and have her take over. When she didn't, I never course corrected. There was no setting of expectations. I didn't do regular check-ins and ensure things were still working for both of us—I just assumed things were going the way I envisioned they were. And I paid for it.

That was an expensive lesson for me in the form of a massive tax hit. And you should know, I don't blame her for that. I take full responsibility because, at the end of the day, I was the one making the money and, therefore, responsible for making sure the taxes were paid. I had tried to ensure I wouldn't drop the ball on that by hiring someone I hoped would stay on me until I got it done—and it didn't work out that way.

She is not a bad person, nor am I—we just weren't a good fit. Let this be a lesson to know how you work and to actively seek people who can balance you out and keep you on track. If someone isn't a good fit, you're not doing yourself (or them) any favors by trying to make it work when it clearly isn't. It will just keep going until you hit a breaking point, and one or both of you give up. If you're lucky, it breaks amicably.

That means you need to think about what will make this a successful working relationship for you. Do you know how often you need communication to feel heard and supported? Have you identified specific tasks and responsibilities for this role? Do you know what "success" in this role looks like? If any of those questions cause you to pause, it's time to start thinking about it.

Then bring them on for a 60-to-90-day trial run with a specific goal or target. An example for a VA might look something like this:

How we'll measure success for this trial period: by the end of 90 days, the ideal candidate will take over inbox management and be able to prioritize and escalate customer tickets so that everyone is taken care of within one business day if not sooner. Frequently asked questions will be documented and incorporated into the Standard Operating Procedure. I want to be able to step away from the inbox completely and trust that anyone on the team can step in to handle this if both of us are out simultaneously. I need to trust that you've got it and you'll come to me with questions or when new situations arise.

That's just for one task, and if this person assumes responsibility for multiple tasks, then you'll want to think through what success looks like for each of those. The point I want you to note is to drill down to specifics in terms of tasks (inbox management, escalation, FAQs, SOPs) and the ultimate end goal (the owner to completely step away from inbox management).

It's okay if you don't get this perfect—the practice of articulating yourself and setting expectations is more important than the perfect wording.

That practice will go a long way toward preventing frustration. The bonus is, when you frame it this way—that we're taking a trial run to see how well we work together—it greatly minimizes any hurt feelings if you get to the end and discover it's not working as you'd hoped. It also eliminates the awkward "We need to talk" message because you both knew going in that at 60 or 90s days, you'd talk.

I don't want to scare you with this—learning to hire and nurture talent is not entirely dissimilar to finding clients, which isn't entirely dissimilar from dating. You'll have to try people out and see how you like them. You'll have to grow into a leader, which will require uncomfortable conversations with people when you're disappointed, or when things aren't working.

But I want you to remember this: It's all figure-outable.

Your Inner Game

Having a strong inner game is critical for your long-term success. Some would argue that cash flow (or lack thereof) is the "make or break" point for many business owners. It's very important, but the bigger business killers are insecurity and anxiety. Unchecked, those two will take over in the name of "self-protection" and lead you to make irrational, fear-based, and counterproductive moves that could sabotage everything you've built.

Many folks shut down their businesses during the pandemic—and I'd be willing to bet that decision was based on a combination of money fears and insecurity. And yet, given the record-breaking stock market growth and the multiple stimulus packages, there was lots of money flowing around (albeit not at ALL efficiently).

So, what happened? Why did so many businesses thrive while others struggled and shut down?

My take? The thrivers said to themselves, "Okay, this sucks. What do I do now? How do I keep this running?" Many of them added new offers or even changed directions entirely to keep the money flowing.

This is that voice of inner authority. It is often what people think of as "confidence." What it really means is that I take responsibility for my choices and the consequences (for better or worse). No matter what happens, I have faith in myself and know I will figure something out.

Insecurity, on the other hand, leads you down a path of uncertainty by constantly bombarding you with unanswerable questions. Let's break it down further:

"What if X happens?" is not an answerable question because there are infinite possibilities. "Why did this happen?" is not an answerable question because it assumes that if only you discern the meaning or cause, you can move forward. Often, we'll allow ourselves to get stuck in these loops because it feels productive like you're analyzing and planning when what you're really doing is worrying.

To quote Van Wilder, "Worry is like a rocking chair—it gives you something to do but doesn't get you anywhere."

"How will I do this?" is a much better question to ask yourself. Other options include "What can I do?" or "What are my options?" Those questions move a challenge away from endless pondering and anxiety loops and back toward action-taking mode.

Another form of anxiety (and one I'm super prone to) is worrying whether people will hate this thing you created.

Look, it's not my job (or yours!) to control how people receive and experience my work—nor is it my responsibility to keep doing things the way I've always done because people like the old way and hate the idea of change. All I can do is put my best work out there and try to connect, then move on to the next thing. You can't worry about how people will react or what they'll think about your decisions because then you're listening to everyone else's voice but your own.

You will never please 100% of the people 100% of the time. Might as well focus on the people you CAN please MOST of the time—and by the way, YOU are one of those people.

Every successful business out there has haters. Their leaders get attacked, and raked over the coals in public. The strong ones melt down in private, process those feelings, and then they get their game face on and figure out a way forward.

Now, that doesn't mean you should ignore all criticism. Constructive criticism has a place because we can all stand to do better. And it's not a bad thing if you feel a little shame or like you could do better from time to time. It keeps you on top of your game. You just can't STAY there.

But remember the people who are in your corner, and have your back. Those people can remind you of who you are when you feel a bit less-than. They can give you invaluable perspective and challenge your assumptions.

You don't have to let the inner anxiety demons screech at you about how everything you're doing is wrong. You get to choose your path forward.

Chapter 16: Angie's Law

If Murphy gets to have a law, then I get to have one, too (especially since Murphy's Law is pretty shitty).

Here's Angie's Law: people who know how to create and maintain relationships can achieve anything they set their minds to.

Bet you didn't think you were signing up for a relationship book, did you? Yet here we are…

Unless you plan to run off to the woods and live off the land, you're going to have to deal with people eventually.

Especially after the pandemic, I get not feeling very "people-y," but the good news is when you surround yourself with good people, you don't have to spend a whole lot of time entertaining assholes.

Since we're making up laws, I might as well drop a few more on you.

Don't go it alone. Everyone you respect and admire—from Broadway stars, movie stars, musicians, inventors, owners of companies, and everyone who has a business or something that's worth having, fought for it. And they most certainly did not do it alone. They surrounded themselves with people who could help them, had the humility to ask for help, and had the grace to accept it.

Get comfortable with being vulnerable (at least with your trusted support group). There's this illusion out there in the business world that you must be tough as nails, show everyone that you've got your shit together, have no weaknesses, and never have down days or make mistakes. The day my business changed for the better was the day I realized I wasn't the only one struggling and that maybe if we struggled together, we'd all get further, faster.

Don't step on toes. Don't burn bridges. You can shut doors, but you never know when you need to open them again, so don't slam them in someone's face. You may need to go crawling back to a job. You may need to reach out to a client and ask them for a reference. You may run across a person at a different company in the future.

Feel the feelings and then let them go no matter how angry or hurt you might be. Don't take it personally... because with a lot of the shit we get all wound up about and offended over, the other person doesn't have a clue how much we've suffered.

Handle it like an adult and leave those doors open for future connections. Even if you never want to work with them again, it doesn't hurt to be nice when cutting ties. I make it a practice not to step on toes, even if that person is "beneath" or "behind" me (I kind of hate those terms, but some folks think like that). You never know when someone will make a massive leap forward. The toes that you step on today could be connected to the ass you have to kiss tomorrow.

Don't lose your cool. I once was a hothead. Given the amount of swearing and sass in this book, I'm sure that's hard for you to imagine. There are so many situations that, looking back, I'm embarrassed by how I handled myself… even though, at the time, I was smugly satisfied with putting people in their place and showing them just how pissed off I was.

Nine times out of ten, the situation wasn't what I thought it was, but I was quick to offense and often blew things way out of proportion. Then the strength of my reaction (read: tears and red face) would have colleagues and clients baffled, going, "Whoa, whoa, what the hell just happened?" I'd gone from zero to pissed in about five seconds. And frankly, I was choosing to be upset over a perceived slight that had no basis in reality—it was purely my imagination, one of those two-sided convos I was having inside my own head.

It really helped me to have someone with some distance and perspective in my corner who could point out where I was jumping to conclusions and when there might be another angle I couldn't see. I can tell you I haven't gotten anywhere in my career without the people that were willing to look me in the eye and tell me I was being really fucking dumb. I appreciate them so much.

Don't be reactive and angry like I was because you're burning some serious bridges and building a reputation as someone who's a pain in the ass to work with. I used to love throwing my weight around and proving to everyone that I was the smartest person in the room—but if I'm honest with myself, the only reason I did all that posturing was because I was deeply insecure, paranoid that I'd be found out as a fraud at any moment.

I figured the louder I blustered, the less reason they'd ever have to question or judge me. I've since learned that if I'm the smartest person in the room, I'm in the wrong room. I don't need my ego to be stroked. I just need results, and I don't care if I'm the person that gets credit for an idea or if I'm just one small part of the master plan. I do care about the impact I'm making and whether I'm helping people and adding positivity to the world.

Don't trip over your ego. It's easy to believe your own hype whenever you get to a certain level of success. As you rack up win after win, you may start to fully believe that you've got some special knowledge or advantage others don't. That's a dangerous trap—because success attracts a very dangerous breed of people known as "Yes People."

Those are folks who are so excited to be in your world that, in their eyes, you can do no wrong. That means they won't push back on you when you're on the verge of making a mistake. They won't point out the pros and cons like a trusted friend or colleague would. They're all aboard the hype train, convinced you are impervious, infallible.

And if you believe those people, you're heading for a fall. They may even be the ones to trip you. "Yes People" and "Hype People" don't care about you. They care about how they look because of their proximity to you. The moment you make a mistake, they will switch sides and become the loudest, most vocally judgmental enemies. They will gladly throw you under the bus if it makes them look better.

Every step of the way, intentionally surround yourself with the kind of "loving mirror" people who can show you what it's hard for you to see… otherwise, you risk losing it all to ego.

Don't pretend you know everything (because you don't need to!). I can't tell you how many of my clients have the impression that I am a super brilliant person. I don't think I'm smarter than anyone else or some savant that everyone in the business world should be watching. But I do tell people the truth.

I've learned the power of saying, "I don't have an answer for you right this second, but I can make a few phone calls and probably figure that out pretty quickly." Or I'll say, "I admit I'm unfamiliar with that situation. I can connect you to someone who knows more about that than I do."

When you proactively look to find answers and solve problems versus defensively making shit up so people never find out there's something you don't know… you look like a smart and resourceful person, not a clueless turd.

Newsflash: no one expects you to know everything.

Trust yourself to be able to figure it out. Even if you don't have the answer, you can find someone who does. You don't know what you don't know, and that's okay. Get curious. It's an opportunity to grow and learn whenever you're facing a question you don't have an answer for.

Don't forget how resourceful you are. You don't get any brownie points for figuring it out all by yourself. Admitting you need help or that you don't have the answers does not make you any less of an expert. If you surround yourself with people who are smarter than you, you have a network of people that can help you find the answers. Isn't this wonderful how brilliant all of this is?

Often, when I've turned to my network with a problem I didn't know how to solve, they came back within an hour and had all kinds of solutions for me. Some of those solutions were so obvious as to be painful, but it's hard to see the big picture when you're in it up to your armpits. That's only natural—there's only so much your brain can handle at any point in time. Your network is like an external mega-brain you can tap into whenever you need a boost. It's fantastic.

Do be kind. Not because you want something from someone, but because we all deserve kindness. You never know what someone's going through and how often the confidence you perceive is them barely holding it together in public long enough to make it back home so they can melt down in private.

Be the support you wish you had. Be the helpful resource that saves someone in a pinch. Be the trusted expert and ally your clients can count on. And be open to a bright, wonderfully unpredictable future full of possibilities and problems you'll figure out how to solve.

You've got this. Now let's go kick some ass.

Further Reading and Resources

As you grow and learn, you may discover you need some extra guidance from time to time. Head on over to permissiontokickass.com. I've got a bunch of free and low-cost resources over there that you can check out—podcasts, presentations I've done, products I've created, recommended reading, and all that jazz. And, of course, if you'd like to become a coaching or consulting client, you'll find my most current offerings available under the "Work With Me" tab.

We've reached the end, my friend. All that's left to do is take some massive action and believe in yourself the way I believe in you.

Acknowledgements

This book has been a massive undertaking, and one of the best learning experiences of my life. While I'm glad after five years of agonizing that it's finally getting into the hands of the people I most want to read it... I'm also glad to have this one in the rearview. All those edit rounds were making me cross-eyed.

This is why we need excellent editors. I happened to have three of the very best –

Dr. Cindy Childress, who helped me take my VERY rough draft – which I had created from nine months' worth of recorded audio transcripts – and turn it into something with a solid structure and purpose. You gave it a throughline and a message that made sense of all the thoughts in my head and I'm still grateful to you for handling the chaos with not only grace, but enthusiasm.

Joyce Hollman, without whose eagle eyes, this tome might have too many wayward commas and errant typos. Thank you for helping me make my ideas clear and my prose tight! Here's to the next iteration for us both, whatever it may look like.

Kathaleen Coyle, who is part red pen-wielding warrior, part book marketing genius. You helped me find renewed enthusiasm for the book when I was worrying whether I'd ever actually get the damn thing done. Thank you for helping me not only cross the finish line, but also come up with an action plan to get the word out. It's not easy being both book coach and therapist, yet you've managed to accomplish both!

To my first mentor (and friend), Kevin Rogers – without whom the name Permission to Kick Ass wouldn't exist. Thank you for giving me permission to help where I could and step into my expertise, and for continuing to support me every time my faith wavered or life interfered with my goals. I owe you so much, and am grateful for that fateful encounter at the Action Seminar. To say you've changed my life for the better is the understatement of the century.

Lindsey Hooper, who was the first to see my vision for this book and patiently took me through nine months of interviews and transcripts, asking me every question she could think to ask on the topics. Without you, this book wouldn't exist!

Brian McCarthy, who talked me off a ledge time and again as my fears popped up and tried to sabotage me. I'm grateful to have a coach and friend like you—everyone needs a Brian in their life!

Alix Penning, my best friend of over 20 years. Who knew how that friendship would evolve, eh? From swimming class in college to living on your couch to becoming Elliot's godmother to all the Disney trips, I couldn't ask for a better adventure buddy or overall awesome person.

Sally Spangenberg, my other best friend, who inspires me every day with her work ethic, her drive, and her wicked awesome dinner parties. I'm grateful we met, and for all the times we get to hang out and party plan together.

To my dad—thank you for always being in my corner, even when (I'm sure) my choices made no sense or sent me down the wrong path. Your faith in my capabilities is a large part of the reason I'm still standing, and continue to get up and fight each day.

To my mom—thank you for always being a listening ear, a problem solver, and the fiercest fighter for me believing in my own worth. I still blame you for my feistiness and my attitude, but it turns out people like that about us. :)

To Becky and Bob—how lucky am I to have the two single best stepparents a girl could ask for? I definitely got bonus parents when you came into the picture, and I'm forever grateful for the encouragement and support.

To Dianne and Justin—thank you for all the love, the silly memes and texts, and the long heart-felt conversations. You have no idea how good the hang time was for my soul, and I will fight anyone who claims they have better siblings.

Ashlee Berghoff, Jennifer Dale, and Amy Harris—you are the best chaos wranglers a girl could hope for. This book wouldn't exist without your superhuman efforts to support me getting organized and getting it out into the world.

To my early readers, without whom this whole thing might be a disaster that limped its way, bloated and rambling, to a forgettable close. Your feedback was tough but fair—and gave me the guts to keep clearing the mud away so people could see the gold. My profound thanks to Brenna McGowan, Belinda Weaver, Shana Story, David Maswary, and Enda Ndungu.

To my blurb writers, who graciously volunteered to read the final manuscript and think up ways to help me convince creative people to take a chance on a sweary business book. Without you, I would have truly struggled to cross the finish line—Dr. Cindy Childress, Lisa Christoffel, Kristen Stelzer, Rachel Mazza, Brit McGinnis, Denise Millet, Ashlee Berghoff, Brittany Herzberg, and everyone from Loretto who pushed me out of my comfort zone in the best possible way.

And to anyone else I didn't mention, I think of you and smile whenever I remember all the good times we've had. I'm grateful to know you—no matter how long or short our paths ran parallel.

I like to think we "trade paint" with the people we form connections with. You rub off on each other in a way that leaves a lasting impression. With all my dents and dings and mismatched colors from all the awesome people I've been privileged to know, I feel like a gloriously imperfect and beautiful human being who's lived life well (and getting better at it every day).

Finally, to you, dear reader. Thank you for sharing part of your journey with me. May we meet again somewhere along the path—I can't wait to see where it leads you.

Milton Keynes UK
Ingram Content Group UK Ltd.
UKHW031126221123
433051UK00015B/662